Once There Was a Farm . . .

THE VIRGINIA BOOKSHELF

The Virginia Bookshelf is a series of
paperback reprints of classic works focusing on
Virginia life, landscapes, and people.

Once There Was a FARM...

A Country Childhood Remembered

VIRGINIA BELL DABNEY

University Press of Virginia
Charlottesville and London

THE UNIVERSITY PRESS OF VIRGINIA
© 1998 by the Rector and Visitors of the University of Virginia
All rights reserved
Printed in the United States of America

First University Press of Virginia edition published 1998

∞ The paper used in this publication meets the minimum requirements of the
American National Standard for Information Sciences—Permanence of Paper for
Printed Library Materials, ANSI Z39.48-1984.

Library of Congress Cataloging-in-Publication Data
Dabney, Virginia Bell, 1919–
      Once there was a farm . . . : a country childhood remembered /
Virginia Bell Dabney.
         p.   cm. — (The Virginia bookshelf)
      Originally published: 1st ed. New York : Random House, c1990.
      ISBN 0-8139-1847-2 (alk. paper)
      1. Farm life—Virginia.   2. Dabney, Virginia Bell, 1919–   .
I. Title. II. Series.
S521.5.V8D33   1998
975.5'465043'092—dc21
   [B]   98-4241
                                                            CIP

TO MY SISTER ALLISON,
WHO LIVED THERE AND UNDERSTANDS.

Author's Note

My daughter looked at me across the dinner table and said, "Do you remember the time I made a coat for a terrapin? It buttoned underneath and I made a tall hat with a feather for him. Every time he'd stick his head out I'd put the hat on it. That would scare him and he'd pull it in and the hat would fall off."

I started to say that he must have looked like Abe Lincoln, but she said in a rush, "Do you remember the fly soup I made and fed to a praying mantis? And the cocoon I found . . ." She looked away and stopped suddenly.

So I quickly said, "And the time I came home and Savannah said, 'Peggy's been catchin' flies all day, tryin' to keep them birds' mouths shut.' I think it was a nest of phoebes you found." She laughed then, and I told her, "I remember. Those are good memories." But we each knew that they were painful—for her because she could no longer do those things and for me because I'd had to take her away from them when we moved to the city.

It was a long time before she stopped making remarks to

me or to her sister like: "Remember how Lucky waited for us every day under the oak tree to meet us from school?" "Remember our old johnny house we gave to the Danielses the Christmas after we got our bathroom because theirs tipped over?"

She was twelve when we moved, a bad age for change, and I had taught her many of the outdoor things I loved, but she had discovered as much for herself. Those four years on a small farm, with fields sowed and reaped by neighbors, and livestock we cared for ourselves, marked her for life. I understood then and even more now; I have been as indelibly imprinted by my own years of growing up on a working farm, close to the earth and its swing of seasons.

Contents

Once There Was a Farm . . .

1

In the Beginning

My parents, living in a comfortable house in the Chicago suburbs, bought sight unseen a 160-acre farm in the center of Virginia. The year was 1917. I don't know why they bought it; by the time I realized it was a curious thing for two non-farmers to do, it was too late to ask. Assured of a farmhouse to live in, my mother promptly moved south with her two children and her father, leaving my father in Chicago, where he worked for an insurance company. From that time on he saw his family only on visits during the summer and at Christmas, an arrangement that both my father and mother seemed to find perfectly acceptable. I was born later, in 1919.

By the time I was old enough to be aware of how we lived, the white farmhouse was peeling paint, leaking in heavy rains, and plaster was falling from the walls. I was not especially bothered by this since no one else seemed to be. In winter we huddled around wood stoves, and in spring, summer and fall a lot of life was lived out of doors. When I slept upstairs with my sister and the rain sluiced down outside, it rained in our room as well. Then we set buckets, old pots and pans under the leaks and fell asleep to the *clink* and *ploop* of slowly filling utensils. My mother, who had grown up on the Iowa prairie before she moved to Chicago, knew what to do on bitter nights when my sister and I, despite woolen covers, could not stay warm in that drafty bedroom. She would come upstairs with a stack of Chicago newspapers and put several thicknesses between the blankets on our bed. The papers rattled every time we moved, but they kept out the cold and we slept. We did not consider this proof of being poor but as a clever way to cope with winter. In our part of the country at that time there were a great many farmhouses as drafty and as poorly built as ours. The rooms were large and square, there was a hall down the middle and a front and back porch. Our house was a T shape; across the front there were two big rooms downstairs and matching rooms upstairs. Extending behind was a single story that was the large kitchen and a porch. Floors were thick oak boards, and on ours my mother put as many rugs as she could to ease the cold. The kitchen had a large wood-burning cookstove, and in winter it was the favorite room, smelling of baking beans or roasting pork or baking bread.

We were not the usual farm family, but it was years before this occurred to me, and it never seemed to matter anyway. My grandfather had been trained in horticulture and animal husbandry in Scotland, bringing with him a set of heavy volumes on the diseases of farm animals. I have only vague memories of him, of sitting on his lap when I was very small, of his white beard, of his deep voice. He died after six years in Virginia, but in the time he had he instructed my mother well. The tempo of the farm did not lessen with his going, though she never achieved the marvel of a garden that was his pride.

When he visited, my father was a man who preferred books to physical work outdoors, though he could walk tirelessly for miles in that gentle country. I don't remember much about his relationship with my sisters, but I approached him only at the urging of my mother, and usually, unless he showed some affability, with timidity and the wish to be elsewhere. This was because too often I had rushed in, bursting out, "Father, I—" and had him slowly turn his head from his book, look down at me over his half glasses and say, "Can't you see your father's reading?" We never became friends.

At that time in Virginia there was a great deal of hired help to be had, so that to say my mother farmed does not mean she plowed or worked in the fields from sunup to sundown. There were poorer white men and their families who worked the fields of larger farms for a share of the crops. One of these tilled our fields, sowed them with corn or alfalfa or grass for hay, and gathered in the harvest in the fall. This was after my grandfather died. Until his final illness he stood on the hay wagon, piling it high with summer grasses as our hired man pitched forkfuls to him. He supervised the cutting of the corn and leaning it into shocks like teepees about the field. He taught young helpers to use the horse-drawn mower he had bought, and the hay rake with its wicked shining tines.

There were black married women who came seeking work in the house and young black men who did general outside work. The man who milked and cleaned the barn, mended harness and fed the pigs, mended fences, gardened and talked with my mother, was paid fifteen dollars a week, and it was considered good pay. My mother tried to explain to my father, who questioned such a munificent salary for hired labor, that Solomon was someone she could depend on; he was intelligent and reliable and worth everything he was paid. On his salary I believe he largely supported a sister, a mother, a crippled brother and the sometime visits of his father.

I lived on this farm until I was eighteen, and returned to it every weekend until I was twenty-one. When I moved away permanently, I remembered stillness, the smells of corn in bloom and honeysuckle. I sometimes woke in the night thinking I heard a muffled cowbell down the street. The sight from a moving car of a path or a dirt road disappearing through fields and trees would haunt me with longing for days.

Three times since, in memory of that first farm, I have bought land to live on, assuaging for a time my old yearning and giving my children some of their own. Twice I have had to move.

Here in the Allegheny Mountains, in my third return to earth, I live on top of a hill, and I hope I can stay, though I miss the sounds of farming that abide in memory. From a farm across another hill I can hear the mooing of cattle; down the draw I hear a saw (chain); in all the woods around there is talk and argument among the ubiquitous crows. The fields I can see in winter when the leaves fall are not mine, though why I should wish to own fields to look out upon is a vagary explainable only by the vistas of my childhood on that first farm.

2

My Mother the Farmer

On the rare days that our hired man Solomon did not come, my mother took over the outdoor chores that must be done daily, help or no help. If he did not appear by eight o'clock, she sighed deeply and put on her old dress, old sweater and lace-up boots and headed for the barn. She did not draft my sister Allison and me for heavy work because, she said, our bones were still growing and could be damaged by carrying buckets of water or being stepped on by a cow. Daphne, our older sister, was at school or at work or married in those years, and escaped all labor. Anyway, Allison was in danger of violent hay fever if she strayed too near the barn. And I was simply in danger from being too young and overconfident. So it was our mother who took the milk pails to the barn and tossed down hay for the cows so they could eat while being milked. She knew how to milk, but probably never wrung those Guernsey teats as dry as they needed to be because she never came back with as much milk as Solomon. (Cow udders must be completely emptied at each milking or milk production will decline.) She gave the horses their ration of corn on the cob—which they bit off with a crunching sound that echoed through the barn—and took the pig his slop of throwaway milk, scraps and grain. Then she fed and watered the chickens, hauling water from the pump near the house to the three henhouses. That was in the morning, and it all had to be done again before sunset.

In the late morning on those days my mother would send me to gather the first laying of eggs. This meant approaching the curtained nests, reaching in and hoping not to encounter a bad-tempered layer. Some hens obliged a reaching hand by slightly raising themselves, but I usually found glaring eyes under red combs and was pecked and snarled at for taking the eggs. (Chickens do snarl, at least hens do. They do it in their throats with beaks slightly open, a warning sound, and to me, intimidating. It says, "Get your hand off my egg!" It is not a squawk, which is done with the beak wider and is a sound of alarm. A snarling hen is threatening; a squawking hen has probably been grabbed, or expects to be.) Still, I liked feeling those perfect warm brown shapes in my hand. I put them in an egg basket made in a shape now seen only in antique shops going for prices my mother would have thought fair for a gravid cow. I knew the people who made the basket. They were an old couple who came once or twice a year to our door to sell what they made. The woman wore a black cap tied under her chin and a long black dress hiding her dusty black shoes. The silent man in black pants and an ancient shirt took the money and carried some of the baskets. They were beautifully made of tough white-oak splints and my mother always bought one or two. Such baskets had to be sturdy because they were used every day. Besides, my mother said, she liked their shape.

For years Solomon had Sundays off between the early and

late feedings of the animals. In August he could come only for evening feedings and milking because of special services at the Rising Sun church. On those days he would pull up in the barnyard about four o'clock, driving a black car with two small American flags flying from the radiator cap. Inside was his mother, a large black lady in a beaded dress, and behind her his paler sister and his twin brother. While Solomon pulled overalls over his good pants and shirt, I was sent up the road to tell Susan, who worked in our house, that his family expected her company. I danced ahead of her as she came back with me, sedate in Sunday black, her hair combed out of its tiny braids into a dark cloud around her face, and her feet in shoes with heels and straps.

The greetings between these friends were warm, high-pitched and rapid. "How you, Mrs. Stacy?" from Susan, and "Right well, Mrs. Coleman, hope you well," from Solomon's mother. Though I was too young to be aware of larger meanings in speech, I noticed that black people carefully addressed each other by respectful titles I never heard whites use in speaking to them. It did not set me thinking then; I absorbed it without question and just once in those years did I glimpse any resentment. That was when I looked down the road one afternoon, saw my mother's car coming and playfully told Susan, "Here comes Mrs. Bell."

She looked at me sharply and said, "It ain't while to tell me her name; I knows how to call her." This stung me to explain that I was only playing, but her injury would let her say only, "That's all right," with a sniff of disdain. I did not understand why then, but I never referred to my mother as Mrs. Bell again.

I did not listen with great attention to what the black people talked of among themselves, though I always seemed to hover on the edges of their conversations. Yet into my heedless grasshopper mind went the way they said things so that even now I can hear them if I listen to memory.

Every Monday morning my mother would have a conference with Solomon. It took place in the kitchen, she leaning against the sink and he just inside the door. Her opening sentence was, "Well, Solomon, what do we have to do this week?" What they talked about was supposed to be what he had to do, but in the course of it she told him most of what *she* would do and why.

He began with seasonal things: "You reckon it time to put manure on the garden?" or "Does you want to take down the old chicken pen?" and "It's gettin' right close to time to put in potatoes—you reckon I ought to do that today?"

All the things he knew he should be about he framed with delicacy in questions so that she could nod or say, "Yes, I expect you ought to do that. . . . You know where the potatoes go this year?" She would tell him she had to replace falling plaster, clean out the stovepipe in the bedroom so the house wouldn't burn down and write my father of all the things that must be done right away.

"The horse needs a new collar," Soloman would tell her. "The chickens got to have they roosts whitewashed. The cow need some more bag balm—her bag's still right sore where it was scratched."

My mother wrote these things down gravely and respectfully as he talked. Then she would speak of long-range plans. "We need to clear a field in the low ground for corn this year. You should plan to start that as soon as you can. It's mostly brush, no trees." Solomon would nod, his eyes looking aside as he saw himself going by horseback the mile to low ground on Crooked Creek, carrying his ax and the lunch that Susan would fix for him.

I was listening, as I usually did, hearing only what I wanted to hear, wishing I could go along to the low ground too, at least on Saturdays. I could take my lunch and eat when Solomon ate, pile up the brush as he cut it and lie on my stomach to watch crayfish and water skaters in the creek pools. There was no use asking; I knew the answer already: "Girls just don't do those things." If I persisted by saying that some of the girls at school helped their fathers clear ground, my mother said shortly, "That's not the same at all—now just forget about it."

Once in a while those Monday-morning talks in the kitchen went from farm chores to politics, or at least my mother's talk did, and Solomon was trapped because it was not proper or respectful for him to remind her that he ought to get to work. He would stand there, shifting feet and nod, or say, "Y-a-a-h?" in a good imitation of surprise, or "Yes, ma'am, that's right," to my mother's Republican opinions. Reprieve came when she glanced at the clock and realized that sounds from outside were the cows bawling to be milked and the pig standing in his trough, banging his hooves on the top rail of his pen and shrieking.

In summer, before the sun was high, my mother put on her old hat (which had once been a fine braided straw), pushed hat pins through it into the bun of her hair at the back, took a basket and went to the garden to pick vegetables. It was a large garden, plowed by Solomon and the horse. My mother set out plants and helped sow seeds. Cultivation was by Solomon and hoe.

In April my mother gathered asparagus, in May rhubarb, lettuce and strawberries. By June her basket brimmed with peas; July and August heaped several with beans, beets, corn and tomatoes. By then the back porch was piled with produce and the canning season was upon us.

In the early years on our farm, canning reduced my mother to a rag by day's end. The wood stove did it, burning hotly, keeping water boiling in kettles where her jars of vegetables sat being processed, sterilizing jars and lids in other pans, and nearly boiling her. She trusted no one with the canning but herself, which she did by the *Blue Ball Canning Book*, but set the rest of us to shelling peas and snapping beans until our fingers were sore. Occasionally now I am visited with the nostalgic remembrance of peas past, pods fat and bursting in the hand, and the smooth bright green beads plopping into a bowl.

In time my mother rebelled against going through another summer of torture by wood fire. She was abetted by advertisements in farm magazines that tempted housewives with the wonders of cooler cooking for those who did not have electricity. Few did. She knew what she wanted, and my father agreed to buy the oil stove that she chose and had it shipped from the factory. The stove was known before it even arrived as the Red Star stove, and the day it came was one of rejoicing. Neighbor women came to see it unloaded from the wagon, its crate removed board by board, its black enamel and red star gradually revealed. It was taken to the kitchen, gently set in place, its tank filled with kerosene and lit by my mother. She primed a burner with a tiny amount of gasoline from a small, thin-spouted container that came with the stove. Then she struck a match and held it close over the burner until it caught with a soft *phup.* When the flame settled into a steady blue ring, she turned the knob that brought in kerosene. The burner purred along quietly and coolly. The ladies exclaimed, and my mother made coffee and served cookies without heating up the kitchen. Mrs. Woodford went home and the next day came back with cash to ask if a Red Star stove could be ordered for her large kitchen. She wanted a bigger one, and my mother felt no envy because Sally Woodford had to cook and can for a family of six. Within weeks another Red Star stove arrived on the train and as many of the Woodfords as possible went to meet it.

The other women who had watched that day murmured their interest cautiously because they knew they probably had no chance of owning such a stove. Even if they yearned for it, their husbands had already said, "Well, you can go over there and look at it, but you got a good cookstove like the one my mama and her mama used. Mrs. Bell come here from the big city; I reckon that's why she wants a fancy stove."

It was a matter of pride with my mother that the farm made enough money every year to cover its taxes in a time when other farmers around were sometimes unable to pay theirs. How much else it paid for I do not know. My grandfather had provided the machinery and livestock to start with, and I am sure my father's salary paid for new buildings, our clothing and Daphne's room and board while she went to high school. But the farm fed us well, and nothing was thrown away; it was fed to animals, preserved, stored, given to neighbors or sold. At one point the price of pork was so favorable that my mother decided to raise pigs for sale. We had a massive brood sow whose reputation was so bad that I was not allowed within ten feet of her fence. She had a surly temper and was known to grab a wandering chicken and devour it, though her size testified to ample meals of milk mixed with coarsely ground grain, called "middlings," corn and scraps.

When she produced a litter of seven piglets, my mother kept them all to raise to full size. But then, as the weather turned cool, the price of pork on the hoof dropped. This news was given considerable emphasis at our house by a visit from Tom Walker, a displaced mountaineer who lived and farmed several miles beyond the farm that belonged to Carl Stevens, who was our newest white neighbor.

Tom never came into the house, although he was always invited. He would ask my mother to show him a new building or ask to see the chickens; he strolled to the barnyard to see the cows, spitting a stream of tobacco juice now and then but saying little. He allowed that he'd like to buy "a few layin' biddies offen ye," and finally said he'd like to see the pigs. He was especially interested because he knew that for the first time we would have pigs for sale. He stood a long while gazing at sizable pigs sunning themselves, pigs scratching their backs, pigs rooting in soft dirt and pigs inquiring if he had anything to eat. After a contemplative silence he said, "Yep. Ye mought git four cents a pound fer them hogs. That's the most ye'll git. Tain't hardly worth feedin' 'em fer that."

Repeating his words later, Mother said she felt a wave of stubbornness come over her, and she told him, "Mr. Walker, I don't intend to sell them for that."

He spit carefully and asked, "How ye aim to do better?"

She said, "I don't know, but I didn't raise these pigs to lose money on. I'll think of something."

He shook his head but said, "I reckon ye kin do it kin anybody."

What she thought of was sausage. Her sausage was succulent and delicious and not too fat because she did not feed pigs too much corn. She asked the owner of the grocery store in Mineral, eight miles away, if he would be interested in a supply of good sausage to sell his customers in November. "Yes ma'am," he told her. "I know your butter, Mrs. Bell, and if your sausage is as good I can sell it easy."

When the weather turned really cold, Mother began sausage production. Normally only part of a hog goes into sausage—whatever is not ham or ribs or chops or tenderloin or pig feet or liver or head cheese. But for this project almost the entire pig became neat packages of sausage, and as always, my mother let no one else handle the meat. For weeks the kitchen smelled of sage, rosemary, pepper and thyme. At the end of the day, her arm ached from turning the hand sausage grinder, though Allison helped grind and so did Susan when she was there. Solomon, Susan, the Marshall family, Aunt Alice across the hill and I don't know who else received presents of pork liver, pig feet for pickling and whatever else could not be put in the recipe.

The finished sausage was stored in a large, heavily insulated chest on the back porch; fortunately the weather stayed cold. At the end of each week another pig was taken to town in small packages and delivered to the store. My mother came home gloating that these pigs were paying well over four cents a pound, her triumph almost overcoming her exhaustion.

After the last pound was delivered, Mother wrote the whole thing up for a contest held by the *Chicago Tribune*, which offered prizes for personal accounts of overcoming adversity. She won the first prize of a hundred dollars for her story. In the 1920s, a hundred dollars was a large sum for a small farmer, and she was amazed and delighted. But that was her only venture into sausage selling. Soon after she sold the sow, who did not enter the sausage grinder because she was too fat and too tough. We never again had so many pigs at one time.

What we had most of was chickens, ponderous birds marked by bars of gray and white in their feathers. They looked rather like they were wearing checked gingham and were a dominant breed on the farms I knew when I was a child. They were called "barred rocks." The "barred" I understand, but why they should be "rocks" is lost to me in poultry history. In the spring, a few of the heavy wide-behinded hens would become broody; their temperatures would go up and they would hog the nests, giving place to no other hens, scolding loudly and guarding their eggs—or some other hen's eggs. If removed to brooding coops with their clutches of eggs, they would hatch downy yellow-and-black-patterned chicks in about three weeks. All of us liked watching those dozen or so miniature chickens running after each clucking hen, and for years most of our replacement layers were hatched and reared in the barnyard. Sometimes half would survive to maturity by running to hide in their mother's feathers at her first warning of danger. She was courageous in fending off cats and other chickens during daylight, but from the opossum's clutching hand in the dark, the weasel's slither and snatch, she could not protect them.

My mother wished to improve the flock and bought a particularly splended rooster from another farm, bringing him home in a box beside her in the buggy. When she arrived and hitched the horse at the barnyard gate, we all gathered to see this glorious bird. Susan, Allison, Daphne and I stood around as Mother opened the box and let him out. He strutted forth, his comb like a flame, and shouted a great challenging crow. Hens ceased their scratching at hearing this Caruso, but out of the dusky barn interior charged the incumbent head of the flock, whom no one had thought to remove. There was fire in his eye and sparks flashing from his spurs. He tore toward the other rooster with head down and feathers standing up stiffly, and the young and beautiful one, though bigger, did not wait. He fled up the road, past the barn, past the machine shed, and veered for the woods, the old rooster pursuing hotly as they both disappeared into the trees. That was the last my mother saw of the prize bird she'd acquired with such hope. The old one returned, chortling to himself, and was greeted by the women of his flock with submissive stoops and bowed necks. He crowed and mounted the nearest ones. My mother, chagrined but helpless with laughter, said she had not taken male psychology into account at all.

When she decided to go into the chicken/egg business, Mother phased out the old flock, cleaned the old chicken house, put a floor in it and turned it into a brooder house. New chickens were ordered from a chicken factory, otherwise known as a hatchery. They came on the train, and the whole cheeping two hundred were picked up at the station. These yellow bits of life were just out of their eggs and hungry. They were brought home and put in the remodeled chicken house, where a kerosene brooder lamp, purring and warm, awaited them. This had a canvas curtain lined with heavy flannel around it, providing a warm dark approximation of the underside of a large hen. The chicks snuggled under it immediately. We put down long gray metal feeders with about a dozen head-sized holes in the tops on each side so that chicks would not trample each other when trying to feed at the same spot. Water was provided in quart jars upon which ingenious star-shaped tops were screwed. When filled and inverted, the water fed down into the hollow star points so that five chicks could drink at a time. One chick, upon finding the feed, would start a sweet piping that brought the others running. Soon contentment spread through the chicken house. When full and sleepy they sat on their feet and formed a solid mat of yellow down under the brooder, eyes closed and sometimes heads tucked under ridiculous wings.

Until feathers replaced their down, Mother had to check on the chicks at intervals during the night. As long as the brooder functioned well, its wick not smoking and its fuel line unclogged, everything seemed well. But many farmers had lost beginning flocks because a brooder lamp flared and set the canvas curtains on fire, or baby chicks froze when lamps went out, or smothered trying to keep warm if it burned too low. The difficulty with kerosene brooders made many farmers bring in their new chickens and quarter them around the kitchen stove at night.

My mother would have none of this; she said the house was already too small to have to cope with two hundred chickens in the kitchen, but the real reason was that she felt there was something distastefully low class about bringing livestock into the house. She would rather trek out to the brooder house in the chill of early spring, and she never lost more than a few of the chickens, smothered by the brooder. Only those too weak to hold their own died.

By the time the first ones grew into hens, bright white with brilliant red combs, they produced more eggs than we had ever seen before. Our baskets overflowed. A truck brought us large crates that each held twelve dozen eggs and picked up those already filled. The driver, the son of a Richmond wholesaler, said his father would take as many as we could supply. So the flock was increased the next year and my mother built a fine new shed for the hens, partly paid for by the first two hundred fanatic layers.

Our hens were happy. I awoke on summer mornings to their singing. Hen song is not musical but it is expressive—of food to eat, soft dirt to take dust baths in, private nests for laying, a sunny place to scratch for worms and bugs and a chance to roam in the grass. Perhaps the greatest difference between raising chickens then and now is that today commercial growers can't afford to care if hens are happy or not. The 1980s hen is an egg machine. She spends her productive life in a cage with all the artificially enriched food and water she can consume, and what she eats makes eggs so that she cannot help but lay. The egg drops onto a conveyor belt and she has none of the satisfaction of feeling it under her, of cackling, "See the lovely egg I laid, perfect, perfect!" Hen brains are preprinted with intelligence about hawk shapes and how to warn and scatter, and not about much else, but they do have the capacity for joy. It is slavery to keep laying hens commercially these days. The layer endures perhaps twenty-four months of caged living, making an egg a day, and after that the guillotine. No lovely cool green grass like ours were turned out on about an hour before sunset so they would not roam too far. No dirt to scratch in, the immemorial right of gallinaceous birds. No soft nest to settle into. Our chicken houses were dusty with the busyness of hens, but the nests were kept clean, free of mites and with clean wood shavings for comfort. When a hen wished to lay, she jumped up into a nest box that was curtained in burlap so it was dim and private. Some other hen might argue for possession of the box, and once in a while a nest would be occupied by two determined layers. When her egg was produced she told everybody it was the best egg in the house and went back to sunning or joined her sisters in pursuit of a grasshopper. Though our hens were also shipped out to meet the ax when they were no longer productive, they at least enjoyed a good life up to the end.

We could not go into the egg business until the roads had improved in our county so that cars and trucks could get in and out. But even before the road was cared for by highway machinery, my mother decided we should no longer live in the horse-and-buggy days; it wasn't good for progress. She bought a car. It was a black Ford with a front seat only, and was called, I think, a runabout. Three could sit in it if one was as small as I. There was no gear in the way; it was on the steering shaft, and I don't know where the hand brake was. It looked a lot like our old horse-drawn buggy from the windshield back, but there were button-on curtains of black leathery material in case of rain. Sometimes we were pretty wet by the time they were buttoned if we went through a summer storm. I seem to remember operating the one windshield wiper by hand. If the rain became too heavy there was nothing to do but stop.

I was the one member of the family who hated it when we got the car because my mother sold the horses. Horses were beautiful; there was nothing beautiful about the car. For years I had had the idea that when I was big enough I could ride a horse every day, and then suddenly we had no horse. "Mother," I argued, "can't we at least keep Nita? If we sell her you won't have any horse to ride anymore." My mother rode with grace and dignity, her back straight, her hands light on the reins; I knew somehow that she liked the way she looked on a horse.

This cut absolutely no ice. "I don't need a horse to ride now," she said. "We're keeping Nelly, you know. Nelly can pull a plow but Nita won't move a step if she's hitched to a plow." Nelly was a heavy-footed white horse with a neck that did not curve like Nita's; in fact her neck sagged like the rest of her.

"Why do we have to have a car?" I asked, petulant.

"Why, don't you want one?" She was surprised at such backwardness.

"No," I said. "I want a horse."

She laughed. "Times are changing, child. You don't want the world to pass us by, do you?"

"I do if we have to have a car instead of a horse," I persisted, knowing it was hopeless.

She gave me the amused look of a woman who has been through two children already. "You'll change your mind in a few years," she said, bending to her sewing. But I was sure I wouldn't—and I didn't.

One thing that the car removed from our lives was home-baked yeast bread. My mother said that she'd learned to make bread when she was twelve years old and had been doing it ever since. I could not remember a time when she had not made bread one day a week, using square little compressed yeast cakes that came regularly by mail, perhaps from Fleischmann's, who still make them. They carried the same yellow label on each that they do now, and I used to stick them on my nose. She made whole wheat bread and called it "entire wheat"; she made white loaves, crusty, yeasty and delicious when eaten hot from the oven.

Most people in the country around us baked large biscuits, and these, stuffed with pork or fried pork fat, were what filled the lunch pails of children at school. My sandwiches were considered a curiosity, and those I didn't like I gave away; Mother had a way of sneaking in healthful mixtures like carrots, raisins and mayonnaise, which were exotic to my friends and popular with them. Their parents did not make "light bread," and when they didn't have biscuits they had corn bread. Even when grocery-store white bread became common locally in the 1920s few large farm families could afford it; such loaves were considered a rare delicacy. My mother held out until she found she could buy whole wheat bread, and then her yeast bread making vanished altogether.

There were ample reasons for our acquiring a car in the late twenties. Roads had been improved—not hard-topped but kept scraped, with some of the worst places filled and smoothed by the county highway machinery. Most of the people we knew by then had cars, though only one was a woman and she lived near a town. It probably took some persuading on my mother's part to convince my father that she was not too frail to steer a car and could have anything fixed that broke. Anyway, Mother was determined to have one. She talked of working part-time to help with Daphne's college costs and the upkeep of a car. Once, Allison, watching my mother's car disappearing down the road, said, "Ever since she bought a car, she never stays home."

Allison expressed the unease that I felt but did not know how to say. There were nights when it grew near and past my bedtime and my mother still had not come home. Susan was with us and watched as both Allison and I peered into the darkness from the kitchen window, looking for her lights to appear on a hill almost a mile away. Those were the years I started to sleepwalk. Some nights my mother would wake to find my bed empty and go searching. She would come upon me curled asleep upstairs on Daphne's bed, but not before fearing I had wandered outside.

But Allison was right. My mother was never confined by the farm again.

The job my mother talked about came to her. I remember when she was approached about it one summer afternoon when a small, well-dressed man drove into our yard in a shiny car and handed her a card.

"I just came from talking to Mrs. Daisy Lewis, the county

nurse," he told her, standing respectfully on the walk in front of the steps. "She said you are the only one she knows who can introduce a new and healthful way of cooking using our Wearever utensils."

Later, describing all this, my mother said that Jim Shands knew how to flatter, but he was so nice about it. Besides, she found out that Daisy Lewis *had* told him that Alice Bell was the only person she knew who could present Wearever and discuss good nutrition with customers.

After that introduction she offered him a chair on the porch and he went back to wrestle a huge sample case from his car's running board and opened it before us. He smiled at me but did not pat me on the head and say, "Is this your baby?" so I liked him right away. I stayed to see what came out of the suitcase and saw him spread shining, heavy hand-some pans across the porch floor around our feet. I had never seen so many matching pots and pans before.

I don't remember how Mr. Shands talked my mother into becoming an agent for Wearever, or how he described the work. It would not have interested me and I only half listened and without much understanding. What it meant to me later was that my mother was away part of several days a week, and Susan, instead of working half days for us, now stayed with Allison and me whenever Mother had to be away. The farm was trusted to Solomon alone on those days.

The first thing that changed was that Mother immediately began using the set of Wearever she had acquired as part of her new job. It gave us our first vegetables cooked with almost no water, a flavor-saving method unheard of and unpracticed in a time and place where most vegetables were boiled to mush with fat meat as flavor. Some of the pieces were our first with cool wooden handles; before then most of the kettles and skillets had metal handles to withstand use on wood stoves.

I don't think my mother made many sales. For one thing, there were few families in that very rural county who could afford to replace the iron skillets and enamel pots most of them had. She did not wish to presume on friendship by making sales calls on acquaintances and neighbors, so she chose those people she believed were prosperous and were barely if at all known to her. This proved to be a select group that she did not mind approaching. She drove up to their doors looking well tailored and handsome in the suits she made herself, and they let her in without hesitation. She came home with stories of houses where there were Persian rugs on the floor and the most primitive equipment in the kitchen. "They say yes, my things are very nice, and they probably do cook better and all, but . . . And when I say they should start out with a few things . . . Well, one woman said, 'If I gave Annie pans like these she wouldn't know what to do with them.' I told her I would come in and give a demonstration of how to cook with them and she told me, 'Oh, that wouldn't help. I leave all the cooking to Annie, and I just know she wouldn't change.' Well, I saw Annie before I left, and I expect she's right. Annie wouldn't take any new-fangled stuff from me, I know."

Mother found herself giving talks on saving the vitamins in food as part of the sales pitch, quite often to women who were not really concerned about carrots retaining their vitamin A, whatever that was. Vitamins were not just ignored in the country then; they were almost unknown.

At one point my mother, in collaboration with Jim Shands, arranged a cooking demonstration at the school. The two of them asked Daisy Lewis to talk about the importance of vitamins to health and growth. The school was in a village, and the attendance was good because there had been rumors that food would be served. My mother got carried away by the subject; she seized a loaf of bought white bread on hand as an exhibit of poor nutrition, tore out its soft spongy inside and balled the stuff up and threw it into the audience. It landed with a solid thud. "That," she told the startled group, "is how this white bread sits in your stomach. Now this"— she picked up a whole wheat loaf and squeezed some of it together—"stays loose and digestible, and it contains things you need, like iron and vitamin B in its brown part." If there was even one convert to whole-grain bread as a result, she never heard about it.

My mother and Jim Shands cooked vegetables that night and served them to the audience. They did it in a combina-tion utensil that allowed them to cook one vegetable at the bottom and steam several others on a middle rack. On the topmost rack were small steamed fruit puddings, and those alone inspired two orders. All food was sampled, admired and eaten, but purses stayed closed. "I'd like to buy your pots," one woman told them. "I'd hang them up in my kitchen just for looks. But all our cash money is going for a radio. Then maybe."

My mother was in this business only a few years. But before she left the Wearever sales force, she found that she made her best sales to some of the husbands who were victims of too much grease and fried foods. She taught their wives how to cook a new way, and they were grateful converts. In later years she said that her message was too far ahead of its time to make a living preaching it.

To the end of her life she referred to her favorite Wearever utensils by their numbers. "Will you get out the two ninety-seven?" she'd say, or "The eighty will be right for a small pudding." If we were baking, "Use the two ninety-two for the smaller layer cake." It was easier than saying, "That little round pan, you know, the one about like this."

During all these years, my father came to the farm for his two-week summer vacation from his work of calculating insurance risks and premiums, and when possible, he came home for Christmas. He was treated by my mother and by us as the guest he was: She cooked the special dishes that he liked and dressed prettily in the mornings; Allison and I were subdued at the table. What we knew best about our father was that he believed we invariably came to the table with dirty hands. The first words he spoke as we slid famished into our chairs were, I believed, accusatory: "Have you washed your hands?"

Allison usually had; she had known him for more years and knew what to expect. Daphne's white hands he never suspected. I suddenly had to look at mine, and of course they were grubby from wrist to fingernails. He seemed always to bend those blue eyes to me and say, "Never touch your food without washing your hands first." Sometimes he followed me to the washbasin to supervise, and this was humiliating because he stopped me halfway through and said, "Use the soap!" when I thought my hands were well sudsed. He didn't touch me but seized the soap, lathered up like a surgeon and then commanded me to do as he did. By the time we returned to the table, he was impelled to speak to my mother about my poor attitude and technique, and the edge of my appetite was much dulled. However, my hands were unnaturally clean.

Of course he moved into the bedroom with my mother, and I, who usually slept in the other bed in her room, moved upstairs with Allison. From my mother's door he emerged in the mornings to have coffee and talk with her. When I appeared and tried to edge by him, my mother said, "Vallie, give Father a good-morning kiss." I went to him and turned up my face as he bent a cheek to me, a cheek scratchy with short white hairs. I kissed it, he put an arm around me, and for a moment I was glad that he was home and that I had a father. But when my mother called me for breakfast, there was the inquisitorial eye again and the voice saying: "Have you washed your hands?"

He brought presents from his office for us: bunches of half-length pencils neatly rubber-banded, each with an eraser cap you could take off and attach by sucking it to the end of your tongue (which he never saw me do), and tiny pocket diaries imprinted with the name of his insurance company in gold. Inside were tables of weights and measures and currencies, calendars, maps, all in miniature. These booklets measured perhaps two and a quarter by three and a half inches and were wonderful to produce from a pocket. I took mine to school to flash before the noses of classmates, but they were unimpressed enough to let me keep it.

My father toured the working centers of the farm beside Mother, from garden to barn to chicken house to pigpen. The pigs he liked to watch as they rooted or slurped supper or put up wet, working noses to catch his scent. Chickens he found dull, and the cows he avoided, probably because of their unpredictable manure-spreading habits. Most of his time was spent reading in the living room, rocking steadily across the floor, across the rug, until eventually he collided with the morris chair on the other side. Then he would look up in some surprise and move his rocker back to the starting point.

While he was engrossed in books, I was outdoors pursuing my usual way at the heels of the hired man or dancing ahead of Susan as she walked home. He and I met briefly at meals, where I tried not to be noticed after the unfailing inquiry about my hands.

My regret for him and for us is that he did not laugh with us more often. The most ringing sounds I ever heard from him were when he sat on the back steps one summer afternoon while we all watched four or five kittens playing. They chased each other madly, tails stiff as brushes, erupting in leaps and sideways prances, grappling, pouncing, kicking stomachs, and sending my father into nonstop laughter. He laughed until he could not get his breath. Before he finally gained control and sat wiping his eyes, we were all doubled up with merriment, infected and overwhelmed by his.

At the end of his two weeks, he would dress in coat, vest, collar, tie and hat, becoming an erect, handsome city man. (Lounging around our house he usually tied a handkerchief around his neck over his collarless shirt.) He hugged us all, me rather gingerly because I was most likely to leave a smudge on his lapels, climbed into buggy or car and was driven by my mother to the train station. There was a slight feeling of relief, never voiced, at seeing him go. The next morning my mother sat at coffee in her old, comfortable bathrobe.

My mother's Wearever business did not survive into the Depression years. It had not been exactly thriving in the best of times, even though it provided her with occasional modest returns. Then, in 1933, another job was dropped into her lap.

For several years she had served as the unpaid president of the Lewis County Farm Loan Association, a tiny branch of a regional Federal Land Bank. Land banks were set up in twelve regions across the nation under a 1916 congressional act, specifically to aid people who farmed or wished to. How my mother achieved this office in an organization of male farmers I can only guess at, but presumably she had first been

elected to serve on the board. To qualify for board member-
ship, one must have bought or improved a farm with funds
borrowed from the Land Bank, to be repaying it on schedule,
and to be demonstrably good at farming.

My mother and father had borrowed a thousand dollars to
buy the farm in 1917, and they were meticulously repaying it.
My mother could talk easily of plowing, harrowing, disking,
egg production, pork production and tuberculin testing of
cattle. Moreover, she looked prosperous in her homemade
softly tailored suits.

While she was president of the Farm Loan Association, she
devoted two half-days a week to helping in the office of Judge
McNeary, an old friend who was the organization's executive
secretary.

Whether the judge had ever occupied a judicial bench or
not I do not know, though he seemed to have read law. He
was a man of florid complexion, circular shape and probably
high blood pressure. My mother was a help in drafting letters,
omitting his favorite Latin phrases so that farmers could
understand what he was saying.

The end of her presidency came when the mortgage on our
farm was paid off in 1933, and she was no longer eligible for
office. Apparently this upset the judge; a letter from him that
she kept is plaintive:

> . . . Am glad for your sake but it hits me very hard and I know
> the Association is a big loser, too. . . . Who will be able to
> handle the work even if we find someone willing to sacrifice
> their time to take hold at a moment's notice? Answer: No one
> in sight.

The judge, however, had a more profound complaint;
shortly after writing that letter his physical condition forced

him to retire without warning and move to his daughter's home in another state. The position he held with the Farm Loan Association was forthwith offered to my mother, and she lost no time in accepting. It paid little, but times were terrible, jobs were scarce and, as she said, "You never know what might happen."

For some reason, probably occasioned by my unsettled entry into teen years, I resented her going off to this work several days a week. I believed she should be at home, content to be a parent and to run the farm. With fourteen-year-old superiority I remarked on the amount of dust on furniture, drawing a visible line through the surface of her mirror and saying, "If you stayed home this wouldn't be so dirty." She gave me a sharp and exasperated lecture that made me ashamed and sulky. I said no more, and within another year I had improved to the point of once in a while dusting her mirror and dresser for her. By this time I had discovered that my mother's small income was enough to allow us to have lunch in the local drugstore once in a while, a delightful development for me, who loved malted milk shakes.

Electricity finally came to the farm in the 1940s. By then there was a newer, better house in place of the old one that had been destroyed by fire. This newer house, built ten years before, had to be wired for the electricity my mother had never expected to have. The house, the barn and the chicken house all glowed with electric light. An electric brooder mothered the baby chicks, and by 1942 my mother no longer had to rise and go forth to the brooder house two or three times a night. Until then she and my father, who was by then retired and now lived with us, rose before five o'clock and lit a dozen lanterns to hang in the henhouses. Unless the hens started eating early on cold days, they used all their food to keep themselves warm and had nothing left over to make eggs. The lanterns were lit and hung again by four in the winter afternoons to keep the hens from going to bed. Electricity meant that my father could go to the kitchen porch and throw a switch at five A.M. and then go back to bed. It also meant that my mother did not have to help light a dozen lanterns in the morning before she went to work in town.

When I came home from Richmond, where I was working by then, I found that my apple-green glass oil lamp had been wired and modernized with a light bulb. I missed the act of striking a match to light it, a personal ritual that had symbolized growing to an age when I had my own lamp and my own room. Turning a switch wasn't the same.

My father believed that with the farm at last entering the twentieth century, the roughed-in bathroom could be finished and used. He didn't reckon on my mother's conviction that bathrooms were needlessly extravagant. "They just waste water," she said. "And we'd have to dig a new well—why, just to take a bath in a bathtub you'd use as much water as the chickens and the cows drink in a day. And to flush a . . . ! I've been getting perfectly clean all these years with a basin and a pitcher of water—and the water gets thrown outside, where it does some good." So my father muttered to himself every day as he went across the yard and garden into a stand of young trees where our privy stood. This was a small building, perhaps five by five, built to conform to standards set by the Virginia State Health Department for "pit privies." In the 1920s the state had begun a campaign to outlaw old-fashioned outhouses because they were open to flies and animals that spread disease.

Hookworm was found in soil contaminated by human

waste, and open privies were the chief culprits for its spread. These parasites thrived in southern states, where people, especially children, went barefoot much of the year; hookworms attach themselves to the feet and from there invade the body. The parasite weakens and saps the energies of its host until he or she has little defense against serious infections. To reduce the hazards of infestation, health departments promoted a new kind of privy.

Ours, built after the fire in 1930, was an example of the proper facility. Others that my mother built before that may have been proper also but they do not stay in my memory. Beneath it was a regulation-depth pit, completely enclosed, with a pipe rising from it to above the roof, venting gases to the outside. This pipe was screened to keep out flies. The inside was clean but not fancy; it had one lidded opening on a tightly built, boxlike seat about nineteen inches high. In summer it was relaxingly close to breezes and birdsong. In winter, one did not tarry.

By the time World War II came, all the eggs that could be produced were needed, so my mother still kept things going with some help from my father. Solomon was no longer our hired hand; he had found a less tiring job with the school system. An older man, Pat Jackson, was now making the rounds of the barn and chicken houses; he walked from his house in the morning and again in the evening to milk and feed. Pat was deliberate of speech and spared my father one of his frustrations in working with Solomon: his inability to understand Solomon's rapid, high-pitched speech. Sometimes I found him in the mornings looking at Solomon with painful concentration, getting him to repeat sentences. Then he would turn to me and say, "What's he saying?" so that I had to translate, to my embarrassment and Solomon's.

Now when my mother went off to her work at the Farm Loan Association, my father gathered the eggs and cleaned them in the basement, grading and packing them in crates for shipping. The garden was smaller and less lush, though Pat occasionally hoed weeds, and my mother's canning tapered off as vegetables from other years still occupied basement shelves. The fields were rented to other farmers, who grew their corn, not ours.

I remember my mother's struggles during the war years with the gas-rationing board. I heard these when I was able to visit the farm occasionally. By then I was married, had a child and was living in a Blue Ridge Mountain town where my husband was teaching.

My mother and the Farm Loan Association considered her travels on farm inspection to be necessary, but the head of the rationing board did not. He took the sour view that Mrs. Bell was doing work that ought to be done by a man, and she was convinced he deliberately refused to allot her gas coupons because she was a woman. It was a new experience for her to hold her tongue on the subject of woman's place in order to avoid offending him. She could not quite refrain from reminding him that she had been running a farm as well as a man for many years. "You just been lucky to have Carl Stevens for a neighbor," he drawled. "I'm sure he had a lot to do with it. . . . I can only approve part of your request this time." And my mother, furious at his contempt, had to force herself to thank him and leave.

When my father died in 1947, Mother stopped farming altogether. She sold the hens and the cow that was left—and then found she could not bear to see good land go to waste. In the end, with none of her children willing or able to come back and keep its life going, she sold the farm to Carl Stevens, reserving only the right to live in a small cottage on our place for the rest of her days. She did not seem to mind the contraction of her life; she was tired, I think, and the changes she saw coming in agriculture appalled rather than challenged her. She wanted no more of the struggle.

3

A Clown in Blue

On this day in mid-March, chill as any January day, there is light snow, fallen in the night. Oaks and dogwoods, hickories and maples, are silver and black, shawled in white. It is like a pen-and-ink drawing out there except for six pairs of cardinals facing my windows, looking for seed. The males are bright-red exclamation points of waiting.

Visiting neighbors, impressed by the brilliant show, say, "Why do you have so many cardinals? What do you feed them?" All the sober-colored birds of winter come to their feeders, they say, but hardly a cardinal.

The answer is I have thickets all over the place; my house is surrounded by thickets. They are mostly blackberry and some stands of tough, wicked greenbrier, all interlaced with young dogwoods. A large, rampant multiflora rose near the garden holds various small bird nests every summer. But the thorny thickets beyond the yard grass is where the cardinals bring up their young. In the first light of dawn the males salute the east while perched above their sitting mates on nests protected by brambles as tough as barbed wire. There is enough tangle around here for all of them, and I hear them answer each other from acres around.

On this March day I throw out sunflower seed and they and their rose-tipped mates breakfast with titmice, a nuthatch, a flock of juncos and one jay.

Jays were the predominant birds on my mother's farm because there were so many oak trees around the house. They shouted to each other, hammered open acorns and stored some of the surplus in holes and crevices for future use. They were big, cheeky birds that seemed to hop on springs, not as endearing as bluebirds or welcome as robins, but tolerated and admired by us for their plumage. Until one day in May.

It was a wet, chilly morning and my mother was out doing chores because Solomon had been kept home, probably by rising creek waters. She came in with her old fur felt hat dripping about her ears and in her hands a rumpled, sad-looking young jay, just out of the nest. He had lighted on the pump handle and clung there, getting wetter by the minute and too afraid or too sodden to fly, even though two parent birds wheedled and coaxed and warned him about my mother's approach. She detached his gripping claws from the handle and brought him in the house. "If I leave him out there the cats will get him," she said, and handed him to me. "Keep him warm," she told me, "and give him something to eat."

I loved him immediately, especially when he opened his mouth for food whenever I petted him. I tucked him into a piece of old flannel nightgown in a box, and put a rubber bottle of warm water underneath the cloth. Since the weather was not good for bug hunting, I took some of my mother's loaf bread, soaked it in milk and offered it to the jay's open beak. He swallowed dripping piece after piece until his crop was full and he went to sleep and I went to school. My mother fed him hourly until I came home.

The May rains that brought me the fledgling jay came every year when the blackberries were covered with white blossoms, and the time was called, at least in my house, "blackberry winter." Rain fell steadily for days, temperatures were low enough for fires to feel good, and small watercourses overflowed. When my mother believed the creek through our farm might have covered the highway bridge, she saddled a horse early in the morning, put on her impervious fur felt hat, boots and long divided skirt and rode out to inspect the road. If she found water well over the bridge she knew the school bus would not reach us, that Solomon could not cross a stream between his place and ours, that the mailman would not be out in his buggy along our road and that she would have the cows to milk, not her favorite chore. But she scooped up a few crayfish in the waters flowing over the bridge and brought them home to Allison and me in her hat, which was never the worse for whatever she put in it. It was a handsome hat, which could not be found today at any price my mother could have paid. She looked stunning in it, even when it was streaming water about her ears.

We played (or I did; Allison, seven years older, was growing beyond such things) with the crayfish on the kitchen floor, watching them crawl backward and swim in a dishpan. When I tired of them they were taken down to the water at the bottom of our orchard hill and tipped out of the dishpan. My mother's hat was also used to bring us newts or salamanders, a nest of baby rabbits that we could only look at, not touch, and a very young box turtle. After the natural-history lesson they were always returned to the spot where she found them.

Mother did allow Allison to keep two box turtles of medium size. Allison named them Andy Gump and Uncle Bim, after two chinless comic-strip characters of the time. Susan, who loved comics and followed them closely, found the

names very funny. Allison kept the turtles most of the summer, feeding them grubs and worms, shining their beautiful
tortoise shells with Vaseline, and finally letting them go
before fall so they could find holes for the winter. Though
they became so tame they'd eat in our presence, they were
pretty inadequate pets and no one minded their going.

It was my mother's intention to let me play with the jay
until his two inches of tail grew out more and he lost the
egg-yolk look around his beak. Then he was to be let fly away
to fend for himself and be a natural jay. Meanwhile the bird
adopted me as parent and greeted my step with glad cries,
eating whatever I brought him. By the time he was flying well
we were perfectly happy with each other, but my mother had
decided we could not keep him in captivity, and on a beautiful day in late summer we all made a procession about a
quarter of a mile to the edge of the woods, everybody but me
saying how happy he would be to fly free. I was holding him
and unable to say anything. My older sister Daphne was
along, trying to make me feel better, and Allison and my
mother were saying it was time for a healthy young bird to
make a living, while the jay I had named Yank was riding in
my cupped hands, looking bright and interested.

I let him go where they told me to, and he flew up into a
tree. My tears brimmed over because I would never see him
again and wouldn't know him even if I did. Then we started
back.

When we walked into the backyard, Yank was sitting on
the roof of the woodshed attached to the kitchen. At that my
mother surrendered, the jay flew down to my hand and we
all marched into the house.

My mother had Solomon build a large screened cage for
Yank in the corner of the machine shed, and we put branches
in there for him to hop about and perch on. I took him to

the house every day to let him fly around my mother's room (which was also mine at the time), the only room in which he was allowed. My mother made a little harness with a long cord so I could take him out to hunt for worms and if necessary jerk him out of any cat's way. We did not trust him to be suspicious of cats.

Yank grew up to be a handsome clown. Against the advice of Daphne, who could see untidy consequences, by fall my mother had another cage built and hung on the wall in our bedroom for Yank's winter quarters. I heard Daphne's opinion when she was talking with my mother over breakfast coffee: "Mother, you know he's going to make droppings all over."

And my mother answered, "Well, but Vallie loves him so, and it's not like she has playmates running in and out the way you and Allison had when you were children in Chicago."

It was the first time I knew anyone considered me deprived because I did not have children to play with. I thought about this a little, remembering when one of the high school teachers and his wife came to call for some reason and brought their son, who was my age. I was told to play with him and took him outside. I tried to take him down to the brook but he refused to go, telling me how nasty the pasture looked from the gate. He did not want to race down the road or climb in the barn loft. "Don't you have any toys?" he wanted to know, and I showed him my green-and-yellow wheelbarrow, which I loved. He kicked it and said, "That's nothing to play with; don't you have a bicycle?"

We finally went back into the house, where he stalked into the living room and made faces and ugly gestures at his parents while they talked to my mother, or tried to. His mother just kept saying, "Now, Edward, don't do that," and his father pretended not to see him. When they all left I hoped

I would never be offered another playmate, a visiting one, anyway.

But back to the blue jay: He stayed in the indoor cage each day until I came home from school and let him out. The first thing he did was fly to my sweater pockets and pull out balls of paper, small pencils and sometimes an apple core, seeking the crumbs at the bottom. Since he usually found something, I must have been in the habit of stuffing sandwiches and anything else in my pockets. Whatever he found he saved a part of to tuck into holes in cushions, crevices in cabinets, under the stove mat or in the backs of book bindings. They shook out of books for several years afterward. If I thought to put in raisins or nut meats, he swallowed several with a delighted sound, filling his throat pouch, which he would unload later.

My sister Allison often had bronchitis in winter, and since her upstairs room was hard to heat, she spent her sick days in my mother's bedroom, where a fire was kept all winter. The jay was interested in whatever was going on in the room, and especially in tray lunches and suppers. He would perch on the curtain rods and fly down to stand on tiptoe and drink from Allison's glass of milk or fly off with morsels of food, usually the ones she gave him, though he wasn't above stealing. Her feet sticking up under the covers made a landing place for him, and from there he would make a bounding hop to the tray set over her outstretched knees. He would look at her plate with one eye, and then turn his head so he could look at it with the other eye before deciding to take something. Once he speared a fresh hot biscuit with his beak and was halfway across the room when the heat got to him. He dropped it with a muffled expletive, flew down and ripped it apart, subduing it to a pile of crumbs.

Yank's trick of stowing things in his throat pouch once

gave Susan some anxiety, which the bird obviously enjoyed. This time I was sick, though not very. Susan was sweeping the bedroom floor. Feeling jaunty, Yank was hopping after the broom and getting very close. Susan kept saying, "Watch out, bird, I goin' to sweep you up." She picked up a slipper and some paper, a book and an apple I'd dropped and put them up on the bed. She reached for a small bell, the kind one puts on cat collars, but the jay saw it first. He snatched it, swallowed it and flew off.

"Jesus, he swallowed the bell!" Susan said, starting after him.

I don't know why I didn't tell her about his throat pouch and that the bell was his favorite toy. He was standing on top of the closet shelf, and when Susan reached for him—maybe to shake the bell out—he flew just out of reach.

"Come here, bird, you goin' to have a stomachache." He hopped toward her, she reached again and the jay flew over her a few feet to the dresser. She chased him for about ten minutes; he was having a wonderful time, and so was I. Finally Susan grew tired and picked up her broom to resume sweeping. The jay landed on a chair and waited for her to notice, but she muttered, "Think I chase you some more, don't you? Well I ain't." Yank promptly flew down on the floor and hopped in front of her so that the bell tinkled faintly from inside him.

"Listen at that," she said. "That bell ringin' in his gizzard." As she stooped to pick up the dustpan he stopped in front of her and regurgitated the bell. It plinked on the floor at her feet.

"How'd he do that?" she said, astonished.

So then I told her. "He plays with that bell that way," I said. "He hops around with it inside his throat pocket."

She sat on my bed and stared at him. "Ain't he some bird, foolin' me like that. He knew it too."

In the spring I took Yank to his outdoor cage. I thought it was a nice place for him, and I suppose my family did too. It was airy and cool and he could hear other birds, even his own kind. I was unable to realize that he identified only with us, and that he was too far from the only companionship he knew. When I went to feed him I was sometimes too eager to do other things instead of taking him inside for his play. I did finally notice that he was not eating, but sitting fluffed and quiet on his tree branch, and I gently called to him. He opened his eyes and I picked him up and carried him to the house. I told my mother and took him into his old room. All that afternoon after school I coaxed him to eat with tidbits of nuts and raisins, but he would not open his beak. I held him in my lap and told him that I would be better to him and we would go hunting bugs again when he was well. I tried mashed hard-boiled egg yolk, a food I believed nourishing. He refused that too, but this time he took my finger in his beak and caressed the length of it with obvious tenderness. That night I forced a little water into his mouth, petted him and tucked him in a box the way I had when he was a nestling. He was still alive in the morning and I convinced myself that he was getting better and went to school.

That afternoon my mother met me at the door and walked with me down the hall to the dining room. Inside she stopped and said, "Honey, Yank didn't make it."

I looked at her and burst into tears. Though I was ten years old, she held me on her lap until I had cried myself into dry sobs. I could not tell her that I thought he'd died because I had neglected him; probably she knew. It was the first death of something I loved, the first grief and the first guilt.

4

Nostalgia, Thy Sound Is Moo

The red sand of my unfinished porch is a pueblo in warm weather. One half of the porch floor is completed, laid with flat gray rocks. The unfinished half is dense with life, a minia-ture canyon, with dwellings set into its six-inch-high walls. On hot summer days if I have an iced drink and languor enough to pin me in a low porch chair for an hour, I will see hunting wasps, like single-engine planes, arriving about every thirty minutes, bearing caterpillars between four of their six legs. The caterpillars are longer than the wasps; the favored color is green. They have been stung into immobility and look like tiny inflated air mattresses.

Each wasp arrives alone. She lands, releases her burden and darts about with seeming aimlessness, climbing the red-sand canyon walls, weaving back and forth. She seems to be looking for something lost, and perhaps it is. No hole is visible in the smooth sand of the canyon wall. Suddenly she stops, digs hurriedly and uncovers an opening. How she has found the right spot is not obvious, but she disappears into the hole, stays briefly, perhaps to check the chamber she has made there, and returns. It takes her another minute of scouting to find the conspicuous green caterpillar she has ferried in. She then picks it up between her legs and drops it in front of the opening. Then she goes into the hole again, somehow turns around, emerges, grasps the caterpillar and tugs it bit by bit inside until the last green bulge of it is out of sight. There is a long pause, and when I've decided she is going to stay in there with it, though she is probably positioning the eggs she is leaving behind, she comes out, nervously kicks sand over the hole with her back feet and seems to pat it with her front ones, and the hole immediately vanishes. She doesn't stay around to gloat; she takes wing and is gone.

Somnolence can keep me here long enough to see another wasp slightly different in color, but of much the same design, coming in for a landing bearing a caterpillar, also green, but this time with stripes. The whole nervous, frantic routine is repeated, except that this wasp has chosen the opposite canyon wall, and has to enlarge the hole to fit her caterpillar. All day, if I have time to watch, I will see wasps come and go. If the porch floor is finished this summer, all those minute, cool caves will be obliterated and the wasps that I hope will have hatched by then will not be able to return to the canyon of their birth. Where will all those frantic mothers of the next generation find the right place to store their captured caterpillars, their urgent eggs? To live here is to worry about things like this.

Once my mother brought home a gorgeous ant in a jar; she had seen him running along a sandy road and scooped him up, putting the jar on the buggy seat beside her. The ant was crimson, roughly an inch long and trimmed in black. I was about eight and wanted to pet his beautiful fur, but my mother said he would probably sting or bite.

She filled a large goldfish bowl with sand, and when she put him in he burrowed into it immediately. We children wanted to keep him and she was curious about him herself, so she willingly set the bowl near a sunny window, where he might bask and we could observe. Allison named him Clarence, in dubious honor of a fat, red-headed neighbor. My mother set us to stunning flies and dropping them not quite dead into the bowl. She left bits of ripe fruit. As nearly as we could tell he touched none of these. Finally she soaked home-baked bread in milk and left it for him, and this he apparently ate at night or carried below. She added a bottle cap of water. He would emerge in time when, worried about his diet, she gave him fresh food, and he allowed her to stroke his body with a cautious forefinger.

Nothing in her small books about insects of that time enlightened Mother, so she wrote to an entomologist at the Virginia Polytechnic Institute describing our crimson bug. He replied that Clarence was a female solitary wasp, also known as a velvet ant, and wingless because of her sex. My mother decided that the decent thing to do was to free the wasp to do whatever she had been interrupted from doing on the hot summer day of her capture. She probably had been deterred from hunting underground bees, but we didn't know that then, and besides, so vivid a creature should be freed. So, attended by two children (Daphne was at summer school), my mother took the goldfish bowl to a hot, sandy stretch of road through our place and dumped Clarence out. The last we saw of her was her bright-crimson body threading through pale grasses beside the road. I have seen velvet ants since but none so large or so richly clad.

In those days our lives were full of other lives. Butterfly cocoons clinging to twigs were placed on a high bookcase to see what would emerge. Wet baby chicks stuporous with cold were wrapped in flannel and set on the open oven door, where they returned to life and to their shrill lost peeping. Fallen baby birds were also warmed and returned to the nests that could be reached. My mother believed that almost any small ailing animal could be salvaged if it was warmed, so even a calf too wobbly to nurse was brought inside, put in a basket near the stove and offered fingers dipped in warm milk. When it rolled out of the basket and stood up shakily, it was taken back to its bawling mother.

The farm we lived on and roamed over had the usual animals of two generations ago. There was always a cow or two, either pregnant or "fresh." A fresh cow was one that had recently calved and was giving milk again after a dry period before delivery. There were horses, a pig, a dog and four or five cats. The cats, except for one pampered house feline, were fed pans of whole milk and nothing else, and expected to support themselves in return for fragrant hay to sleep in. The barn was full of mice and rats. Every thicket had several families of rabbits, and squirrels multiplied on acorns in the oaks around. There was no cat or dog food on the market that we knew about. Dogs and pigs ate table scraps, augmented for the pigs by middlings. In winter the pail of middlings was heated on the stove so that they had a warm breakfast.

We always seemed to be overflowing with milk. The pastures were thick with bluegrass, and cows use bluegrass to produce quantities of white, warm, foaming liquid. As soon as the milk buckets were brought full into the kitchen, my mother or my sisters set out the stoneware crocks. (Later my mother bought white oblong enamel pans that could be stacked.) Into these they strained the milk from the buckets, using scalded cheesecloth over scalded metal strainers. Immediately the milk was covered and put into the icebox. By morning it had a coat of golden cream so thick that it bent and folded upon itself like heavy satin. This we used in coffee or on berries, and it was rich beyond any cream one could buy in a grocery store, then or now.

Milking was done twice a day by hand, and every creature on the farm drank it. We children had it skimmed at each meal and in between; the house cat had a bowl of it. When it soured, the chickens drank it, and for the pigs it was served any style, with floating apple and potato peelings, odd salad greens, leftover beans, bread scraps—anything that now goes into the compost heap. Sometimes the cream, kept for butter, threatened to overflow our wooden churn, and the hired man was sent home with a quart or so of sour cream to make rich biscuits or corn bread.

The yearning for that remembered taste of cold unpasteurized milk joins my sadness for other lost pleasures of another age. Raw milk cannot be bought anywhere in my part of the country as far as I know; if it could I would willingly make a considerable journey so I could take it home, put it in the refrigerator and have the joy of skimming its lovely fresh cream in the morning.

Occasionally I drive by farms here in the mountains where, among heavy red or black beef cattle, there will appear the surprising glimmer of a silver-buff Jersey milking cow, her luxurious udder swaying close to the ground. Several times I have stopped and gone to the farmhouse to ask if the owner would be willing to sell a quart or two of milk and perhaps a pound of butter. Always the woman or man at the door tells me: "Oh, we don't milk that cow; we just keep her to raise our calves on."

"What do you do for milk for yourself?" I ask.

"We buy it at the store—don't have to fool with milkin' it or storin' it or makin' butter." One of them even added once, "My folks don't like butter much anyway, it's too cowey. We all like that margareen."

So I have made a vow. If I ever have two fifty-thousand-dollar bills to rub together, I am going to buy a piece of land with a house, a barn and a small stream on it, fence it and install in it a milch cow. She will have curved horns above her great thick-lashed eyes and a tonkling bell to chime across the field on summer nights. In the morning I will milk her with my head leaning against her clover-scented flanks. I will carry the milk pail to the house, strain the milk and set it in the refrigerator. I will rise at dawn the next day and dip thick cold cream into my coffee and drink it sitting on the back steps or on a bench under an arbor while my cow grazes peacefully in her field. What I will do with all that milk I will decide later. Once one acquires a cow one perforce must buy other animals to avoid drowning by milk.

Though cows move through my memories of childhood and girlhood, it was not until my husband and I bought a farm of our own that I learned the close-up care of cattle. We were about thirty years old when we found a small place we thought we could afford. It lay in grazing and farming land sloping east of Richmond toward the tidal waters of the Rappahannock River. There were great estates there, original land grants from England's kings, and our piece of land had once belonged to a vast acreage held by one family.

Even now that small holding lives in my mind, bathed in a sunlight different from other places I have loved, criss-crossed at evening by late swallows and early bats. The land rose gently as you came into it on a white sand road, and then dipped. In that dip, slightly hidden from the main road, the house was built. From there the fields fell away in two swooping hills, one below the other, the bottom one narrowed by trees circling the lowest point.

The house was extremely modest, even nondescript: four large rooms and a back and front porch. There was a barn, larger and of better construction than the house, and a shed for chickens.

It was early April when we moved, chilly and wet, and the first thing I did was make a fire in the black iron cookstove that came with the kitchen. My children, five and nine years old, were charmed with seeing how one made heat without moving a thermostat lever. They were city children who had played all their days in yards and on sidewalks and sometimes in streets. Perhaps they adjusted well because I was so happy to be back on a farm.

The two girls and I burst out of doors in the early morning that first spring and summer before breakfast, before the school bus came and my husband left for work in the city. We visited the two cows and the ancient oak under which was the same beautiful deep white sand as in our driveway. In the afternoons we wandered down a hill under large oaks hung with catkins, their yellow pollen drifting onto our hair and coating the soles of our shoes. At the bottom was a ravine cut by a spring of clear water. It fell down steps formed of blue marl clay, almost hidden by richly fragrant ferns and mosses. This place was eternally cool even when hot suns burned the sandy loam of the fields above. In blazing August noontides we would leave the small airless house, descend into that coolness and listen to the water falling.

Whenever I could steal the time, I sat on the back steps overlooking the two grassy hills sloping down from the house.

They filled a hunger for unpeopled vistas, for changing light that touched the upper hill before it gilded the lower one, for dreaming.

Down in the deep sand under the old oak, the children were building their fantasy farms, racing and probably breeding their toy horses. Horses dominated their talk and play; they acted out Walter Farley's stories from *The Black Stallion* every day. They longed for horses as I had at their age, and running, they tossed their hair for manes, stamped and became horses at full gallop. Neither felt the need, as I once had, to tie on a fringed-rope tail.

When one of our cows came in heat that June, my husband decided to lead her down the road a mile or so to a large farm that kept an able bull. A cow in heat brooks no delay; she stands at the fence and bellows night and day. She will mount the gate or a barrel or another cow in her frenzy to mate. Gone is her placidity; she grazes barely, if at all. She is no longer content to lower her fringed eyelids sleepily as she chews her cud. Farmers in my time dropped everything to grant her fervent needs or risk her bolting to look for a mate herself. Once she is faced with an eager, snorting, pawing suitor, she may suddenly turn coy and saunter just out of his reach, as if copulation is the last thing she has in mind. Eventually, though, the impregnation is accomplished and she returns, the picture of calm docility, to the pasture.

My husband was the product of city living, and in my own farm years I was never encouraged to know about (that is to say, was kept innocent of) the sexual imperatives of animals. So when he decided to let the children go with him, both of us thought it would be a mild lesson in propagation on a pleasant spring day. They set out, and going down the road the anxious, urgent cow (a large Guernsey) was continually trying to climb on his shoulders. By the time they were halfway, a neighbor in a truck stopped and offered to take them. The children immediately climbed into the truck, glad to be out of the way of the cow's erratic progress. The cow was tied on behind and for the rest of the way was kept too busy trotting to embrace the truck.

The whole thing was an experience for the two girls that they promptly incorporated into their play. They had a toy farm with several rubber cows (though no anatomically correct bulls), and were playing on the living-room rug on a rainy day.

I heard the younger one say, "Cows like bulls, don't they?"

And was answered sagaciously by the other, "Not as much as bulls like cows."

That was long enough ago for toy departments to offer complete sets of farm animals—pigs with piglets, cows with calves, chickens, horses, wagons—and a barn to put them in. So much has changed in the farm scene since then that the old barnyard toys are as out of date as the Noah's ark of my own childhood.

Four years of those sunlit fields and open skies changed us so that we were no longer the same people who had moved there. My older daughter discovered her kinship with animal lives, wandering the fields and paths freely, usually attended by her smaller sister. She cradled toads, examined snakes, beetles, worms, caterpillars, butterflies, nests of birds and rabbits. She and her sister together found spectacular moths: the royal walnut moth, with orange fur and blue-gray veining, and the deep rose female promethea, among others. One of them brought home a strange caterpillar on a Friday in her lunch box, and by Monday, when I opened the box to fill it, the occupant had finished the leaves he was imprisoned with and spun himself a cocoon.

In those years their curiosity prevented their cringing at

things with six waving legs, or bugs that buzzed and thudded into or near their plates. School friends lived too far away to visit, we had no television in the early fifties, and their afternoons were spent outdoors in unconscious intimacy with whatever hopped, ran or flew.

In the end we had to move back to the city because I could not support the family, the farm and a car for transportation to the job I had to take. Peggy, nearing thirteen, suffered a cruel wrench from the farm to sidewalks, noise and too many people. Her sister, sitting at the table months later in apparent good cheer, would sometimes grow big-eyed and break into tears, saying, "Let's please go back to the farm."

I was changed too. By then thirty-five, my husband gone, I was sobered by the struggle to save the farm from foreclosure, then selling it, and by the necessity of going to work in an office.

I said good-bye to the barns and fields and the gate swinging open on an empty pasture. I permitted myself a last cup of coffee, gazing from the back steps over the two hills below me. In a kind of resignation I viewed the farm as something that had been lent to us just long enough for us to carry its benison within for life. The only one it did not change was my smallest daughter, who had been born there, and was not quite three when we left. She alone was hardly touched by our farm and grew into a lover of cities.

5

Conversations

The idea that talking to oneself is evidence of loosening mental screws seems to be imbedded in human belief. In earlier centuries women who mumbled to themselves were feared to be muttering incantations, at the very least, and were likely to be hung as witches. People who walk along with their lips moving in a mostly interior dialogue are today considered dotty, if harmless. No matter that they may be working out a theory to explain the motion of galaxies; they are probably judged to be unstable. I've been told many times, "It's OK to talk to yourself, but when you start answering . . ."

I reflect upon this—aloud. There is no one here to reply. My dog and cat are accustomed to speech not addressed to them and do not raise their heads to stare at me. As usual, I come to no conclusion; I turn to something else, and the discussion, if you can call it that, stops.

This is not a development that has come with age. I cannot remember a time when I did not hold lively conversations with myself. When I was small and underfoot my mother sent me somewhere else by saying, "Go out and see if the road is still there," or just "Run along now and play." Of my two sisters, one was away at school and the other was just enough older that she disdained holding any polite verbal exchange with me at all, so I played alone. Once out of my mother's hearing, I began talking to myself.

"Where shall we go?"

"How about down by the stream?"

"No, it's too close to lunch."

"Let's go climb on the gate."

So I—we—went to climb on the big gate to our driveway. At those times I had a sense of not being alone at all, and yet I did not see myself as two people but as one. When I climbed the great rough post to which the gate was hinged, the wood feeling warm and friendly, I intended to sit there with myself and sing my made-up songs.

I have tried to analyze that child, but it is hard to do because instead of examining her from outside I feel her from inside. I can still grow warm from the remembered sun of those years and see the brown scuffed shoes on her feet, and they are still my feet. I know her as she danced through sunlight or rain commenting on things she saw. I am there again as she says, pointing some three hundred feet away, "I'll race you to that tree," and runs, feet pounding, hair flying, to beat herself to the tree.

Whenever that child who was I was alone she talked to herself. Around other people she said very little, and the "you" of her conversations retreated inward without a trace. As she walked toward the house to go inside, she no longer talked, and she did not start again until she was where she could not be seen.

I was still doing this when I was ten or eleven, and once got caught at it. I was kneeling in a garden patch of my own, planting some pansies, probably giving myself directions: "Not that way, dummy, you have to put them farther apart," or some such.

On his way to a chicken house, Solomon came down the path and said, "Listen at her just talkin' to herself!"

I stopped and sat on my heels, terribly embarrassed, though I smiled as if it didn't matter. After he was out of sight I whispered, "Can't do that anymore." But I did, of course, only now I whispered if there was any chance I might be overheard. Out in the fields, down by the stream, sitting in an apple tree in the orchard, I still talked out loud, but only when no one was in sight.

By the time I was fourteen I began talking with men—not boys, men. These were not men I knew; I scarcely knew any except neighbors my mother's age, living as I did on a farm miles from any town. They were men I made up out of romantic scraps of heroes in books. From men seen in movies I took the voice of Nelson Eddy, the face of James Stewart or Gary Cooper, and once Charles Boyer—but I grew tired of his French accent because it was too hard to talk for him that way.

All of my conversations with them went on in my room, whispered to a mirror so I could practice my expression. By holding a hand mirror higher than my head I could tell how I would look if he were six feet tall. Then, by tilting my chin upward, I invited a kiss, a very chaste one, but it was all I could imagine then and quite enough. (Once a classmate asked me if I knew what a French kiss was, and I didn't. She wouldn't tell me, and later I realized she didn't know either.)

Within my small bedroom I walked in blossoming apple

orchards or down lanes rich with honeysuckle, holding hands with several Jims, one Douglas and lots of Marks. They all came closer and closer, wanting only the kiss I was prepared to give. I was unable to imagine anything beyond that except a proposal of marriage. Sometimes they invited me to dinner on a hotel terrace, and then I managed to make tea and toast taken to my room substitute for dining by candlelight.

These were fantasies, practice sessions for what I foresaw as the real thing, and I knew this perfectly well. However, they did not prepare me in the slightest for men who took a glance from under eyelashes as an invitation to the backseat of a car. None of my imagined men had been so crude because nowhere had I learned about sex. It was not in the books and magazines I read and it was censored out of the movies of the thirties. One film my mother and I saw managed to convey a sexual encounter between the young hero and a fan dancer by having the camera zoom in on an upper corner of what was obviously a bedroom, with the voices of a man and a woman rising from below. No rustle of bedclothes, no heavy breathing, just conversation. I was not impressed and did not wonder about what was happening. Afterward my mother said about the scene, "It could have been in poor taste, but it was handled very well." I said, "Um-hummm," not especially interested. It looked pretty dull to me.

My fantasy conversations with men were put away with other childish things when real experience came along. One discovery that I made was that the flirtations learned in front of my mirror could send messages I did not intend if used across a table, and one experience with that cured me. But it was probably a hangover from my fantasy days that later made it easy for me to fall in love for the first time with Todd. He not only looked like James Stewart but he drawled in the

same way and had the same diffident air. It is likely that both
he and his look-alike movie idol cultivated this abashed man-
ner, though it seemed natural enough in Todd, who was
nineteen, tall and slightly awkward. I was eighteen, living in
a rented room in Richmond, and at that time I had met only
a few men I would go out with. Each could barely get through
an evening before requesting sexual payment, which I refused. I had picked up a lot of information about sex from
friends since I left home, and I had no taste for experience.

Todd played a French horn in a WPA orchestra. The WPA
(Work Projects Administration of the Franklin Roosevelt era)
sheltered, among other things, a number of artistic endeavors
that saved artists from starving during the Depression. Under
its aegis, writers wrote now-classic accounts of how people of
the time lived, photographers were paid to document life in
small towns and on farms and musicians received bare subsist-
ence wages to bring great musical works to backwaters of
culture.

I met Todd when I visited a friend at a rooming house
several blocks from me in Richmond. It was at a time when
I had no regular employment, as much leisure as I wanted and
almost no money. It was understood then that nearly all single
men one met in the thirties had no money either. I never
asked, but Todd probably received no more than twelve dollars a week, if that, and most of it went to pay for a room,
whatever he ate, and cigarettes.

When we were introduced, he lingered longer than necessary at the door of Thea's room, asking me where I lived and
if we would like to go down to the corner for a drink. We did,
and when I found out he played the French horn, I asked if
he knew the signature melody for Wagner's *Siegfried,* a nota-
ble part for his instrument. The *Siegfried Idyll* had been

bought by my mother at a record sale a few months before and I loved it. Todd responded by singing the melody right in the middle of drinking his Coke. He was the first man I'd met who knew anything about the kind of music I listened to. When we finished our drinks we walked back to his rooming house, where Thea left us, and he went with me along the old brick sidewalks to mine. He kept his hands in his pockets except when smoking, and did not once leer.

We began a friendship during which we walked through the city and into the parks three or four afternoons and nights a week, sometimes more. Since the park we frequented most was at least three miles away, and we walked around within it, we had a great deal of exercise. Our silences were easy, but we found much to talk about besides, little of which I remember now. Mildly flirtatious exchanges and silly jokes were part of it, and Todd did tell me of his hometown in North Carolina. He impressed me by saying he played chess with his father by mail; the two of them wrote their moves on postcards. We kissed chastely and leaned against each other on park benches, holding hands. Then we walked again to find a place open where we could sit over coffee (five cents a cup) until midnight, when he walked me back to my rooming house.

All through the rest of that winter and into spring we walked and talked. If the winds were bitter, we sat at coffee somewhere. Once in a while he would take me to a third-run theater, but that was a luxury. At the time I received three dollars a week from home for spending money, and sometimes I paid my own way.

His engagement with the orchestra was over in May, and he had to go home. On his last night with me, he must have spent everything he had to take me dancing at a hotel that boasted an orchestra. I asked him about such extravagance and he said, "It's all right; I know somebody in the band." We rode a bus to the hotel downtown, I in evening dress and he in the black-and-white attire he wore in the orchestra. I can't remember that it was a tuxedo; I can't be sure it was not. He did wear a black tie. We rode back at midnight and he asked to come in with me to say good-bye. As we came into the hall, we could hear my landlady's husband snoring upstairs. In the living room, he was overcome to the point of pulling me close. For the first time our closeness and his kiss stirred me down to my boots, and I drew back in surprise to find that he was as astonished by it as I. He stared at me and touched my cheek, smoothed my hair, did not smile.

"Would you?" he whispered. "It would be the first time for me."

I caught his hand and in a moment shook my head, overwhelmed that so suddenly a friend had become desired and desiring. It was not because I didn't want him closer, but because I was afraid. So was he. Backing away from each other with sorrow, we parted virgins.

Todd left the city and we never heard from each other again. I have remembered him with a wistful, girlish love for fifty-odd years.

Through the years of marriage and motherhood, the "you" of myself rarely emerged. The days were full of seemingly constant talk with children, husband, friends, pediatricians, dentists, orthodontists, teachers and other parents. The hours alone were so rare that I felt no need to clutter them with words.

But now I live alone and find myself addressing a "you" who may have valuable insights to contribute. Our talk is desultory but companionable. Sometimes when an old regret visits and cannot be readily shaken, I can count on her to say, "Well, you did the best you could," or "You can't do it for them; they have to find out their own way." She is handy with commonplaces, but they are comforting, and I would miss her if she were not there when needed.

6

Sisters

During the summers of my early childhood, our farmhouse was filled on weekends with people coming and going; there were cars in the yard, sometimes a horse or two with reins dropped over fence posts, laughter up and down the stairs, the hand-cranked phonograph playing and feet dancing.

I knew the visitors were there because of my sister Daphne, who, at seventeen, was twelve years older than I. Her classmates were the ones who enlivened our house: girls who looked like women to me, and boys who dressed like men. These youthful swains, often in pants buttoned just below the knee above long socks, and wearing sleeveless sweaters over white shirts, stood about in the house or in the front yard, talking to girls. The girls were draped on porch railings or up and down the porch steps. Some of them wore their hair cut even with the lobes of their ears (as Daphne did); a few had long hair still, knotted behind their heads. Their dresses were bright pastels with deep flat collars, so shapeless that they did not hint of bosoms or waistlines. I do not remember that any of my sister's friends wore the flapper skirt length we now associate with the twenties. Their skirts covered their knees and the round garters upon which they rolled their hose were out of sight.

The tallest boy was Quinton, and he sometimes wore riding boots with tan pants tucked in their tops. He called me "Baby," a name he conferred on me when I actually was one. He was the most at ease in our house because he lived only a mile and a half away and was there, I think, whenever Daphne was. He had been coming to our house since she was barely into her teens.

On Saturdays he usually rode up on his shiny brown mare (on Sundays he had the family car if no one else needed it), and as his boots stepped onto the front porch, Daphne came down the stairs in knickers and riding hat, with a tassel dropping over her ear to one shoulder. Quinton would watch her descend, then follow her to the kitchen, where my mother was usually making something. He was always superbly polite to my mother and asked after her health and about Allison, and whether she needed his help with anything. My mother treated this as the formality it probably was.

Daphne and Quinton told my mother where they were going, undoubtedly a parental requirement, then went out to the barn, where he led out our little horse Nita, saddled her and helped Daphne up. I always wondered why, since Daphne was in the habit of swinging herself easily into the saddle. Together they would canter out of the yard, through the gate and into the road that went one way to Frederick Station and the other to the village of Jouett. I would watch them go, terribly envious. My greatest longing was for a pony or a horse of my own, and when they were out of sight I got on my favorite long stick and cantered about on it for an hour, being seventeen.

Quinton was there, of course, when the others were, and was one of those putting records on the phonograph while couples danced from the living room into the hallway, down the hall, into the kitchen and back into the living room. At some point the records would stop and all of them would squeeze into whatever cars were there and drive off with a great deal of laughter and shouting above the motor racket. They would be back before dusk, and some went home, but there were always a few who stayed, Quinton among them, filling plates with food my mother had prepared and eating on the front porch.

No matter what was happening, I had to go to bed by eight o'clock. One night when Daphne had a special party, Japanese lanterns were strung up on cords running from one big oak tree to another. The candles inside glowed with soft mothlike colors around the yard. I was allowed to turn around in bed and put my pillow in the windowsill near the foot so I could watch what was going on. Somebody—probably Daphne—was playing a ukulele, there was singing and a couple was trying to dance in the yard. I fell asleep before I could find out what else happened. In the morning there were leftover tiny cakes decorated with real violets that my mother had candied, some paper hats and party favors. Daphne and a friend were still asleep. When they both finally came downstairs I hung around listening, smelling their perfume, looking at their satin slippers, drinking in the way that girls looked when they grew up, what they said, how they said it.

I closely watched my oldest sister move through those days that in my memory are always summer. To me, Daphne was beautiful. Her teeth were white and even, her smile wide and warm. Her hair was bright brown with a slight burnish of red, and her skin was cool and white and untanned. I, who wished to be like her, had the darkest hair in the house and was in the sun so much that she called me "Tarbaby." Her eyes were the only ones blue-gray like our father's; she had a slight dimple in one cheek when she laughed and a faintly cleft chin.

I hardly associate this girlish Daphne in my memory with winters at all. During her high school years I was very young and when I try to picture her then she seems to flicker in and out of my consciousness. I was told later that she had to live with a minister and his family during the school year. From their house she could walk the distance to school easily. My mother took her there in the buggy in September, Daphne's trunk strapped on behind and the little horse Nita hitched to the rear of the buggy, wearing her saddle. She was stabled at the parsonage for my sister's use in riding home on nice weekends. The distance was nine miles and became too difficult for Daphne to cover on horseback once winter deepened and the days darkened early. Then my mother fetched her home for Thanksgiving and Christmas holidays, driving with the buggy top up and ample lap robes for warmth.

But summer was different. I seem to remember her at home in the long summer days and how life picked up and danced.

My mother was the happiest I ever knew her to be during those summers of Daphne's girlhood. On the weekends she wore her most attractive dresses, though she covered them with an apron and spent most of her time in the kitchen. She expected Allison and me to clean ourselves up as well, especially on Sunday, and used this as a way to keep me from underfoot in the afternoon. Just before Sunday dinner, she would call me into the house and say, "It's time for you to take your bath."

If there was a friend of Daphne's in the living room, she would hear us and look into the kitchen, saying, "Is that

Tarbaby?" I did not like anyone but Daphne to call me that and would have an attack of shyness, standing mute.

"She's getting ready to go upstairs and clean up a bit," my mother would say, meaning that no matter how I looked now, I would undergo improvement. "Run along," she'd add. "There's something you'll like for lunch."

Upstairs in my sister Allison's room, the washstand would be waiting for me. I would drop my dirty dress, socks and underwear in a heap and pour warm water out of the pitcher into the big china basin. I liked the smell of soap and the oilcloth covering the washstand and of fresh water, liked making thick suds and creaming them on my skin. I would wash my face and on down, hitting most of the places I could see. Then I would put the basin on the floor and step in it so I could wash my legs. The water would be mostly suds by now, but I didn't care. When I stepped out and wiped the suds off with a towel, my skin felt taut and clean. Then I would go to the door as instructed, open it an inch and yell, "I'm through."

From below my mother would answer, "All right."

There would be a pause in the talk of visitors who heard my yell and I would listen to it pick up again, trying to understand what was said.

As I was putting on a clean thin vest and drawers, I could hear Allison coming up the steps. She carried the tray with my lunch on it, and would set it on a shelf out of my reach.

"Let me see if you've washed first," she'd say, not with enthusiasm but because she'd been told to do it.

"I did wash," I'd say as she lifted my arms, but even I could see that there were dirty places left.

"Look at that. You're not clean."

I hated having Allison check me over, but she didn't like

doing it either. She would have been reading, drawing, helping in the kitchen or sitting in the living room with the others
when Mother sent her upstairs.

"You didn't touch back here," she'd tell me, looking at the
back of my neck and applying chilly water. The washcloth
scrubbed up into my hair, not gently.

"Hurry up," I'd say. "Everything's getting cold."

"It's dirty here too."

"Ouch!"

"Stop yelling. If you weren't such a dirty kid—"

"I am not. Hurry up."

Finally Allison would have rewashed much of me, except
the front of my legs, given me the tray and left. I would
inspect the tray's contents with pleasure, feeling no resentment at having to eat alone. It usually had on it fried chicken,
a roll, some fruit and a slice of cake, pie or whatever dessert
my mother had made for the guests. The tray cloth was a fine
linen towel, embroidered, and there was a cloth napkin for
covering my clean underwear. I looked forward to these solitary meals on Sundays; I could not say why, but they made
me feel quite loved. When I was finished I was supposed to
take a nap, and sometimes I did. If sleep did not come I looked
out of the window and across the fields, listening to birds
singing, humming to myself. The naps in my life were mostly
taken before I learned to read.

I would always wake up when Daphne's friends began calling back and forth as they were getting ready to leave in the
cars. I had learned not to press my face against the screen to
watch because then someone would see me and point. Suddenly I would remember I wasn't supposed to be seen in my
underwear and retreat to watch them from deeper in the
shadows. Daphne and her friend Grace were usually in Quin-

ton's car, Daphne with a band about her hair and laughing. Three more of her friends would be in back. Quinton would spin the crank protruding from the front of the car, and when it shuddered into sudden ignition, he would rush around to the steering wheel to feed gas to keep the motor turning while he vaulted over the closed door into the driver's seat. The whole business made a dreadful din and sent up a cloud of partly burned gas. Then they would back and turn those ugly vehicles across our yard and drive off down the road, raising a great deal of dust. The silence left seemed empty, and so did the afternoon ahead. But then my mother would come in with the dress I was to wear, either the yellow one with a row of chicks embroidered in black, or the pink one she had smocked. I would have to change underwear for these; she had made matching undergarments like rompers with drop seats. I suppose it was fashionable; all the dresses she made for me for several years had matching underwear with elastic in the legs. Modest but hot. With these Sunday outfits I would wear black strap shoes over long white socks, but only when I was not likely to be running full tilt anywhere. For every day I was the only girl in the world made to wear hightop, dull brown shoes. Other children went barefoot in the summer, or at least their shoes didn't lace up over their ankles. My mother believed my ankles were weak.

"Where did Daphne go?" I would invariably ask.

"Just for a drive," my mother would say. "They're taking Lila home." Or Ruby or Edith or Lucy.

A drive. I would wonder each time what that was like, and when I was released clean to the outdoors and told to stay that way, I would convert the big wheelbarrow into an open car. I would sit at the front with a made-up friend much like Daphne's friend Grace, and steer and make motor noises. In between bursts of the engine, I would tell her, "There's Charlie-the-bootlegger's house," and "There's where Mrs. Emlaw lives; she has a buggy with mirrors and vases in it." We soon ran out of places to go because I had not traveled enough to imagine more. Besides, my mouth was tired from making Model-T noises; they were much more strenuous than the sounds of later models.

Tennis fever swept the nation in the twenties; Helen Wills's bare knees under her tennis dress flashed from front pages in a time when photographs were not lavishly used in newspapers. Helen Wills at Wimbledon, Helen Wills at Forest Hills, Helen Wills at the White House and Helen Wills slamming the bejabbers out of her opponents.

Tennis racquets were what my sisters wanted for Christmas, though no one around had a court and they couldn't play until spring. My father sent a net too, and in April it was strung up over the grass and balls were batted over it. But of course this was not acceptable, and by summer Daphne and her friends pined for a real tennis court. Quinton approached his father, but Mr. Painter was a horse-and-hounds man and thought tennis somewhat effeminate.

There was much talk about making a tennis court under the trees, and I heard Daphne say, "If we have it here, Tar-baby can run after the balls." When enthusiasm reached a suitable pitch among their friends, Daphne and Quinton went into the house to talk to my mother. She came back out with them, drying her hands on her apron, to listen to excited plans for the broad space between two large oaks.

"We can do all the work, Mrs. Bell," Quinton kept saying, joined by a chorus of yes indeeds from the others. There was no thought of a hard-surface or clay court. They would pack

the dirt hard, they said, and it would be just fine. My mother,
I'm sure, saw this as another way of keeping daughters enter-
tained at home with wholesome activity; anyway, that's what
she wrote to my father. Quinton immediately brought a load
of sawdust from a sawmill on the Painter land, and he and
Solomon used it to build up one end of the regulation space
until it was level.

Daphne and her friends did do all the rest. They cleared
the weeds from a large area. They shoveled and hauled wheel-
barrows of sand (our land was quite sandy, and there were
patches of it along our driveway) to cover the sawdust. Bumps
were leveled, dips filled in, and the space was raked to even-
ness. Finally it was packed down by the boys, who rolled a
large barrel full of rocks back and forth over it until it barely
registered a footprint. When Daphne and Grace filled the
lines with whitewash, a cheer went up. In front of my mother,
Allison, Susan and me they opened a new can of tennis balls
in celebration. I remember keenly the wonderful smell of
uncanned tennis balls even now.

They played to exhaustion that first afternoon; my mother
sent me out with lemonade and cookies but no dinner invitation. They did not go home until it was too dark to play. I
was given my supper, but no mention was made of food for
anyone else. Not until they had all limply climbed in cars to
go home did our family finally eat. I suppose my mother
thought the tennis court was enough to provide; she did not
propose to feed the players every weekend.

This homemade court was used for all the summers that
Daphne was home. There seemed nothing incongruous to us
in our having a tennis court filled with young people with
good racquets in front of our seedy-looking house, which by
that time badly needed several coats of paint. Evidently my

mother believed that it was important to give us some experiences of the more affluent young when she could. Her theory seemed to be that her children would not then be country-unsophisticated when life required them to move into a larger world. Meanwhile our white house could go gray, the yard unshorn by sheep (a local method of mowing), and the barn door could sag off its hinges.

When Daphne went off to college, life changed for all of us. That was when my mother bought the car, partly because she believed she should earn an income to help with Daphne's expenses. Perhaps life was suddenly taking a quieter turn for her; all through Daphne's high school days she had been immersed in whatever play or party was planned or given by Daphne's class. When scenes from *H.M.S. Pinafore* were put on to raise money for seats for the auditorium, my mother created costumes from the trunk of velvets, silks and other scraps she had been accumulating for years. Both she and Daphne were clever with their needles, and they giggled together when creating something out of scraps. If a sudden skit was proposed to entertain the school board, over a weekend my mother, proud that Daphne had a lead, would produce a dress for Martha Washington, a uniform for a Red Cross nurse of World War I or a modest harem costume of opaque materials.

All plays were scheduled in the fall and spring, when roads were passable for parents. Audiences were small because the high school, set in a village bordered by farms, served a region of low population. Some of Daphne's classmates boarded where she did or with other families. The rest walked and a few came by horseback. Teachers boarded locally too, even into my high school years. The few who had cars could not afford to use them to drive to work over the terrible roads.

Most of the teachers were from towns and cities, and they introduced their students to books, plays and music. A few served in quiet frustration trying to reach the brain centers of children unacquainted with any books except the Bible and Sears, Roebuck catalogs. The school's library was almost nonexistent. When told about this dearth of books, a friend of ours who was a teacher in Chicago sent boxes of used readers, old classics, histories, and math and science texts, and for years these were the core of our school library. Pupils were forced by determined and exasperated teachers to listen to *Little Women, Tom Sawyer* and *Gulliver's Travels* read to them in class.

My mother's years of being active in school functions almost ceased when Daphne graduated. Much of her time not devoted to the farm had been absorbed in being Daphne's mother and costumer. Neither Allison nor I could give her this joy in such full measure—not then, not later. Whatever it was that Daphne had we did not have.

To Allison and me, Daphne's absence was nothing new; we had seen little of her when she was in high school. Now when she came home from the college seventy miles away she came on the train to Frederick Station and my mother picked her up in the car. If the roads were impassable with ice, snow or mud, my mother took the wagon and plow horse, and they drove home wrapped in blankets.

My sisters were changing subtly. Only I seemed to stay the same. Allison was fourteen and growing tall and too thin; my mother probably never realized how her way of calling Allison "Lanky" gave her pain. Her brown hair waved over her shoulders and down between her shoulder blades nearly to her waist. Some days she could barely breathe and stayed in bed wheezing, propped high on pillows. My mother would drive several miles to ask Dr. Chiles to see her. He came when he could, listened to Allison's chest, teased her a little and told my mother to feed her well on milk, eggs and cod liver oil. "If you'd get rid of that cat," he'd say to Allison, "you wouldn't have so much trouble breathing." The cat slept on her bed and was her only companion through tedious hours.

"He says that," Allison told my mother, "because he doesn't like cats." The doctor also thought that living on a chicken farm might be partly to blame. He left her a bottle of medicine and told my mother she might outgrow her constricted breathing. In my memory, Allison seems to have been in and out of bed during all my childhood years. She was subject to attacks of asthma and her wheezing was the evidence clearly heard in the lower hall and in my mother's room below hers. When the attacks passed she was up and helping around the house, going to school, planting seeds that grew and bloomed with a profusion no one else could coax out of flowers. While her bouts with asthma persisted, she had the characteristic dark circles under her eyes and the the wan, white look of patients who fight for breath. By the time she was ready to leave home, her asthma seemed to abate, and she blossomed into a pretty young woman with pink-and-white skin, short brown waving hair and brown eyes flecked with green, the color of my mother's eyes and of mine.

Dr. Chiles, who in those years spent so much time at our house, liked my mother, but he was one of the people she treated with formality and never asked to dinner. He used to drop by to "see how Allison is," first in his trim, shiny buggy and later in a shiny car. If no one was sick, my mother met him on the porch and did not ask him to come in. He was a small man, trim, dapper and attractive, but considerably shorter than my mother. I remember him standing for an hour talking, one foot on the path and the other on the first step, and my mother on the porch above him. The gleam in his eye was more than amusement, and she did not miss its meaning. Her auburn hair was slowly darkening to brown, she was still slim and graceful, and she had the self-contained carriage of her independence. His admiration, which he hinted at in a low voice, made her uncomfortable, and even when he was making a professional call, she moved steadily toward the door before him when it was over. My mother was not without coquettishness, but she did not practice it—in fact, kept it under strict control—whenever a lone male visitor was in her house.

In those years Allison and I hardly ever enjoyed each other's company. She was safe from me, "the Pest," when she was in bed, and did not suffer me gladly when she was up and about. I asked silly questions and enjoyed stupid things, things she had outgrown. She slammed her door when I wanted to come in and told me to go away and let her alone. I'd stand outside and yell insults, and once, when tried beyond her short endurance, she jerked the door open, slapped me and slammed the door again. I am not surprised now, but I was then.

Allison could not have been more than fourteen and I seven when our mother came home one summer afternoon, staggered from the buggy and retched into a flower bed near the porch. She had left the horse and buggy in the driveway without hitching them. Pale and queasy, she made it to her room by holding on to things in the hall and then she collapsed on her bed. I followed her, frightened and astonished; I had never seen my mother sick before.

"Go get Allison," Mother said, and closed her eyes.

I was afraid she was dying and I do not remember going for Allison, but she was probably upstairs. When she went into Mother's bedroom I hovered near the door.

"What's the matter, Mother? Are you sick?" She bent over to remove my mother's shoes.

"I'm terribly dizzy," Mother said. "I can't raise my head without getting nauseated."

"Oh, Lord," Allison said. "We'd better get the doctor."

"No, no, I'll be all right after a while. It must be something I ate." I could hardly hear her. "But ask Solomon to put the horse and buggy away."

Allison went to find Solomon and I tiptoed up to the bed. "Mother?" I whispered to her closed eyes.

She opened and shut them immediately. "You run along, honey, and help Allison. Mother's sick."

I stood, not moving, afraid her paleness was terminal. "I'll fix you some lemonade," I said.

A look of revulsion swept her face and she half groaned, "No, please. Just run along and let me sleep a little."

That night Allison undressed her as well as she could, and my mother, by lying flat with eyes shut, was able to undo her corset. Getting her into a nightgown was a slow process, done between Mother's seizures of vertigo every time she sat up.

The next day Mother still could not raise her head. When she opened her eyes it was to find everything spinning. She could not drink or eat, and Allison had to take over the kitchen to prepare her own meals and mine. Solomon, as concerned as anyone, went for Dr. Chiles. Susan was away, off making her annual visit to Ashland, Kentucky.

When the doctor came, he found that my mother's blood pressure was far too low. "No wonder you feel dizzy," he told her. "It won't kill you, but it will make you wish you were dead." He took out a large bottle of dark medicine, probably iron-and-liver tonic, and told Allison to give her ice chips that she could dissolve in her mouth lying down.

"I can't possibly swallow that," my mother said, waving at the bottle.

"Yes, you can. Lie still, keep your eyes closed and I don't think it will bother you." He asked for a spoon and demonstrated. She grimaced, but that was all.

During the time that my mother lay there—I remember it as weeks, though perhaps it was one—Allison had to contend with my brattiness as well as meals. I did not take her reign in the kitchen with good grace. When she told me to wash my hands, bring in water and dry dishes, I marched up to my mother's bed and complained of her bossiness. When she told me not to bother Mother and to go outside, I refused. She pulled me by one arm and I hit her with the other. She repaid me with a harder punch and I ran crying for the bedroom.

My mother managed to put an arm around me and say, "Vallie, you must stop acting like a spoiled little girl. Allison has to do everything right now. You can at least try to help her."

I turned away uncomforted, feeling blamed, feeling mean. I did not like myself.

Gradually my mother improved. On a day that she could sit up and eat something besides milk toast, Allison produced a wonderful pie made with cottage cheese, eggs and lemon rind. She received praise from my mother and even from me, and I discovered how good it felt to be nice to her.

I would like to remember that I became more helpful and less churlish thereafter, but I don't think my disposition improved noticeably until my mother reappeared in the kitchen. When she did, my dislocated world slipped back into place and I could admire what Allison had done. Of course I did not go so far as to say so.

By the time I was eight years old, we no longer had to go to a tiny two-room elementary school; the county began providing school buses. Roads were graded and scraped, though still unpaved, dusty in summer and fall and awful in winter. We rode nine miles each way to Apple Grove High School, grades one through twelve, a large wooden structure heated by stoves. Behind it was a sort of cottage, on one side of which classes in home economics were held, on the other, shop and agriculture instruction for boys.

Sisterhood was hard on both Allison and me in the close confines of the school bus. In adolescence, she was regularly embarrassed by my loudness and overactivity. If I got into trouble and was picked on by others, she could not come to my rescue because she was physically frail and probably thought I'd brought it all on myself anyway, which was as least partly true. She could only turn her head and pretend that I was no relation when I slammed books on the heads of my tormentors. Older boys would eventually grab the younger ones in a straitjacket embrace when they were going after me and the situation would calm down.

At home Allison told Mother what a disgrace I was, and I would say indignantly, "But he was trying to take my lunch box," or my books or my shoes.

My mother sighed and looked off into the distance. "You could sit up front," she said.

But I said I couldn't. "The older girls get on first and they sit up front," I explained, knowing this was not necessarily true. What I couldn't say and probably didn't know was that I liked fighting with boys; it was a lot more fun than sitting properly in a row of girls. Usually we girls rode along the benches on the sides, facing a backless center bench, where the boys sat, along with a few girls who found no other spaces.

It was not uncommon for shoes to be thrown out of the bus window, or for someone's cap to be heaved into bushes along the road. The victim would yell, "He threw my cap out!" and the driver would stop and turn around in his seat. Everyone grew quiet under his stare except for a few giggles.

"Who threw it out?"

Silence.

"You, Eddie?"

"It won't me."

"Jake?"

"Me neither."

His eye settled on one boy shrinking behind a larger one near the back. "Benny, you git out there and git that thing you threw out."

"Me?" Benny was astonished.

"You."

So Benny went back and retrieved whatever it was, and then was told to sit up front near the driver, sometimes between two silent Woodford girls. The Woodfords, I know now, were not humorless, but Allison and I thought they were. They just did not find amusing anything that happened on the bus. There were three of them, all with uncut brown hair in braids down their backs, all in dresses longer and fuller than anyone else's, and with sturdy, opaque underclothes. Their land bordered on ours to the northwest and they were excellent farmers. Their house was big and white and smelled year-round of mothballs. At the beginning of cold weather they did too. I had to grow up to realize what fine, rugged, kind, dependable people they were.

Allison was growing up and away from us. She stayed in her room studying, reading or drawing when the weather was warm. Her drawings were becoming quite skillful, I heard my mother say. I remember some of them; there was a hint of laughter in her pictures of me reading with my black stockings wrinkling down about my shoes, in her portrait of our doctor, in her sketches of cats and my pet blue jay. I liked watching her draw, though she allowed that rarely; usually she was upstairs with her door closed.

Mother called her each evening at milking time to strain the milk, and less and less did she do this readily. I suppose it was a point of discipline with my mother, but the milk would sit there and she would call Allison three or four times, the last with much irritation. She may have understood that Allison was declaring her own independence, but apparently thought this could not be admitted or permitted. Finally my sister would drift down the stairs, her expression a "Don't speak to me" one. My mother would say, "Let's have a nicer expression," and Allison would scowl and turn her back. I don't remember what was said next, but it was loud and scathing. These arguments were painful for me and I hated them because they were often settled only by my mother's quick, hard slap and "Don't you talk back to me." Allison would turn and run upstairs to hide her tears and Mother would have to strain the milk after all. I learned not to go up softly and call to Allison in sympathy; at these moments she hated everyone in the family.

"Allison," I tried once, whispering through the keyhole.

"Go away."

I turned the knob, determined to go in anyway, and she stared at me, her eyes red, her mouth hurt, and said, each word stressed painfully: "You get out of here and don't ever come in here again."

While I was dancing more or less happily through those days, I was aware that Allison was often miserable. She had no use for my talk, my table manners ("Don't mupple so!" she used to say furiously to me as I chewed next to her) or my opinions. Sometimes I would indignantly report what she said, but mostly I did not. Any punishment of her was so uncomfortable for me that I covered my ears and went outside.

My mother's disciplined childhood had taught her that parental dicta should never be questioned, and she did not know how to cope with Allison's rebellion. Both of them wanted—insisted on—the last word. The best last word was a slammed door; they both used it, and both ended up feeling miserable afterward.

There was ample reason, I suppose, for each of them to think the other was wholly unreasonable, but I believed, as did Allison, that our mother was sometimes too harsh with her. It was not anything I could have expressed at the time even if I hadn't been afraid to say anything. Allison was a sensitive child, a fact that my mother, though essentially kind, never seemed to acknowledge. Apparently my mother had spent many nights holding the infant on her shoulder during Allison's early attacks of asthma so the baby could breathe and sleep. Her own exhaustion may have made her unwittingly resent a child who required so much of her. It is hard to know how she could have done so when one looks at the photographs she made of Allison at three and four years. They show a clear-eyed, pure-browed little girl with long waving hair catching the light until it becomes a halo. Her face looks out, grave, faintly shadowed and lovely. While Daphne's early pictures are of an engaging, smiling child, and mine are of a small, suntanned girl nicknamed Tarbaby, Allison's are of an ethereal being.

My mother's authoritarian voice reduced my own rebellion to pliability (I never heard her argue with Daphne; they seemed to coexist as friends), but it made Allison stand up for herself until forced down. Mother took umbrage at any back talk and believed in putting uppity children back in the Victorian place she considered proper. Beyond that, it is probable that she and Allison were so different in temperament that they could not help but wound each other.

7

Baptism

I must have been about eight years old when I first saw a Bible, and I was astonished by its vivid and dramatic pictures. It wasn't ours; if my family owned a Bible it was kept out of sight, or perhaps with reference books no child would have explored. The Bible I saw was in the little two-room house that belonged to Susan, the black woman who stayed with my sister and me whenever Mother was away. When it was time for her to go home after our mother came back, I often went with her to stay for an hour or so. I fetched water for her, fed her chickens and pulled weeds for her pig.

Susan's Bible was very new. She had bought it from a salesman who stopped regularly at our house with a great suitcase full of flavoring, spices, unguents and creams. My mother rarely bought anything from him, and rather discouraged him, but he had managed to come when she was not there and opened that splendid display of wares for Susan's wonderment and ours. He assured her the Bible was a great bargain—only five dollars and worth more, and she could pay him a little each time he came, a quarter a month for a beautiful, holy book. She made the transaction with painful hesitancy, but the Bible became her treasure and justified the sacrifice.

I had a passion for books and I had never seen one like this, except my book of fairy tales. Looking at it with me, Susan tried to explain that it was the word of God and that I would know about it if I went to church.

Allison and I were regularly invited to church and Sunday school by the Woodfords. They drove a superb black carriage with three seats, oval windows and a black fringe all around. I think they used it only on Sundays, and to attend funerals and weddings. It was my heart's desire to ride in it, and I asked my mother to let me go to church with them just once. "Why can't we go?" I wanted to know as that lovely vehicle with its two dark horses rolled out of our gate after the tenth invitation.

"I've told you, you wouldn't like it," she said. "It would mean sitting still for a long time. Maybe when you're older and more dignified."

"But they might not have a carriage then."

"Is that the reason you want to go?"

"Well, and I'd like to see what church is like." But it was really the carriage and she knew it.

I was unclear about why we did not go to church the way our neighbors did. My mother always thanked the Woodfords for inviting us, and always refused, giving no reason. It was to become evident years later that she did not want to incur the wrath of my father, who believed that churchgoing would fill our young minds with myths and lies. I suspect now that there was more to his proscription than that. I think it lay in our possible exposure to stories of sexual transgressions and to words like "adultery" and "covet" (as in "covet thy

neighbor's wife"). My mother would have agreed with him;
both dreaded our thinking about, and even more, our asking
questions about, words they did not want to define.

When I discovered Susan's Bible I was astonished at what
I'd missed. In it were large colored pictures of men and
women with great white wings, sometimes outspread and
sometimes furled behind them, curving above their heads
and shoulders. I thought how marvelously one could swoop
and glide on those magnificent wings, and could imagine the
rush of air, the marvel of flying.

"I wish I had wings like that," I told Susan.

"People like us don't have wings," she said.

"They're like us," I said, pointing, though I remember that
all the faces in that Bible were white, a fact that seemed not
to bother us at the time.

"No, honey, them is angels. You have to die and go to
heaven to be an angel."

This was completely new to me, and I was full of questions.
Susan had to start by explaining God to me as "who made
you and me and everybody." She said He'd made the earth
and sky and sun and moon and all the animals as well. "And
if you be good, when you die He will let you be one of His
angels." At that point I thought there was nothing I would
rather be than an angel, and as soon as possible if there were
some way it could be accomplished without dying.

All that summer I imagined myself with wings, spreading
my arms as I leaped down the hill, from the tops of gates, the
woodpile, anything. And all that summer I begged Susan to
tell me about the pictures in her Bible, and she read some of
the text with me leaning against her shoulder, reading along
with her pointing finger. There was a picture of a man in
something that looked like my nightgown, his gold-brown

hair falling to his shoulders, his eyes looking upward. Susan told me he was Jesus, and then she had to explain him too. He was shown healing sick people, sitting at a table with men on either side, and ascending toward heaven barefoot on a cloud.

If I had kept all this to myself and pondered it in my heart I would not have found myself in trouble. But I insisted on telling Allison with some superciliousness that she would not go to heaven if she didn't stop whatever it was I wanted her to stop. An eight-year-old telling this to a fifteen-year-old brings on herself nothing but scorn. "Where do you get that heaven stuff?" she asked.

When I told her she asked me how I knew it was true. "It is true," I said, offended. "Susan says so."

"Go ask Mother," she told me and turned her back.

In some agitation I sought out my mother, who was kneeling in the bean row of the garden. Indignantly I told her that Allison had laughed at me when I told her about Susan's Bible, and had asked how I knew it was true. "It is true, isn't it?" I demanded. "Susan says it is."

My mother did not answer right away. She pulled off her gloves and laid them in the basket of vegetables. "The Bible has many stories in it," she said slowly, "and they are thousands of years old. They have been told and retold so many times that they were probably changed and added to. Most of them were told over and over long before people could write things down."

"But Susan says the Bible is the word of God."

My mother sighed and put a hand on my shoulder. "There are other religions besides Christianity," she told me. "They all claim that their writings are the word of God, or at least of divine origin." I was not following her well, but I understood the drift. "When you are older you can read about them yourself and decide what you want to accept. But don't tell Susan what I said. Her feelings about her Bible are important to her."

My feelings about Susan's Bible were important to me too, and were now confounded by my mother's words. I knew without her saying so that she found the subject painful and hoped I would never mention it again, and I did not—to her.

My pursuit of this fascinating new knowledge went underground, spurred on by the hope of qualifying for wings. Whenever I could I asked Susan about the stories in her book, and it proved as rich a mine as my book of *Grimm's Fairy Tales*. Into my head went images of David with his slingshot (I knew about slingshots; boys at school made them out of forked sticks and bands of rubber cut from old tires); Samson and a woman Susan called Dee-ligh; Mary, Joseph and Jesus, who was their son; foot washing, the eating of loaves and fishes, and turning water into wine.

As I am remembering this, there is a sudden shift of scene in my mind and I am instantly present in another year, when my mother-in-law is suffering the long speech of a Methodist relative on the evils of alcohol. Finally my mother-in-law says, "But Aunt Jessie, if it's so bad, why did Jesus turn the water into wine at the wedding in Cana?"

Tight-lipped, Aunt Jessie shakes her head and answers like one betrayed: "I don't know. I just never could understand how He could do such a thing."

Two of Susan's favorite exclamations were "Jesus, I do know!" and "Well, Jesus!" the last said with her voice rising at the end. These words seemed to give her much authority, and I thought she might know a way to my heart's desire. I think I asked her again how I could be an angel with wings;

neither one of us considered that I was interested in dying.

"You got to be baptized, honey, baptized in water, if you want to go to heaven and be an angel."

There were certain Sundays in the summer, Susan said, when her church, the Rising Sun, held baptisms. I wanted terribly to go but realized it would never be allowed; there was no use asking. The matter of color did not occur to me, and she was probably aware that my going would never be a problem. Her description was all my imagination needed for a full-color picture to play on my internal screen.

"The preacher's all in white and he wades out in the river to where it's right deep," she told me, and I saw him moving heavily through water the color of creamed coffee. (All the creeks and rivers were tinged by red clay soil in our part of Virginia.) "He prays out there and the people he's goin' to baptize wait on the creek bank. They's all dressed in white too." I saw their dark heads above their white robes (long, like nightgowns) all bent as the preacher prayed. "The choir is singin' real soft," Susan said. "He reaches out his arms for the first one to come to him. When she gits close he catch her hands and lay her back on his arm and ease her down under the water. The choir starts singin' louder: 'Halleluiah, I'm a child of God, I been washed in Jesus's blood. Halleluiah, I'm sweepin' through the gates.' That's what she hear when she come up out the water. It's a joyful time."

I went about singing this gospel tune and brooding on my own baptism or lack of it. I could not understand why being immersed in water was so important. Finally Susan told me, "You has to be baptized to wash away you sins."

Sin was never spoken of in our house. After listening to some of the Bible verses on sin I understood it to be something you did even if you knew you shouldn't. Probably kicking my sister was a sin, and lying, but was getting up on a horse in the stable sinful? Or trying to ride the pig around the pigpen? I didn't know but thought it would be a good idea to be safe about this. In my desperation I devised a plan for my own baptism and hoped it would be acceptable. One afternoon when my mother was away and Allison was in bed with a slight fever, I asked Susan, "Could you come down the hill with me? I want to show you something."

Susan went to the stairs and called to my sister in her bedroom, "You want anything, Allison? I be out back for a while."

My sister's muffled voice came back, "No, I'm asleep."

Susan laughed and told me, "She talkin' in her sleep now," as we went out back into the hot sunlight.

She followed me down the long sloping hill behind our house, I leaping ahead, she calling as usual, "You watch out for snakes." At the bottom there was a wooded area thick with poplars, young pines and maples.

I sat Susan down on an old cedar tree trunk that twisted near the ground and told her, "You watch that part of the water there." Then I went into a little thicket of pines, took off my dress, put on some old white curtains I had found in a scrap box that morning and brought down the hill. I wrapped one of them around my waist and another around my neck, crossed and tied in the back. From there I went down to the stream, waded a short way and stepped out into the pool that Susan was watching. I heard her say, "Well, Fathers . . . !" and then I dunked my whole self. I had to squat under the water to do it because it was not very deep. Quickly I stood up, squeezed shut my eyes, which were full of water, folded my hands and said, "I am now baptized in the name of Jesus Christ. Amen."

I opened my eyes and looked at Susan to see her in deep prayer, her face completely hidden in her apron. I stepped out of the water, walked in my squishing shoes up the bank (I had orders never to go barefoot) and, dragging the wet curtains, went up to her bowed figure. Her shoulders were shaking.

"Susan?"

"Hmmmmmm?"

"Am I baptized now?"

There was a brief spasm of her shoulders and she raised her head, took off her glasses and wiped her eyes. Then I understood that she was not praying but laughing so hard that she could not speak. Her laughter was always contagious for me and I stood there sopping, unable not to laugh but not sure that I thought anything was funny. When she did gain a little control Susan said, "You go put on you clothes before you catch col'." She was laughing again, in a special way she had, bent over with one arm slapping her knee.

"Susan," I said.

"Don't mind me, honey, I just . . . What you want?"

"You better not tell Mother."

She was trying hard to stop. She wiped her eyes again and sighed, "Father, I do know," and put her glasses back on. I trailed the sodden curtains behind me into the pine thicket, dropped them and pulled my dress on. It felt warm and dry to my chilled body. I gathered up the curtains and went back to her. By this time she was calmer and put her arm over my shoulders. "Don't mind Susan for laughin', honey. That was real nice, real sweet. You done the best you know how and the good Lord will understand."

"Maybe He will think it's funny too." This was not the effect I had expected my baptism to have.

Susan held on to her laughter and said, "He will under-

stand, honey. He will. I reckon He bound to smile, but He
sho' understand."

We walked back to the house, I quiet and slightly hurt, she
shaken by fits of silent mirth. I asked her not to tell Allison
about it either, but I didn't think she would. Once inside she
said, "You give me you shoes and I put them to dry in the
sun. That way you Mama won't be wonderin' what happen."
She took the curtains too, and hung them on a fence where
they dried well before my mother came home.

Susan did not tell anyone in my family about my baptism,
but she did tell Solomon. Doubtless she had to tell someone,
and she knew he would not repeat it to my mother. I walked
with her to the barn the next day and we found Solomon
bent over washing the cow's udder in preparation for milking.
He smiled up at me and said, "Hear you been sanctified." I
was immediately too shy to answer and found something to
run after, but I heard Susan laugh and looked back to see her
doubled over and Solomon's high-pitched merriment joining
hers.

Though I wanted my baptism to be acceptable on earth and
in heaven, Susan's laughter slightly dimmed the glow I had
first felt about it. Hope that it would by some magic make me
eligible for wings still lingered. All that summer I kept trying
to fly, believing that at some point I would flap my arms and
find I could swoop and soar and float above the farm. For a
while I was nicer too, and quicker to help, enough to make
Allison say to Mother, "What's got into *her?*"

They did not waste time looking for reasons; farm work was
too pressing in the summer. My mother dropped her voice
and said, "Be thankful for small favors," which I heard because I was listening, though for praise, not a verbal shrug.

I visited the scene of my baptism nearly every day. Actually, I had spent a lot of time there before my immersion. It was the most beautiful bit of woodland I knew, divided by a quiet stream, lush with moss and with great tree roots making steps down to the water. I was always happy there, alone or with our collie, Mac. He went along on most of my walks, a rough-coated, unaristocratic young dog, tan, white and black. I sat on the bank of the stream, an arm around his neck, soaking up peace and sunshine, watching the water striders (Susan called them "Jesus bugs" because they walked on water), which dimpled but did not break the surface tension of the stream. Three years later this dreaming spot was to vanish in a forest fire that swept down on our farm from four or five miles away.

My mother never said anything at all about her own beliefs and I was never sure what, if any, she had. I think if I had asked she would have told me, but there were a lot of things I never learned about my mother because—I now tell myself—when I was a child her answer to some personal question was "Never mind that, it's something you don't need to know." I learned early where not to tread, and it stayed with me in later years when she might have needed to talk about things with a sympathetic adult.

Almost the only brush I had with the religions of mankind until I went away to college was through Susan and her Bible, and the chapel exercises we attended one day a week at school. I learned hymns and sang, but I have no recollection of anything the visiting minister talked about to his restless and inattentive captive audience. We were marched to chapel and marched back, each grade herded by its teacher. Chapel was never questioned by any parent, not even mine.

The school bus I rode was full of farm children, some of whom had come to that part of Virginia from the mountains with parents looking for better land for farming. I was an innocent among children who knew more of the struggle for life than I. Most of them went to local churches and bore an ancient, violent hatred of Catholics. They did not know why, and probably their parents also had a bred-in-bone distrust of popery so old that the ancestral meaning had dropped away, leaving only the hate.

Unacquaintance with church caused me some pain when an aggressive boy asked me on the bus, "What church you go to?" When I said I didn't go to church, his sneer was waiting. "You're an old Catholic, that's what you are."

"I am not a Catholic!" I said loudly.

"You are too a mean old Catholic. I seen you at the Catholic church."

When I said, too smartly for my own good, "What were you doing there?" he shouted me down, "Catholic, Catholic, Catholic!"

I was near to tears when I got home and asked my mother what a Catholic was. She told me and I said, "Then I'm not one, am I?" and she said, "Of course not." For some time whenever the kids who rode the bus needed an easy target they called me a Catholic, until I moved up near the driver and sat looking stonily out of the window. As usual, Allison was forced to pretend she did not hear what was going on.

Churchlessness was one of the barriers to my acceptance by other children, but this probably wouldn't have mattered if I had not been a smartass who did not know when to keep quiet. What I said, and I said too much, was with a Yankee accent (actually midwestern), still the mark of an alien sixty-six years after the Civil War had ended.

Also I never learned one necessary bit of southern manners that every one of my classmates knew without being consciously taught. When Mrs. Elmira Duke called on me in class and I, inattentive, said, "What?" she paused and looked at me, waiting. More faintly I asked, "What did you say?"

When she said, "And what else do you say?" it threw me into total confusion. No teacher had corrected me before, but Mrs. Duke was an older southern lady. Around me was the silence that descends on a classroom when one member is catching it.

Mrs. Duke was still looking at me. "I don't know," I barely got out.

"Didn't anyone ever tell you you should say 'ma'am'?"

Oh. That was it. "No," I said.

"No what?"

I was caught again, and there were sniggers. "No ma'am," I mumbled.

Then she said, "Don't you say 'ma'am' to your mother?" This time I shook my head. Mrs. Duke pursed her lips and told me, "You will be expected to say it in this class."

When I reported all this to my mother she was not surprised or indignant, as I thought she should be. "Daphne had to say 'ma'am' to a few teachers, I remember, and it didn't seem to hurt her. Allison probably does too. I think you can do it if it makes Mrs. Duke happy."

I had years of difficulty remembering to add this regional courtesy, which was strictly required in grade school. In my head it became mixed up with the Civil War we studied and the Thomas Nelson Page books that were read to us. There were a lot of "ma'ams" in those stories of the Confederacy.

From fifth to seventh grade we knew of no war in history except the War Between the States, and it was taught as if it had happened yesterday. Some of our teachers had grandparents who had lived through it and who passed on their bitterness about lost husbands and brothers and possessions. As vividly as if they themselves had gone through it, teachers told us how silver was buried in gardens to keep Yankees from taking it, of nothing for families to eat but moldy cornmeal, of never having real coffee, of horses stolen by soldiers of both sides, of women's despair when they heard that Richmond had fallen, of going to church, where there were no men except old ones, of men limping home after defeat so broken that their wives had to carry on the farm work for them.

I listened to these accounts with sadness and pity, never daring to say that my great-grandmother had cousins who fought and were killed on the Union side. It was safe to tell them that my grandfather came from Scotland after the war was over, but not that the mother of the woman he married had once boldly ridden her horse, bedecked with a Union flag, through Confederate lines in Missouri, sure she would be treated with courtesy, as she was.

When I was eleven my history class was taken to Richmond to see Battle Abbey, an edifice built to keep alive the memory of that war. I remember only the enormous murals towering above our heads. The battles they depicted horrified me, not just because of the wounded and dying men in blue and gray (preponderantly gray), but as much again because of the mortal agony of the horses shown. I had never realized that those lovely beasts were also slaughtered by bullets on the battlefield, or left maimed and screaming in pain. Before the end of the tour I could not look at those paintings without crying, so I did not look at all. I moved with my class and kept my eyes at a point below or between the great panels and blurred my focus.

Battle Abbey is now part of the Virginia Historical Society, murmurous with hundreds of people who daily come there seeking the paths of ancestors or researching the histories of family land ownership. Everybody I have met there has been from outside the state. The murals I saw at age eleven are not readily visible, though one may still see them. Today they would affect me in the same way, and I could not face them even now.

8

Daphne and Robert

Suddenly, during her first year at college in 1925, Daphne began to be courted by men with marriage in mind. It began with her Thanksgiving holiday, when the first of them called to take her out for an evening of cards at his sister's. The laughing swirl of young people through the house had disappeared. The girls who used to arrange themselves on the porch and about the tennis court were scattered, some engaged, one at college on the West Coast, and one moved with her family back to New England. And Daphne came home with more invitations then she could accept between written assignments that she had to complete.

By her spring holiday I was getting used to awakening when her high heels clicked up the porch steps late at night and she stopped to talk to Mother before she went to bed. I'm sure my mother and Daphne herself would have been surprised at how much I was learning about the shortcomings of her suitors.

"Well, his mother's nice," I heard her say about one of her dates, "and I like his sister. But Mother, I don't think they ever read anything over there. I couldn't stand a man who doesn't read. . . ." Or after a night out with Quinton: "We drove to Ashland and saw that Clara Bow movie. He was crazy about her; you might know Quinton would be. I'd rather have seen Barrymore, but you know he can't stand anything serious." Then her scorn for an impetuous youth who drove with one arm around her: "I told him I would be too busy to *ever* see him again."

The next morning Daphne would come downstairs about nine o'clock in a pink robe and satin mules. She would sit and drink coffee with Mother, talking more about the night before. They were like a couple of sisters laughing together when I came in from the April morning, having been to the barn, run the length of the road twice, played with the dog and acquired the first layer of dirt for the day. Daphne would reach out a white hand sometimes and say, "Hello, Snub Nose." I liked to catch her cool hand with my hot one, but she always withdrew it—I thought then because my hands were dirty, but I learned later when my own hands grew cool that you don't like to have them held by hot ones.

By summer my mother had chosen her favorite of the men coming to see Daphne. He was a lawyer somewhat older than the rest, and he always brought candy and flowers. He waited in the living room and tried to be polite to me, who for some reason felt an obligation to entertain him when Mother had to be in the kitchen. He did not find this easy; I brought out some of my father's books to show him and he was terribly uninterested.

There were two tall glass-doored bookcases, one on each side of a window, filled with books collected by my father. I do not know why he chose to keep them at the farm unless in the hope that we might read them. I don't think any of us

did—certainly not my mother, who preferred magazines. I
think he considered them proper for a cultured man and I
believe he intended to read them all someday.

Many of them were thick and dark, and did not attract me.
But a few I wanted to read when I could because they looked
interesting and had pictures in them. I remember only a few
titles: some of De Quincey's works, Nathaniel Hawthorne's
Twice-Told Tales, poems and stories by Longfellow and Gib-
bon's *History of the Decline and Fall of the Roman Empire.* Few
if any showed signs of use; the bindings were stiff and the
pages seemed never to have been turned. The ones I chose
to display to visitors were large volumes of Brady's photographs made on Civil War battlefields. Even I knew they were
remarkable, probably because some adult had said so.

Quinton still came to see my sister, still called me "Baby,"
was now selling cars—and driving them fast. Daphne said she
told him she would not ride with him unless he slowed down.
"He said, 'I don't drive fast; this car doesn't go fast,' but I
said, 'I have to hold on with both hands when you turn a
corner, and that's fast.' " My mother murmured that John
Ayres, the lawyer, seemed a nice stable sort and Daphne made
a face. "Mother, he *asks* if he can kiss me. If he didn't ask and
just . . . anyway, he has bad breath." I had discovered the
latter myself, but was more interested that Daphne could tell
my mother about his request. I knew I never would.

Carl Stevens, the farmer-teacher whose house was down
the road from us, was snatching time from his cows, pigs and
sheep to see Daphne once a week. What they did for enter-
tainment is impossible to imagine now and I don't remember
hearing. Livestock showings? Barn raisings? Church socials?
Carl still taught all elementary grades in the little two-room
school I was then attending. Near the close of the school day

he'd read to us from Joel Chandler Harris's Uncle Remus stories, difficult to do unless one has mastered nineteenth-century black dialect. He made it live for us and for himself; once he had fallen out of his teacher's chair because he laughed so hard.

Around Daphne, Carl was subdued and mindful of his manners. He really talked more easily with my mother about crops, contour plowing and pig diseases. My mother liked and respected him but told my sister it wouldn't be easy living in the house with his old mother and father and his perfectionist spinster sister. Anyway Daphne probably never gave Carl a matrimonial thought, even before a new suitor appeared on the scene.

She decided to complete college in three instead of four years and was going to summer school. Her new roommate for the term was Annie Laurie McClough, who also came off of a farm, who planned to teach as Daphne did, and who had an irreverent sense of humor. As soon as she could, Daphne brought her home on a weekend and we all had a wonderful time listening to her stories of her five brothers. "I want Daphne to meet Rob; he's my youngest brother," Annie Laurie told us. "He's never met a girl he could really talk to."

Daphne met Rob in September, when she finally had a weekend free to visit Annie Laurie's family, and we met him a month later, when Daphne was home. They had been writing back and forth, and when he arrived at our house on Saturday they knew each other with the intimacy of people who can say on paper what they cannot in conversation.

Rob was a farmer, but unlike any others we had known. His speech was an engaging amalgam of Virginia southern and highland Scottish. His parents had come to Virginia from Scotland, and of all his four brothers and one sister he alone had a dark gypsyish look. I remember his smile; it would be called crooked, I suppose, because it curved up one side of his face. It showed very white teeth in his sun-darkened face and flashed suddenly under his slightly hooked nose. His hair was heavy and black, and so were his intent eyebrows, but the eyes were a surprising, blazing blue.

That winter their courtship was almost entirely by letter because Rob could not risk driving the roads in his old car. I don't think Daphne said much about him when she was home, though I used to take her letters, sealed with sealing wax, to the mailbox, and I took them often. I brought his to her too, since I usually ran for the mail first. She had stopped seeing anyone else; she needed the time for study, she said, if she was to complete work on schedule.

By summer, though, Rob seemed to be visiting every week-end. I used to come upon them walking in the orchard, sitting on the bench near the tennis court, strolling through the long grasses of a field I liked to run through. They would be talking and laughing. I knew better than to join them, but I would stand at a distance, looking and learning what a young woman looks like walking under apple boughs, carelessly catching a spray of leaves, the grass parted by her fluid walk. Daphne often carried a wide hat and her dresses swayed about her young body. Sometimes I saw them holding hands, but they dropped them self-consciously when I appeared, and Rob stuck his in his pockets.

I suppose my mother could see that things were growing serious between the two of them. She had wondered aloud a few times about how Rob could take care of a farm and yet spend most of the weekend with Daphne. Finally she asked him.

"I do the morning chores and the Da takes care of things when I'm not there."

"The Da?"

"My father. 'The Da' is Scottish for Dad."

"But how about the plowing and planting?"

He gave her his lopsided grin. "Well, I've been out there a few nights when I got home." She didn't say she didn't think that was any way to run a farm; she didn't say anything.

Later, though, as she and Daphne were fixing berries for a pie, Mother said, "Evidently they don't have any hired help. That means they do all the farm work themselves. That's hard and demanding, you know."

Daphne nodded.

"Any woman Rob marries won't have an easy time."

Daphne said, "Yes, I know," her smile creasing a dimple. I saw my mother glance at her and away; she must have been worried then, as she had not been before, that Daphne had almost no acquaintance with what farm wives had to do. Our farm had been where she stayed when she wasn't going to school and where her friends came to visit, but not where she rose to make breakfast, feed chickens, wash clothes, bring in wood, cook, clean and help with outside work.

Sometimes Daphne and Rob would drive off in his old car to visit a high school classmate at Frederick Station, Mary Anne, who had come back from California engaged. Her euphoria and my sister's were well matched, though Daphne wasn't officially promised. They came back from those rides in high spirits, always before supper. Rob managed to eat at least once at our house every weekend. His mother, he said wistfully, had never learned to cook—certainly not the chicken with noodles or roast pork that Mrs. Bell could put on the table. He ate hungrily; when he was there I got only the backs of fried chicken.

During the week Daphne was supposed to be teaching me the fundamentals of arithmetic, and as I sat in her room bent over exercises she was writing letters. She forgot all about me, and if I was quiet I could spend most of the time instead reading the stories she thought I should know. *The King of the Golden River, Hans Brinker and the Silver Skates,* Lamb's *Tales from Shakespeare,* and *Poems Every Child Should Know.* After the letters, she worked on a white negligee she was making, embroidered with wisteria, back and front. I watched; I liked being in the room as she worked. The negligee was a major work and took most of the summer. Sometimes she thought about checking my multiplication.

One August afternoon Daphne and Rob returned from a drive before suppertime, and she went into the house immediately. He came over to where I was swinging.

"What are you doing?" he said, though it was pretty obvious. I slowed to a stop, and before I could answer he said, "Would you like to have a brother?" I looked at him and he laughed, and I understood the laugh. It was from happiness, and he had to do it. I just stared and he said, "I'm your brother now," and he picked me up and hugged me.

I thought it was wonderful and fell in love with him on the spot. I had always wanted a brother, and here was someone handing me one. But he had to explain that it was because he had just married my sister.

I was about to tear madly into the house and shout out the wonderful news to Mother, but Rob put out a hand and said, "Don't go in yet. Daphne is telling your mother."

"When did you get married?"

"A little while ago in town."

"It would be nice to have a wedding—I mean with a cake and everything—wouldn't it?"

He smiled that sideways smile. "Is that what you'd like?"

"Ye-ess. I thought Daphne would get married that way."

"We thought about it, but we decided this way was best. I have to be in the fields all day soon and couldn't see her at all if we put it off."

"Will you take her away?"

He hugged me again. "Isn't that the way it is with brides?"

I was temporarily overwhelmed with what I was hearing, for the moment immobile while thinking about it. Then Daphne came out on the porch and called Rob. He hurried up to her and I heard her say, "She wants to see you. I think she's having a hard time with this."

I was so full of excitement that I went galloping off, skimming bushes and leaping stumps, running through the pasture and startling the cows chewing cuds in the shade. By the time I had made the circle from machine shed and holly tree to barn to woodshed, down the road and around the mailbox and back I saw Daphne and Rob come out on the porch. I tore around to the back door overflowing with goodwill and said to my mother's back, "Mother, Rob said that now he's my brother." I went up to her and she turned slowly, making no attempt to hide her quivering chin and flowing tears.

It was the first and nearly the only time I saw my mother cry, and I was undone. Before I could stutter out anything she turned away and said, "Please leave me alone," and was gone. Her bedroom door closed very quietly and the lock clicked. I burst into tears myself, miserable with the sight of her face and the frightening realization that she was not magnificently strong after all. I went out to the barn and sat in the hay, feeling abandoned and disowned. She had never ordered me away before. It was the worst thing that had happened to me . . . no, that was not true; the worst was knowing that she herself was crying and alone.

I sat there hearing Rob's car start up and drive away and thought: "Daphne's going; he's taking her away." I snuffled up my leftover tears and went back to the house. It was very quiet, and I went softly up to Allison's room. The door was closed as always, and I barely tapped on it. There was a muffled "What do you want?" When I tapped softly again the door jerked open.

"Please," I said, "let me in. Just a minute."

"What's the matter?" She was suddenly without anger, looking at my red eyes and puffy face. I told her; I told her the whole story, leaning against the inside of her door and almost whispering because our mother was in the room below. I assumed that Allison had been in her room all afternoon and knew nothing.

"I'll be darned," she said, looking out the window. "Daphne told me after she told Mother, but anybody could have guessed. . . ."

"But what made Mother cry?" I asked.

"I think she wanted Daphne to marry John," Allison said. John was the lawyer. That wasn't all and I knew it wasn't all, but I could not understand what it was. There was a long silence and then I opened the door to go, and Allison told me, "Don't say anything more about it to Mother." But I wouldn't have; I wouldn't have risked seeing such pain in her face again.

When Rob and Daphne came back from wherever they had been for an hour or so, my mother was back in the kitchen, composed and gracious, her face freshly powdered, her hair carefully done up. After a late supper, which was rather stiff for us all, Rob and Daphne went upstairs together to spend their wedding night under our roof. My mother was able to suggest this arrangement with outward calm and iron control, though her children were not fooled. They recognized her terribly erect back, her higher-than-usual chin.

The next day the newlyweds drove off to live with Rob's

parents in their big house thirty miles away. They were given a bedroom, a living room and a large back kitchen (there were two kitchens in the house). At home, I missed the clack of Daphne's mules on the stairs in the morning, her lift of laughter, her "Hello, Snub Nose," her talk with Mother. There was a loneliness that had not been there even when she was away at school. But I was given her room that summer to sleep in, a considerable consolation. I reveled in being able to close the door at night and light my own candle. There was a lamp in the room, but for a while I preferred candles. The room still smelled of Daphne; there were still traces of her powder on the dresser. Her writing desk against the wall was still full of her letters, and the inky tracks of her cat, lost when I was very young, still marked the drop leaf. Under the bed was a pair of her suede shoes, turned on their sides, and in the corner closet hung winter dresses and a dark robe she'd used at school. The soap she liked was in her soap dish, her pitcher was half filled with water and the china basin with its blue forget-me-nots had her fresh scent. I disturbed nothing. Eventually, feeling sentimental, I used the rest of the water and thought of her.

Mother had it harder. I did not know it then, but her grief over Daphne's choice was made more acute because she had lost her only congenial companion in that house, and in the country around, to a man who expected and would take full possession. My mother had no other close friend or confidante. Her loss shadowed us all, though I never saw her in tears over it again. The house became quiet as it never had been when Daphne was there. The tennis court sprouted weeds; there were hardly ever any cars parked in our yard on Saturdays and Sundays.

A few men called on Allison occasionally and they went out casually, but Allison was looking for something better. She was not attracted to most country-reared males; "I certainly don't want a dirt farmer like Rob," she said. Perhaps the caliber of suitors had declined from those who courted Daphne. Sometimes Allison said, "I hate little towns and small pale villages," a mysterious quotation that I later found scribbled in the back of the English literature book she left me. It may be that she wrote it herself. She *did* hate them; she felt there was nothing there for her, and she left for the city in 1930. She had changed in the months near her departure from a too-thin, hollow-eyed girl to a pretty and slim young woman. Chicago changed her even more to one who wore small, smart hats and becoming, inexpensive clothes and used city speech. As I grew into adolescence I admired the changed person she became and wrote her letters that she answered; gradually on paper we became friends.

9

Early Scenes and Night Pieces

The very early scenes of childhood that I remember are like snippets from a film: a brightly lit sequence appearing now and then out of the darkness, though I know the camera was always running. In one frame I am standing in my crib chewing paint off its iron rails, doubtless ingesting a little lead. I know that I am waiting to be taken out, and I chew paint because I am bored. In another, I am under the front porch, and since I can stand up I am probably no more than two and a half years old. I am furious and crying. I am also butting my head against a beam that supports the porch. A man's face appears; he is bending down to look at me through a door in the latticework around the base of the porch. He speaks to me, smiling, and it is something like: "What's the matter, honey? Don't hit your head like that." I don't know him; I drown out his voice with my angry one and butt my head even more. I am mad because he is looking at me, because I can't tell him or anybody why I'm angry, and because I wet my pants when I knew well enough to go in the house in time, but didn't. End of scene.

The man was Carl Stevens, who had recently moved into the big white house down the road with his parents and sister. In later years he was fond of recalling that moment as the first time he'd seen me, and his amusement at my butting my head. Whenever he did, the same feelings I had that day would sweep over me, and for a tick in time I was again that angry child, embarrassed that he saw me with wet drawers and unable to express myself except by banging my head. I knew my mother would find out and tell me again not to wait next time, her tone a little scolding so that I cried in anticipation. Her quick hand frequently checked my seat for dampness whenever I went up to her and leaned on her knee. It was an automatic move on her part. I was her third child, and damp bottoms were all in a day's work. I suppose they were for me too when I had children, but I don't remember making the same check.

Carl had probably come over that day to pay his respects to my mother the farmer. He was a man of perhaps thirty or thirty-five years, I would guess in looking back, but his brow was furrowed with responsibility even then. When I was a few years older he came often, sometimes in the middle of the night, riding up on his horse in a considerable hurry. When he knocked, my mother would rouse, call, "Just a minute," light the oil lamp by her bed and carry it down the hall to let him in.

"I sure hate to disturb you," Carl would say, "but the old sow's in trouble. I wonder, could I—"

"Certainly," my mother would say, going into the living room and lighting the hanging lamp there. "I'll get the books."

She would come back to her bedroom, find me sitting up, frightened at being left alone. "Sit tight a minute," she would tell me and lift some heavy books off a shelf to take to Carl. Then she would come back, wrap me in a blanket and carry me into the living room, where I sat sleepily on her lap while he read. The books were encyclopedias of animal diseases brought from Scotland by my grandfather. They would discuss what Carl read for a few minutes, he might take notes, and then he would leave, disappearing into the night. She would take me back to bed, slip off her robe and get in herself.

I liked getting up to join these late conversations in the glow of a hanging lamp shaded with ruby glass. But it is only now, thinking of it years later, that I realize it was my mother's sense of propriety that was responsible—it was improper for her, still a young woman, to be seated alone at night with a man not her husband, and to that I owed my pleasure. I was the only other person awake in the house.

Other things woke us at night—rather frequently, I think. It is possible that my mother felt herself and her children to be vulnerable and alone, but I never caught any feeling of fear from her. I do not remember the black people on our place saying anything about things being unsafe, and since I listened to much of what they said, I would have reacted.

There was a man living somewhere in the woods beyond our house whose considerable thirst drove him to the bootlegger on Saturday nights. When he had drunk to stupefaction, someone at Charlie's place would hoist him onto his horse and slap its rump. An hour later his horse would stop at our gate, but Henry was in no shape to open it. He was conscious enough to yell, not words but a rough shout that roused our dog and my mother. She would put a coat on over her gown, take a small revolver she kept under her pillow, grab a lantern and go out to open the gate. Then she would lead the horse by the bridle to another gate beyond the barn, with Henry limply sprawled on the mare's neck, not even holding the reins. There she would open the second gate, see them through and close it. There was never a word from Henry, but she felt the horse's gratitude. Then she would come back to bed, where I was lying awake, fearful until she returned.

"Henry doesn't have half the sense his horse has," she nearly always said the next morning. "He'd have been dead in a ditch long ago if it weren't for that mare. She knows exactly what to do with him; she probably takes him into the stable with her."

One night when I was sleeping upstairs with my sister, we were awakened by terrible screams right outside our window. To me it sounded like several women were being strangled at once. Allison was sitting bolt upright, saying, "Oh, Lord!" I added my own screams to the uproar. My mother came upstairs forthwith, lit the lamp in our room and told us the shrieks were coming from owls sitting in the trees close to our house.

We could not believe this. "Just listen," my mother said. "They're really talking to each other." We held our breath and did not like what we heard, so she stayed with us until the screams moved farther out in the yard and finally stopped. It is the only time I have heard more than two owls at once and so close. Now I occasionally hear the small screech owl; his quavering cry in the night sounds like notes played on a musical saw. In these mountains people will tell you that if you hear the screech owl in late summer, it means there will be frost in six weeks. Weather forecasting by owl is as reliable as by groundhog or woolly bear caterpillars.

Once in a while in winter there was a knock at the back door, and to us who awoke from heavy sleep it always seemed like midnight. My mother rose, of course, and went through the cold house from bedroom to hall then through the kitchen to unlock the back door. In the light of her lamp there would appear the pale face of John Nicholson, who plowed and reaped our fields on shares. It was an unshaven haggard face, for John had a penchant for drink that marked him with blear eyes; he also had more children than he could care for, and this branded him with pain.

"No ma'am, I cain't come in," he'd say, lisping slightly because of few front teeth. The time I remember best he said, "It's Gordon, Mrs. Bell. He's got lung trouble terrible and we's run out of rags for him to cough into. I'm right sorry to bother you all like this, but my wife is 'bout wore out. . . ."

"Please come in, Mr. Nicholson, it's too cold for you to wait out there. You don't want pneumonia yourself."

John Nicholson edged in the door and stood there, miserable in his abjectness, his old felt hat turning in his hands. I had opened the kitchen door a crack to see what was happening and was shivering with the cold and curiosity. My mother almost bumped into me as she came to hunt for old towels and soft clean rags for nineteen-year-old Gordon Nicholson to cough into. Kleenex was not yet common and John Nicholson could not have afforded it anyway.

Since I was up Mother put some old towels in my arms and dug ripped pieces of underwear out of a chest under the living-room window. We went back to the kitchen with the bundle.

"How will you carry these?" she asked John.

"On my back, I reckon."

So Mother found an old pillowcase to put everything in. Before he left she asked him what they were doing for Gordon. "Ain't much we kin do," he told her. "We just got to wait for the crisis, the doctor said."

"Is he sweating?"

"No'm, he ain't yit. He's just lyin' there a-burnin'. But Dr. Chiles said when the crisis come, if he come through it, all that stuff in his lungs gonna break loose. That's why we need the rags."

"Is Dr. Chiles there now?"

"No'm. He tole us what to do. Said if he . . . if he . . ." Then Mr. Nicholson dropped his head, trying to hide the struggle in his face.

"I know this is hard for you and your wife," my mother said softly.

"Ye know Gordon's been a good boy. Ye know that. We don't aim to let him go to heaven yit. Not kin we help it." And he picked up the pillowcase of rags and slipped into the night. When he had gone we realized how cold the kitchen was, and how cold it probably was at the Nicholson house.

"Tomorrow," my mother said, "I'll have to send some old sheets over there. If Gordon passes the crisis he'll be sweating and they'll have a time keeping dry covers on him."

"What's a 'crisis'?"

"It's the point when, if his fever breaks, he'll start to recover. If not—"

"Will he die then?"

"Honey, you've got to get to sleep now. No more questions tonight." But I was sure Gordon would die, and soon, because it was in Mr. Nicholson's face and because my mother would never talk to us about death.

After what struggle in that poor household we could not know, Gordon shook the infection from his lungs and by summer was back in the fields, as gaunt and pale as his father. The family seemed unlikely to survive all that they had to, and yet they did.

Gordon had four younger brothers and a sister—pale,

meek children constantly sniffling. The girl, Lena, was near my age, and as she grew might have been pretty had she more spirit. It did not occur to me then that life had leached color and joy from her. Her hair was lank and dispirited also, her bare knees rough with cold. She and her brothers walked to our house every weekday morning because that was as far as the school bus came. When it rained or was cold, the Nicholsons waited inside, sitting quietly on our chairs, sniffling or coughing.

By the time I was thirteen and full of baffling new prejudices explainable now only by the uproar in my hormones, I was offended every morning by the sounds of vague illnesses that emanated from those harmless children waiting in our living room.

"Mother," I finally asked, "can't you let them wait on the porch? I can't stand listening to them snort and sniffle all the time."

I am ashamed now of saying it; actually, I was ashamed of it then, but was not yet in touch with my uneven sensibilities. I wish my mother had told me no, that we had to be kind to Lena and her brothers, who had so little, who had to walk a mile to the school bus while I did not—and besides, I should think of someone other than myself. Unaccountably she did not; she told the Nicholsons that they had to wait on the porch, and I was confirmed in my snottiness. Lena did get a warm coat I had outgrown, so Mother probably felt some remorse too. She even made a hood for it so that it was not too recognizably my old coat.

In another year I was recovering from being thirteen and discarding some of the ugly thoughts I had then, becoming more charitable and thoughtful. When Lena turned fifteen, she became engaged to a young farmer and quit school. Perhaps her family pushed her toward marriage to reduce the strain of feeding so many. She had been married a year when her new husband decided to join the navy. He went in soft, overweight and pork-fed. He came out trim and compulsively neat after the war and started a furniture-making business with skills he'd learned in a navy shop. The business prospered, and at last Lena had a warm house of her own, high heels and some soft color in her cheeks. I saw her once in her yard with her children and she was smiling.

John Nicholson's appearances at the back door were usually ordinary enough, but one other was not. It came one evening when we had just finished supper. Allison was spreading her homework on the table and I was trying to understand long division and having difficulty with Mother's explanation. When she opened the door to a brisk knocking, there was John, but in addition to his gaunt self he had with him a small thin woman who looked very unhappy, her brown hair pulled back from a plain, high-cheekboned face, her hands twisting together.

"Mrs. Bell, I brung my wife. She needs a woman to tell her what to do. She ain't listen to me." He took his wife's arm, pulling her into the kitchen.

Mrs. Nicholson looked at my mother and said painfully, "Don't you pay him no mind, Mrs. Bell, he's been a-drinkin' again."

John rocked slightly on his feet and said loudly, "Naw, I ain't neither. I ain't drunk and you ain't gonna git out of it thataway." This was certainly not the meek, spiritless John Nicholson we knew.

My mother showed them into our new dining room and then said to my sister and me, "You'd better go to my room."

We recognized the tone. Picking up our books, we left, but without words between us we dropped them in the bedroom and quickly sneaked back to the dining-room door to listen.

"Go on, tell her," Mr. Nicholson was saying to his wife.

Nobody spoke. We wondered if she was shaking her head or just sitting there. Then my mother said gently, "Would it help if we talked alone, Mrs. Nicholson?"

Again silence.

"I reckon I got to say it if she don't," John said, his voice still louder that we had ever heard it.

Mother said, "There's no need to shout. Just speak quietly."

John dropped his voice a fraction but it kept getting louder. "What it is, she done tole me I cain't sleep in my bed no more. It's her duty to me, ain't that so? You a woman, Mrs. Bell, and a wife, and—"

Evidently Mrs. Nicholson could keep quiet no longer. "Don't you listen, Mrs. Bell. He got no business comin' here and talkin' to you like this. I tried to keep him from comin', but when he gets the drink in him I cain't do nothin' with him." Even with the door closed we could hear her embarrassment.

"Mrs. Bell, she said she gonna leave if I . . . you know, you know what I mean. It's her duty to her man, the preacher said so. I ain't askin' a thing but what a husband's due. If she's gonna eat my bread and meat—"

"What you don't drink up first!" Suddenly Mrs. Nicholson was louder herself. "Mrs. Bell, I done give him six children. We cain't feed the ones we got and I ain't a-gonna have no more. I made up my mind. If he cain't let me be I ain't a-stayin'."

Allison apparently knew what this was all about. "Come

on," she whispered urgently. "I think we'd better go back to Mother's room."

"What are they talking about?" I asked in a whisper, not moving. "What's he mean when—"

"Shhh, they'll hear you. Come *on.*" She pulled my arm hard, which was guaranteed to raise my resistance. I opened my mouth, but she knew what was coming and clapped her long fingers over it.

Then, very clearly, we heard our mother say severely: "I think you had both better go. This is not the kind of thing you ask a lady, Mr. Nicholson, and I realize you've been drinking, but since you asked me," and her voice had a scolding tone we knew very well, "I don't think your wife should be expected to take care of your needs when she doesn't want to. Your needs aren't more important than hers. And she's right: You do have enough children."

We heard her walk into the kitchen and open the door. There was a moment of suspense and then chairs moved and John and his wife followed her. If anything more was said we didn't hear it because we had headed to the bedroom, from which we could hear Mother locking the back door. When she came in, I was lying on my stomach looking at a magazine and Allison was writing in a notebook, her history text open beside her.

"What did they want this time?" Allison asked.

"He'd been drinking," my mother said, "or he wouldn't have the nerve to come for . . . It was pretty embarrassing."

"Why, what did they want?"

"Never mind," our mother said. "The whole thing is best forgotten. He didn't know what he was doing or it would never have happened."

The episode seemed to trouble Mother for several days. We

would see her standing staring out of the window, a habit she had only when bothered. I don't think she was as offended by it as embarrassed, and she may have wondered how she could have handled it more kindly.

When I could, I asked Allison what Mr. Nicholson meant about his wife not letting him sleep in his bed. "Never mind," she said, sounding exactly like Mother. "You're too young to understand." I was about nine or ten and knowledge seemed a long way off.

I thought about taking the question to Susan, but the suspicion that if I did I might find out something I didn't want to know kept me silent. That and what Mother had said about forgetting what had happened; I was afraid she might find out I hadn't.

10

Places

Live alone long enough—or perhaps just live long enough—and you will find yourself trying to remember with exactness the places you loved long ago: the kitchen of your childhood home, a schoolroom of your sixteenth year or roads you once traveled day after day. Perhaps you will end up sketching them as I do: a square or an oblong for a room, a window here, a table there, a stove and chimney in this space . . . What was on the shelf in the corner? Sunlight came in this window and lay across the rug in the morning; the cat used to sit in its warmth and wash her face. An orange tabby with white paws, she had just had warm milk . . . and I remember suddenly that sometimes when I was sick in bed, my mother used to bring in one of the kittens and give it a saucer of milk so I could watch it lap and forget my sore throat.

Unexpectedly and without my willing it, as I write a letter or plot a garden, a mental door swings inward and I must enter and draw what is there. For a few minutes I am in another age, watching from under the jacquard spread of my mother's bed, or simply present, conscious of no age, a disembodied sensibility in another time.

Several times I have found myself sketching an odd little apartment that my husband and I lived in shortly after marriage, just before World War II. It was in a southern city in the mountains near a large army base, and living quarters were scarce. The living room had an overstuffed chair, a table, a brown sofa of furry material like my old teddy bear and a bed in the wall behind cream-painted wooden panels. Of course no veteran apartment dweller would have been impressed with a bed in the wall, but I had never seen one and was intrigued that it could so completely vanish. The rest of the apartment is what has kept it in my memory. The passageway to the kitchen had a table that one had to fold against the wall and secure with a hook to get by. Two chairs folded up beside it. This was where we ate. Potatoes and canned goods were stacked in an alcove beside the table, but the floor under them was a door to the basement.

The kitchen had a low oilcloth-covered table hung from chains at each end; raised, it revealed a bathtub underneath. Another small table in the corner could also be raised; under it was the toilet. There was an old gas range and a 1920s kitchen cabinet. The sink served as washbasin and kitchen sink. The back kitchen window looked out on a magnificent sweep of Tennessee mountains. The living-room window viewed streetcar tracks twenty feet from the door; the last one to town clanged by at midnight.

It was in that apartment that my husband became ill with pneumonia. The bed stayed out of the wall for weeks; the entire place smelled of his profuse sweatings and of illness. The teddy-bear sofa was my bed. A young doctor, whose name I picked from the phone book, came to see us and proved young and gentle. He knew, I'm sure, even before we told him, that we had very little money and no hospitalization

insurance. He told me that my husband's recovery really
would be a matter of good nursing, though possibly a new
drug would help. He prescribed sulfadiazine, and after two
doses my husband's high fever dropped and he slept. Later
his fever climbed again and his urine turned bloody. The
doctor shook his head. "We will have to watch carefully," he
told me. "The kidneys are going to bleed, but it's important
to continue the sulfa if we can." He ordered lots of liquid, and
I poured tea and water and lemonade into Monty day and
night, rousing him from sleep that was close to unconscious-
ness. When I went into the kitchen to fix broth, the smell of
meat juices mingled with sickroom odors until I had to open
a window and let in air smelling of burning coal instead.

I think the doctor came every day at first; it was a time
when this drug treatment was precariously new and scary.
The sulfa was continued and the bleeding continued too, but
gradually my husband's fevers lessened, the drenching sweats
ceased and he could sit up. After weeks of confinement with
him in that tiny apartment, a day came when I was surprised
by his saying, "I'll be all right for a while. Why don't you go
out, go downtown or something." With unseemly willingness
I caught the next streetcar heading down the mountain and
went first to the library, breathing in the smell of books and
sauntering (sauntering!) among the shelves. After that I
walked around the streets just looking—at budding trees,
crocuses in the grass, wash on lines, dogs in doorways, children racing from school. Then I rode the streetcar back,
bringing news of flowers and spring to cover my guilt for
leaving.

I recall too the room in our old farmhouse where I was put
to bed for a nap every afternoon when I was very young. It

was Allison's room, and her bed was a cot with a drop side that was raised to make it full size. It sagged nicely in the middle so that the sleeper could snuggle in a hollow, with the mattress rising comfortably around her.

In those years Allison's dresser was half of a large black metal wardrobe trunk with drawers in it; doubtless it had been used in the move from Chicago. Her washstand, as well as all the others in the house, was made of a wooden packing crate covered with white oilcloth and curtained with a skirt of muslin. Oilcloth was indispensable before plastics were invented; it was a firm cloth coated on one side in shiny white waterproof material, and it could be wiped clean. Coming from a city house with a bathroom, Mother may not have known about the marble-topped walnut or cherry-wood washstands of large country houses of the time; even if she had, she probably would not have spent money on them anyway. When she had any money for the house, it went to put pictures on the walls or to buy records of Caruso singing, or of piano music and a few operatic selections—the overture to *Madame Butterfly*, songs from *Carmen*, *The Mikado* and *H.M.S. Pinafore*. We grew up knowing bits of great opera, snatches of symphonies, but none in its entirety. For years I believed composers wrote only selections.

In the ceiling of Allison's room there was a large hole where plaster had fallen and the supporting lathe had broken. Looking into it from the bed I could see darkness in and beyond its edges. I asked my mother what was up there and of course she said, "Nothing, it's just a hole." But to a child as young as I a hole was not just a hole. It was a mysterious and dark cave and might have all kinds of things in it waiting until grown-ups were gone to come creeping out.

At first this was an interesting idea, and I watched the dark opening until I fell asleep, thinking of tiny horses, tiny people, thimble-sized dogs and cats that might show themselves if I watched long enough. But then one night I dreamed that a family of bears lived there, bears that were large, black and frightening. Dreams were as real to me as anything else that happened, and I told Mother about the bears above Allison's room.

"What?" she said. "Bears?"

Hearing me, Allison laughed and said, "Where did she get that idea?"

"But I saw them," I insisted.

At the next nap time, my mother found that I was afraid to be left alone with the hole in the ceiling, that I couldn't look at it without feeling terror. "Honey, there's really nothing at all up there to be afraid of. Just close your eyes and go to sleep."

But it was no use. To quiet my hysterical crying she had to move me across the hall to Daphne's room. When or how the hole was mended I don't remember, but it was not long after my announcement about the bears. When the ceiling was smooth and white I returned to my naps there. Allison, who scoffed at my bears, was nevertheless relieved not to have the hole hovering darkly over her head at night.

One winter when I was older and sleeping with Allison in that same room, we both awoke to hear something falling and bumping down the stairs outside our door. While we lay holding our breaths, we heard Mother get up to investigate. She found a cob of popcorn on the steps and realized that a rat had stolen it from our supply in a box under Allison's bed. She came up to tell us, knowing that we were probably rigidly awake.

"Be sure your door is shut," she told us, "so the rat can't get back in." Then she went out and brought in the cat from the woodshed. Carrots, a golden-orange knobby animal, was a stray that originally came to our house seeking a place to have kittens, and birthed her litter of six orange-and-whites in a nest of chips in our woodshed. She was no welfare case, it turned out, though she did drink some warm milk we gave her that first morning we found her. She proved to be a phenomenal rat catcher, able to climb the walls of our barn to catch large shrieking rats trying to escape Solomon's stick as he poked it in our corn crib. Carrots would kill one rat, drop it and catch another, until rat corpses littered the barn floor. She was petted and made much over for this, and accepted hands on her prominent backbone with stoic patience, then licked smooth all the fur rumpled by praise.

My mother put her in the upstairs hall that night and she immediately understood why she was there; the smell of rat set her whiskers twitching. She settled down, watchful and alert, her instinct telling her that sooner or later a rat would appear. Then Allison and I went to sleep. Later we were aroused by vigorous gnawing sounds under the floorboards.

"That rat is coming up through the floor!" Allison said, sitting up in the cold air.

"Let's get Carrots," I said. She slid out and lit the lamp, shivering. I followed her, and all our stirring silenced the gnawing. Allison turned the doorknob, and Carrots must have been pressed against it on the other side listening to rat sounds, for she pushed into the room and started sniffing along the floor.

"I guess we scared him away," Allison said, standing uncertainly and chilled in her nightgown. Since we were both cold, we left Carrots on patrol, blew out the light and went back

to bed. Sometime in the night the gnawing began again and
Allison and I both were immediately awake, listening for the
momentary meeting of cat with rat. But the floorboard
proved too thick and the gnawing went on and on and on.
Finally we slept anyway. At daylight Carrots, her front paws
neatly tucked under her, sat, still waiting. The rat, though,
apparently discouraged by its all-night work, was no longer
heard from. Carrots was put back outside temporarily; my
mother knew enough about rodent habits to say, "He'll be
back tonight to try again."

Sure enough. This time Carrots was installed in our room
before we went to bed. All was quiet, and Allison and I
believed the rat had taken himself elsewhere in defeat. We
were curled in deep slumber when a loud thump and a pierc-
ing squeal brought us upright. More thumps, a growl and a
scuffle. My sister said, "I'm afraid to get out of bed; I might
step on it." Then my mother opened the door, holding a
lamp. In its light we saw Carrots gripping the neck of a rat
nearly her size, its hind legs kicking, its hairless tail thrashing.
She paid us no attention but set the rat down, holding it with
her claws so she could get a better grip with her teeth. This
time she bit down, bones snapped and the rat was immediately still. Carrots dropped him, pawed at him to be sure he
was dead, and then went to Mother and rubbed around her
ankles.

"You're a wonderful kitty," my mother told her, and we
got out of bed to join in the praises and to pet old Carrots's
bony back. She knew she had done her job well and accepted
her due. She never gave the rat another look, and my mother
took her downstairs to feed her milk and find some tidbit for
a reward. Carrots returned to the woodshed peaceable and
content. When I went out to see her in the morning she

yawned in my face, blinking her golden eyes, then smoothed a wrinkle in her fur, turned over and went back to sleep.

In 1925, my mother decided to tear down the old back porch bordering the kitchen and make it into a dining room. The porch was old, its floorboards sagged and Allison's bantam chickens roosted under its roof every night with messy consequences. Besides, it was full of unused and unwanted objects that no one would miss.

My mother found a carpenter, a Canadian displaced for some reason to the small town of Mineral. Later someone told her he was hiding from the law because of stealing or bigamy or perhaps even murder—who knew? But Mother refused to believe it, for by then Mr. Bennett had completed her dining room and charged for nothing but his labor.

He came to us in June and was given the old schoolhouse on the place (this was before it became Susan's house) to live in; his home until then had been a boardinghouse in Mineral, and he had no way to commute eight miles to and from work each day. He ate his meals at our table, and probably that was part of his pay. He liked to relax before dinner by sitting in the kitchen so he could talk to my mother as she cooked. She fed him well on whatever we had, and he ate with enjoyment and moderately good manners. I hung about him raptly, breathing in his smell of sweat and wood shavings, and he usually ended by taking me on his lap, where I leaned back in bliss, listening to the rumble of his voice vibrating through his bib overalls.

Mr. Bennett was skilled in cabinetry. He not only constructed the dining room with a fireplace at one end, but made high, small-paned windows that slid in their tracks as if on silk, and also most of the furniture. My mother designed

a long table with matching benches for each side. He made
them graceful but sturdy, planing and sanding them until
they felt as smooth as stroked hen feathers to my hand. Out
of a blown-down oak tree he fashioned a kind of sideboard,
though it was not heavy in appearance, with drawers for silver
and table linen. The furniture was simple in design and restful
to the eye. My mother stained these pieces dark brown, set
them against white walls, and made rose-colored curtains and
pillows. One bench stood against the wall opposite the table,
with pillows at its back.

Over the fireplace at the west end of the room, Mr. Bennett
mounted a simple, heavy oak mantel the width of the room.
It was stained too, and had asparagus ferns trailing in front
of the high windows that flanked the chimney. The ferns
glittered with late sunlight and threw pale shadows on the
floor. It became the room where Allison and I studied on
weeknights, and my mother sewed or read. Five years later,
when our house burned, Mother tried to find Mr. Bennett
again, but he had gone, no one knew when or where.

The room Mr. Bennett made was the one where Daphne's
mules tapped cheerfully across the floor at midmorning, and
where she sat to drink coffee with our mother, her knees
crossed so that a satin slipper dangled from one white foot
and gave me, watching from my tanned and scuffed-shod self
on the bench, a sense of her porcelain femininity that is still
a part of that room, though it be ashes, and Daphne herself
dust.

11

Drought

The last rain in these mountains this summer was about July 11. It is now the twenty-first day of August and it has not rained for one month and ten hot days. All of us who live here think some computer glitch has been made in weather deliveries and we are getting Arizona weather by mistake. Days that usually have a high of eighty degrees now reach into the parching nineties. Thunderheads rise in the west, look us over and then go somewhere else to rain. Grass crackles underfoot, the birds quit singing after the sun is up. Many have packed it up and left; the indigo buntings are gone and the wood thrush has taken his flute to damper places.

I sit limply on the porch with a cold drink; the dog lies at my feet eyeing my glass. Finally I give him an ice cube and he crunches it, licking up the tiny ice puddles. I give him another and he wants it, but not now, so he takes it over to a dusty bush and buries it. It is the first drink the bush has had in forty-two days.

A wind comes up in the afternoon, leaving the dogwoods limp and the poplars yellowing prematurely. There is a smell in the air that I remember from another time; it is of green leaves hot and burned in the sun. I keep watching the horizon and sniffing for any faint whiff of fire starting in the woods, presensitized for all time by what happened when I was eleven.

On a Sunday in April 1930, my mother was pacing from the yard to our upstairs hallway back window and then down again. She was watching a column of smoke rising beyond our woods to the west. I caught her nervousness and watched also, but without her added awareness that there had been very little rainfall during the winter and early spring. There were new leaves on the trees, but on the forest floor the old leaves were as dry and separate as cornflakes.

I heard Mother report to Allison that the smoke seemed to be moving our way. My sister was in bed, feverish and coughing. She wanted to get up and help us, but my mother said, "Only if necessary," and started gathering possessions we could take with us if the fire came nearer. I was sent at a run to tell Susan, living then in the old schoolhouse on our place, that she had better take our horse and buggy and leave as soon as she could. Our tiny car could not hold more than three people. I raced back to our house to pack my two new dresses. Allison was coughing more; the smoke was bothering her. Mother was dumping drawer contents into a box. I lugged down books I wanted to save and Mother told me, "There's no room in the car for those, Vallie."

Carl Stevens drove into the yard and my mother met him on the porch. There was a tense conversation. "Mrs. Bell, you and the girls better get out right quick. That fire is picking up fast. You all better come over to our house. It's got so much plowed land around it I think it will be safe."

"Allison is sick in bed," Mother told him. "You can take the girls and I can come behind you."

But she had hardly finished when I burst into tears. I

grabbed her arm and said, "I won't go unless you go too!" I was sure she would be caught in the fire if we left first.

Carl looked at my stricken face and said, "I'll just take Allison." He went into the bedroom with my mother, picked Allison up in her blankets and carried her out to his car. We all saw Susan setting Nellie the plow horse at a fast trot, turning the buggy into the main road out front, heading away from the fire toward her old house, a mile away.

The wind picked up; smoke was bluing the air around us and the smell of burning leaves stung our noses. My mother pulled her Model T near the porch and put a box with our silver, her photographs and her handmade linens into the tiny trunk space. She had already put our suitcases on the running board. Now she hastily gathered up some new Wear-ever pots and pans packed in salesmen's suitcases and flung them on the bare sand of the tennis court beside a box of my father's choice books. Burning ash was flying over us. "Get in," Mother yelled at me, and I did so only because she had her foot on the running board herself. She backed the car out, and as we fled through smoke growing thicker every minute, she leaned out of the window and called Mac, the dog. He came running. "Lean out and call him," she told me, and I did. He ran easily not far behind us; he had never followed the car before but understood this was a crisis.

I thought but didn't ask about the cows in the pasture and the chickens in the chicken houses. There were new chicks under the brooder, and I told myself that the brooder house was off by itself and maybe . . .

At Carl's house my mother parked the car near their drive and asked Carl's sister if Allison was in bed. "I put her in my own room," Miss Lou said. "I'll watch out for her—don't you fret."

We all ran toward the open field on the north side of the Stevenses' big house to watch the fire. I could see our house standing calmly among its oak trees. Behind it to the north the fire seemed to be going away, though the smoke was so thick it was hard to tell. We could see great rolling balls of fire in the treetops and I thought I could feel the heat on my face.

"If the wind just doesn't change . . ." my mother said.

We stood there until I couldn't stand the tension and began to cry, but Mother said, "Hush, that only makes things worse," and I stopped, wanting to watch and at the same time afraid to see what would happen. The whole woods beyond our house, our orchard in its grassy clearing, were in flames. There was a crackling sound as branches broke and fell from trees like burning logs in a fireplace, showering sparks. Over our heads birds were flying from the fire. Our house stood peacefully silhouetted against the orange-and-black swirl of smoke and flame.

Suddenly I heard my mother say tightly, "The wind's shifted," and we watched as a great ball of fire, tumbling and rolling on the wind, came toward our house. It caught first in the highest oak-tree branches, and they flared like torches. I thought of our house cat Brownie for the first time and clapped my hands over my mouth. My mother turned away and said, "That's it." I stared long enough to see burning branches drop on our roof and the entire scene obliterated by smoke that had tongues of flames roaring through it.

My mother and I walked back to the Stevenses' back porch and sat on the steps, she silent and her face white. After a while Carl came over and said, "It's not coming here. Your fields just burned over and it stopped at the road."

"The house gone?" she said, looking up.

"It's gone," he said. "All those trees dropped fire on it."

As soon as she could, Mother stood up as if very tired and went inside to tell Allison. But my sister knew; she'd known before she was out of the yard at home. "When Carl was carrying me to his car," she told Mother, "I looked back and I saw that our house was nothing but a pile of cinders." She did not know why she saw it this way, but she knew it was true. She said nothing to Carl as he turned the car around and headed for his house.

He thought she was weeping because she was scared, and he kept saying, "Don't worry now; you all will be safe at my house."

I can remember almost nothing else about the rest of that day. My mother could not go back to our place because some of the old trees were still burning and the ground was still hot, but she drove off to send a telegram to my father. Carl offered to take her, but she said, "I think I need to be by myself for a while right now. You've all been so kind . . ." She came back in time for the supper we had at the Stevenses' big table. After supper, Miss Lou took me upstairs to a tiny room under sloping eaves and showed me a bed with a feather mattress. When I sank into it, its billows rose around me. It was warm and cozy and I snuggled in deeply. Only when my mother came in and kissed me good night did I ask her about the cat.

"I don't know," she said. "We'll just have to hope. But don't expect too much."

I was still asleep at faint daylight when Mother, unable to rest, went to the kitchen and found Carl, Miss Lou and Carl's mother fixing breakfast. They gave her coffee and a hot biscuit and then Carl went with her to look at the smoking ruins of our farm. There was one large, slightly charred tree standing at the far edge of our yard, and curled up asleep on one of its roots was Brownie. At my mother's touch she rolled over, yawned and stretched; there was no figuring out how she had escaped. The barn was gone, the machine shed vanished, the woodshed and its attached room where my mother kept her equipment for developing photographs were ash heaps. One of the chicken houses was a mass of hot melted asphalt roofing over incinerated birds and twisted metal feeders. Another still stood, the new one set off by itself and built for the largest new brood of chickens, which were now gone with the brooder house.

My mother and Carl walked down the pasture hill, seeking the cows they believed might have escaped. At the bottom, up to their knees in the stream, the devastated woods behind them, both of them stood, their udders distended with milk. Carl went back to his house to get milk buckets.

Neither Allison nor I was allowed to go back to view the ruins. We stood with Miss Lou looking across the fields at the black skeletons of trees around the dark pile of rubble that had been our house. We stared numbly, trying to sort out what had happened. Miss Lou kept shaking her head and saying, "I just can't take it in that your house is gone."

Solomon came the long way around that morning; he dared not walk through the still smoldering woods. He came very early, while Carl was gone for the milk buckets, and found my mother standing alone in the center of her lost buildings. His joy and relief at seeing her was so great that he grabbed her hand and shook it. "We thought sho' it was goin' to hit you, we thought sho'." Then, looking around, "Ain't much left, is it?"

And my mother said, "Not much but one chicken house."

Two families of black people, Solomon told her, had lost their houses in the woods near ours. The Jacksons had fled on foot to their friends. Our near neighbors, Mary and John Marshall and their six children, were homeless for the second time in six months. Their old house had burned in the fall and they had built another. Now that was gone too.

"Where are they now?" my mother asked.

"They went to that little house over the hill," Solomon told her. "Ain't much room, but it keep the rain out."

"How can they possibly get eight people in that tiny house?"

"I don't know, but they does it."

My mother was walking from one pile of rubble to another, feeling, she said later, in a daze, when the Woodfords drove up in their wagon. Their own house and buildings were safe but they had lost some good forest. Mrs. Woodford put her arm around Mother and said, "We've been praying for you and the girls. Now we want you all to come stay with us until things are straightened out. We'll be so glad to have you, you know."

Her earnest goodness touched my mother, but it was not her way to turn to others. "I'm not sure yet what I have to do," she said, "but it's wonderfully kind of you to offer." She laid a hand briefly on Mrs. Woodford's arm. "I just have to work things out."

Carl came back with the buckets and gave them to Solomon, who went down the hill to the cows. Carl and Mr. Woodford stood around and talked about the fire as each had seen it moving across the landscape the day before, speculating on its origin. Mother and Mrs. Woodford moved from ruin to ruin, picking up pieces of things, trying to identify them. One was a darkened dish with a garland of roses; looking at it in her neighbor's hand, Mother said, "Those were my best dessert bowls." She carried it as they walked around, and after the Woodfords were gone she met Solomon and the full milk bucket to get a dishful for the miraculously escaped cat.

Carl called to her, "Mrs. Bell, you might's well pour that out. We have plenty milk over home." So she filled the cat's saucer and the rest was poured out. The white puddle filled with black cinders as it sank into the ground.

Before the day was half over, people from miles around were coming to find out what had happened to the Bells, to ask if they could help and to wander about the stricken farmyard. Tom Walker came on foot and asked my mother what she was going to do now. "Ye ain't wantin' to stay here, air ye?"

"I don't have any other home, Mr. Walker."

He spat with no change of expression. "I tole my wife that's what ye'd say. Ye ain't no quitter, I tole her. We remember about them pigs."

Quinton Painter's parents drove up, bringing a telegram from my father. Mother read it aloud: "TERRIBLE NEWS. GLAD YOU AND CHILDREN SAFE. CHECKING INSURANCE. NEED DETAILS."

Claude Painter knew how the fire started. A caretaker at the Cross Corners lumberyard five miles away—"been hitting the bottle right heavy," he said—decided it was a good day to burn off some fields for plowing. After he lit the match the fire swept through the grass. "He couldn't have stopped it even if he'd been sober," Claude said. "Lots of folk were at church, you know, and there weren't many around to do anything. Couldn't anyway—too dry."

The Painters also urged my Mother to move in with them until she could decide what to do, but she thanked them with the same words she'd said to others. She did not say that she had already decided what to do; she was probably not ready to put it into words. When the Painters, Tom Walker, the Martins and the Youngs had offered help and gone, she asked Carl to come with her to look at the chicken house that had been untouched by fire. It still smelled of recently poured cement and new wood. As she opened the door she said, "You see this little room we set off for feed? I think I can stay in here while a place is fixed up for all of us."

"It's right small . . ." Carl said doubtfully.

"But look, I could put a cot over there, and some kind of stove here. And a table and chair. That's all I need right now."

He shook his head. "You know you can stay with us. You'd be comfortable and real close by."

"But Carl, I need to be *here*. I'll have the dog, you know."

That, of course, is how it was. I was sent to stay with Daphne so I could finish out the school year. Allison, still running a fever, was put to bed at the home of a friend who was a nurse. My mother may have thought she had tuberculosis and did not dare leave her with anyone else. As she had already decided, Mother moved into the feed room of the chicken house, from which she directed and helped with the cleanup of all that was left of our house, barn and sheds. She kept finding remnants of her life that she turned over and over: a solidified aluminum puddle on the tennis court where the pots and pans she'd tried to save had melted (she eventually replaced them all); the handles to her bread mixer and meat grinder, the wooden parts burned off, the machines twisted and useless; fragments of rose glass from the shattered hanging lamp in the living room. (To this day I think of that lamp with love. It could be raised or lowered on a chain in the center of the ceiling. Its bowl was filled with kerosene and set into a scrolled metal base. Its clear wide shade had bubbles caught in the glass that made rose-colored dimpling shadows on the walls around.) Before they were hauled away, she touched the warped brass bedsteads, the broken shards of pitchers and basins, and the cracked, streaked pieces of my father's plate collection that had once shone from a plate rail in our new dining room.

Mother did not allow herself to sigh over these things for long; there was too much to do. One of the first things she did was to walk through deep ash in the ruined woods to see what was left. The young silver-green white pines were gone, and the hollies, once so thick, were unrecognizable. But the trunks of the large blackened oaks and maples still stood, two or three large barren branches left pointing upward. Walking behind my mother with an ax, Solomon cut a notch here and there in the charred bark; underneath there was solid, un-burned wood.

"There's a lot of timber here good for building if we can get it out," my mother told Solomon.

"Certainly is," he agreed, looking around.

"Enough for all of us," my mother said thoughtfully.

No rains fell in the weeks that followed and there was wholesale despair among farmers. Mother and Solomon re-planted a garden, though little grew. But she was laying plans that kept her from always watching the skies and listening for rain.

12

Starting Over

Several days after her inspection of the burned woods, my mother went to the law office of Harrison Floyd, an old acquaintance. I don't know if she had in mind what she wanted to do or if Harrison told her what she should do. In any case, her next move was to go to the Cross Corners lumberyard to see the owner, Jeb Hensley. A large man with heavy jowls and hair oiled flat to his skull, he was sitting at an untidy desk inside a door labeled OFFICE. She introduced herself and said she would like to talk to him briefly. He did not get up from his desk. "You want to order lumber?" he asked. When she hesitated his eyes swept over her, from narrow tied shoes and her one suit saved from the fire to her dark hair knotted neatly on her neck, then he pulled out a pocket watch. "I got only a few minutes," he told her curtly.

"Then I'll come right to the point," she told him, sitting down by his rolltop desk though he had not offered her a chair. She crossed her legs and sat very erect, gloves in her hand. "Mine was one of the houses burned by the fire started in your field here on Sunday the thirteenth." She looked him directly in the eye, she said later, and he wasn't prepared for what she said.

He fumbled the watch back in his pocket and shifted in his chair. "I'm sorry to hear that. Awful dry this year, awful dry. I reckon you will be needing lumber for rebuilding?"

"That's why I'm here," my mother said. "Since it was your employee who set the fire that destroyed so much property, I believe you—"

"Wait a minute, Mrs. Bell. I was not here when that happened. I had nothing to do with you losing your home."

My mother kept her voice cool and even. "Your man was working for you that day. He set the fire. Three families lost their homes as a result."

Mr. Hensley stared at her. Finally he said, "Well, I fired him—he hadn't ought to of been drinking. I'm not responsible for him drinking. I told him before never to come to work if he was drinking."

Mother went on to say that the least he could do was furnish lumber for the rebuilding of the Jackson house, the Marshalls' house and ours. He did not look at her as she talked, but his face grew red and he finally stood up. "Mrs. Bell, I hate to say this to a woman, but you're a fool if you think I'm going to give you and those others all that lumber free. I'd lose my shirt."

My mother said, "If you come out and cut the usable timber from our burned-over woods, you can do it. There are hundreds of large trees that are burned only on the outside, and they'll make good lumber. That way you could replace what we have to get from you to build our houses. I would ask only half price for the timber to replace yours, and a fair price for the rest that you can sell in your yard here."

"Mrs. Bell, I don't buy burned timber; I don't mill burned

timber. I can't talk to you anymore; I have other people to see and my work to do." He stalked to the door, opened it and waited for her to leave. She was angry, she said, but she did not let him know it. She rose, drew on her gloves and walked out slowly. On the platform she stood looking at the great piles of cut lumber in the yard. Mr. Hensley started down the steps, then saw that she was still standing there, turned and came back.

"I'm willing to do one thing, Mrs. Bell: I'll let you and those other people have the lumber you need at a good price, just what it costs me. No profit."

She shook her head. "I don't think you understand," she said. "The Jacksons and the Marshalls have no money and no insurance. They lost everything."

He turned away impatiently. Over his shoulder he told her, "You know coloreds never have any money. What I just told you is the best I can do, and that's a lot more than you'd get anywhere else." And he walked away.

My mother got in her car, drove to the courthouse and reported the conversation to Harrison Floyd. "Sounds like Hensley," he said. "The only way to get him to do the right thing is to sue him."

My mother looked at him in dismay. "Oh, dear," she said. Then, "What if you talked to him?"

"I will talk to him—at least I'll try. But he's slammed the door in my face before and he won't want to hear what I have to say this time."

Mother told us she had not considered the idea of taking Jeb Hensley to court, and she wondered if she was getting in too deep. There was a long silence while she thought about where it all would lead and Harrison swatted a few flies on the windowsill. (He was always swatting flies. I found this out when I went with Mother two times that summer and he'd mutter, "Screens have holes in 'em.")

Mother finally told him she would have to talk to my father. He was coming down soon, she said, and perhaps he would want to talk to Harrison himself.

So my father came by train to Virginia on the next weekend instead of later, as he had planned, and when he saw the bleak, blackened land where his green acres had been, he could hardly speak. He held my mother tightly and said, "I had no idea, no idea."

And she answered, "I know."

My father was further appalled when he saw where she was living. "In a chicken house! My God, you don't have to live here; the neighbors must think we're destitute, no better than poor whites. You could stay at a Frederick Station boarding-house I know."

"But hon," she mollified him, as she told Allison, Daphne, Carl and me several times in recounting how she kept her independence, "this is quite cozy. I have everything I need right now, and it's only until they finish the little cottage and the girls can be here with me." She served him coffee and a pineapple upside-down cake that she'd made on top of the stove, and told him all the details she had not had enough time or paper to write about: how the fire looked, how it smelled, how it was to see the great old trees go down with their crowns ablaze. She took him to look at the beginning framework of the small house we were to stay in until a real house was built. It was to be of unfinished boards and have a small screened porch for sleeping. She said he grudgingly agreed that it would do, but was not happy about it.

On Monday they drove to the courthouse to talk to Harrison Floyd in his office smelling of old law books and ink. As usual, my father looked like a Chicago businessman: gray suit, dark blue tie, stiff collar and shined black shoes that laced up over the ankles. Harrison was in shirtsleeves because the temperature was nearly ninety, and his shirt was wet in back. No matter what he wore, my father appeared never to sweat.

"I talked to Hensley," Harrison began, after shaking my father's cool hand. "He told me what he told you and said we're crazy if we think he'll do more than offer you lumber at cost. I asked him if he was prepared to say that in court and he called me a few names and said we couldn't prove he was to blame. I'm of the opinion that he's something of a coward and that if we call his bluff he will settle out of court."

My father wanted to be sure Harrison thought he could win the case in court; Harrison answered, "Mr. Bell, I can't promise that; I can say I think there's a good chance." But what he said wouldn't have mattered much, my mother told us later, because my father was angry enough at what had happened to his land to sue anyway. It was my mother who wanted to know what losing a court battle might cost and my father who showed impatience at the question. Harrison settled it by saying, "I want to do this, and I will not accept any fee from you. All I need is your authorization to go ahead. Also the authorization by the signatures of the other people who lost property, which you can get for me, Mrs. Bell."

For the remainder of his lamentably short life, Harrison Floyd was to receive eggs and fresh cream from our farm every week.

It embarrassed my mother that for quite a long time after the fire there were people who would not charge her for service. Dr. Chiles was one; no matter what he did for us— treat sore throats, wrap up sprained ankles, give shots—he refused to let my mother pay him. This bothered her so much

and went on for so long that after her children left home she
sought another doctor. Mr. Evans, the garage owner who did
all the work on her car, would charge her for nothing except
parts. Notaries, deliverymen, even bank personnel would
wave away proffered cash or checks.

After they left Harrison's office, my father decided to cut
his visit short, probably because it was uncomfortable sleeping on the daybed in the chicken house, and certainly because
looking at acres of destroyed property depressed him. He
joined my mother briefly in studying designs for houses, but
gave this up when it became obvious that she had very strong
ideas about what she wanted. All he insisted upon was a
bathroom, and he departed under the assumption that this
would be in the plan. We had a small amount of dwelling
insurance, a pittance by today's standards, though many
country people did not. Even the several thousand dollars we
had would go far. The Depression was beginning; skilled
workers were hunting for jobs, any jobs, and prices were
dropping.

When the little temporary house was finished, Allison and
I came back to the farm. She arrived first, looking less
pinched and thin and no longer coughing. Edie, the nurse in
whose home she had stayed, believed she'd had a bout with
bronchitis, not the tuberculosis that my mother had feared.
Rob brought me home the next weekend; Daphne could not
ride with us. I was not told it was because she was pregnant,
but guessed that it was. We had to stop at least twice where
the road crossed streams so that Rob could pour water in the
radiator and cool the engine off. It seemed an interminable
trip.

When I first saw the small rough house where we were to
stay until a proper dwelling could be built, it sat squat and

black on our barren land, covered outside with the same dark asphalt roofing material used on our chicken houses. The inside walls had exposed studs and boards and the low roof had nothing between its peak and us. There was one large room, where we were to cook on a two-burner oil stove, eat at a plain table and wash dishes on a long shelf holding a dishpan. At one end of the shelf was the bucket for drinking water; underneath was another for waste water. There was a smaller room adjoining that was really a screened-in porch. It held an old rocker given to us, an open-out day bed where my mother and I were to sleep, and a cot for Allison. However, this makeshift house was home because it smelled of my mother's coffee and the oil stove, and our cat Brownie was asleep in a chair.

I don't know how the farm looked to Allison, but I had a hard time adjusting to its barrenness, its burned smell and the loss of all I'd known. First I walked over the raked and cleared ground where our house had been, saying to myself, "The back door was here . . . no, it was there. This is where the kitchen was," and not really being sure. I kept trying to remember everything as it had been, making it exist whole in my mind. "The bookcase was here in the living room. Here were the two rockers. The morris chair was there. The chest was under the window here."

I didn't talk to anyone about this process of re-creation; it was only for myself. My mother was busy, driving back and forth to the courthouse to consult Harrison Floyd, trying to find a house design she liked, checking fences with Solomon, ordering fence posts and wire, agonizing over the garden (she finally decided this was a waste of time). Most of the nation suffered drought that year. Dry spring had given way to dry summer, cloudless skies, almost constant sunshine. Once in

a while there was distant thunder and a cloud would rise in
the northwest. But my mother would eye it and announce,
"It's a wind cloud." Indeed this was what it usually was, and
it rolled over us, whipping up dust. Perhaps once in three
weeks there would be a five-minute shower, nothing more.

No vegetables grew in our garden that summer except
cabbages, and those because they received all our dish- and
bathwater. We bathed by putting an enamel basin on a chair
and asking for privacy. It was a soapy business; we were afraid
to be lavish with water. All used water was poured carefully
into a bucket for watering plants.

Our cows had to be pastured on Carl Stevens's farm because we had little grass and no way to keep the milk cool;
there was no room in that cottage for anything but a small
icebox. I asked about the horse when I came back from
Daphne's and my mother said, "Nellie never seemed to recover from the run from the fire. Susan was keeping her but
she just grew weaker and weaker. She lay down in the pasture
one evening and by morning she was gone. Don't say anything to Susan about it; she feels bad enough now. Anyway
Nellie was old and it was probably her time to go."

It saddened me too: our last horse. I believed she'd died of
homesickness. I thought she probably remembered her barn,
the nice smell of hay and the long hill she had always grazed.
"Well," Mother said when I told her this, "she was spared
coming back and having no green grass or stable. It wouldn't
have been home to her anymore."

The cottage, as we called our rough little house, was partly
furnished by neighbors and friends, who held a "pound
party" for us at a local church. People brought a pound of
whatever they could spare. There were jars of jam and canned

vegetables, pillowcases, a side of bacon, an old table, several chairs, plated silver, odd dishes and an enormous walnut bedstead we had to save for the future house. There was also a beautiful old spoon holder that we used as a sugar bowl. My mother was touched and grateful. I am not certain how she thanked the anonymous donors but the time-honored way was to send letters to the church and the county paper, and she probably did this.

While I went about silently grieving over lost things, Allison was having difficulty living in close quarters with Mother and me, and trying to decide what to do with herself. Back in the winter she had talked about going to college, but now she was not sure she wanted to. She and my mother used to talk about it across the table when I was out on the porch, supposedly asleep.

"I just don't want to be a teacher," Allison said.

"Not everybody who goes to college has to teach," my mother answered.

"What else is there? I mean that I have to have a college degree for?"

There was no immediate reply. The options open for women were limited: teacher, nurse, secretary, store clerk. Even I knew Allison was not suited to these.

"I'd really like to study art. You know that's all I'm any good at."

"Honey, we've talked about this before. You can't make a living that way."

"Some people do," Allison said. It was a time when all magazines, and there were many, were illustrated not by photographs but by drawings and occasionally by paintings.

"Well," said my mother, "it will be all right to study art, but you need a skill so that you can eat while you do it. Your father would never agree to just sending you to art school."

That summer my sister was often left alone with me in the stifling heat of the cottage because Mother was off somewhere nearly every day. Allison sniffed, "She never stays home; I think she just likes to drive around." Mother was looking for a used sewing machine, she was talking to carpenters about the house plan she had finally chosen, she was seeing the lawyer, she was sending off urgent mail—and as Allison probably knew in a way that I did not, she was keeping herself hectically busy because she could not bear to stay at home in cramped quarters with us except when she had to.

In happier times I would have been outside playing, but there was no shade left, no tree putting out leaves, though a few tiny bushes were trying to grow and bring forth foliage and the grass was coming back. Only the deep-rooted sprouted and only the tough survived. The sun burned down every day. I stayed inside to escape the heat, talking to Allison, who did not want to be talked to by me, making it impossible for her to be alone. I sometimes complained and then we ended by quarreling. It was no wonder that she wanted to leave, and as soon as possible.

In June, Harrison Floyd entered suit against Jeb Hensley as owner of Cross Corners Lumber Company and employer of one Samuel Hickman, who set a fire in Hensley's field that he was unable to control, in consequence of which the plaintiffs' property was destroyed by fire and they suffered severe discomfort and dislocation. The suit asked either cash compensation for timber destroyed and buildings burned, or that Hensley furnish lumber for rebuilding to Alice and Emory Bell, Jane and Patrick Jackson and Mary and John Marshall, and further, that he buy the usable burned timber at fair compensation.

We had just finished supper one evening when a large car drove into the yard and parked behind Mother's. Taking off

her apron and smoothing her hair, she said, "It's Mr. Hensley
. . . you and Allison better go out on the porch." Then she
went to the door.

"Evening, Mrs. Bell," we heard him say.

"Good evening, Mr. Hensley."

"Nice little house you got here."

"Would you care to come in?" my mother asked, opening
the screen door. Allison and I could hear the sounds of a big
man stepping inside and shaking the floor as he walked across
it. He stopped near the table, but did not pull out a chair to
sit down.

"How you been gettin' on?" he asked. Even Mr. Hensley
could observe the southern custom of making small talk
before getting down to the real subject.

My mother said, "Quite well, thank you," and waited.

"Mrs. Bell, I know you're alone and all, and your husband's
not here to advise you. I hate to see a lady like yourself taking
on something you can't succeed in and will just cost you
money."

"I don't understand," my mother said, though she understood very well.

His voice rose: "I mean, I don't care what Harrison Floyd
has told you, what kind of lies he used, but suing me isn't
gonna do you and those colored people one bit of good. No
jury in this county is gonna make me pay you and those
niggers for a fire I didn't set and had nothing to do with."

My mother started to reply and he cut her off by raising his
voice. "I told you I was willing to let you all have that lumber
for a good price, a good price, lower than I'd sell it to anybody
else. It's a good offer, and if you want my advice you'll take
it because it's the best you'll get."

As we listened we could imagine my mother drawing herself up, standing beside the table with its dirty dishes and remnants of our supper. Her voice was chilly: "I will wait and see what the jury will do," she said. "And if you have anything more you want to say about this, Mr. Hensley, say it to Mr. Floyd."

He must have stared at her for a moment, and then we heard him start for the door, where he stopped. "You're a Yankee woman, Mrs. Bell, and most folks around here don't have much use for bossy Yankee women. I think you'll be sorry you started this." He opened the screen and stepped down.

Mother, of course, did not allow him the last word. "I was not the one who started it," she said to his back, but he didn't answer. He got in his car, slammed the door, gunned it and backed over a rosebush my mother was trying to nurture. On the way out his car went fast enough to raise a great deal of gray dust.

We came out of hiding immediately and asked her, "What will he do?"

Standing at the door, Mother shrugged without confidence. "I don't know. Mr. Floyd says he's all bluster and no action. . . . I don't know."

13

Gates

The gates of my childhood clanged shut the year that I was eleven, going on twelve. Nobody heard them but me. In the months after the fire I was unable to return to the heedless, running, vaulting child I had been. I found I no longer wanted to run flat out down the orchard hill or gallop madly along the road. I can't remember the day a stick became simply a stick, no longer chestnut-colored with a mane and flowing tail. I dropped childish things right and left, not even bothering to put them away.

At school I was shut out from the group I longed to join with their newly pointed breasts and occasionally painted mouths. I had never felt so much on the fringes before, but suddenly all the girls seemed to be growing up faster than I, and sharing a knowledge that I lacked and didn't know how to acquire. They whispered behind their hands, standing around the big stove in our classroom in the mornings before classes.

"What?" I would say. "What are you talking about?" I knew better than to ask but couldn't help it.

The question triggered significant glances among them and finally one would say, "Shall we tell her?" She leaned over, put her mouth near my ear, her hand hiding it, so close her breath caused almost unbearable tickling, and said, "Grace Terry is pregnant." She drew away and said, "You know what that means?"

I said of course I did, but I had not learned the word at home. I guessed; it was what Daphne was. But Grace Terry was in high school and I saw her on the bus every day. I started to say "When—" and they shushed me violently.

Then one of them whispered, "Do you know how she got that way?" and I had to say no.

"How?" I asked, and they laughed so hard they couldn't stand up and fell against each other in helpless merriment. I was the only one left standing upright, though I wanted terribly to be able to fall against them giggling with hilarious knowledge. I knew that "no" was not the best answer for social acceptance, but I was sure I would be quizzed if I said yes. It took most of my grade-school years to learn painfully that when I lied my imagination was never equal to the truth of some of the things they knew and I didn't.

They were the girls who went about with linked arms, singing songs I didn't know and doubling over at private jokes. Once in a while they would grab me around the waist and carry me along with them for a brief moment of belonging. It did not happen often; usually I went about the schoolyard alone, trying to look as if I were going someplace important or coming from somewhere else, smiling. It fooled no one but it saved my pride.

Shortly after Jeb Hensley's visit to our house, my mother received a note summoning her to Harrison Floyd's office.

She went immediately and was told that Jeb had signed an agreement to supply without charge enough lumber to replace all the buildings destroyed by the fire, and to buy the usable burned timber at a fair price. She came home as close to jubilation as she could let herself be, and carrying a rare treat: ice cream for us all that she had the drugstore clerk wrap in newspapers so it wouldn't melt on the way home.

"After all that Jeb had to say about no jury making him do anything, partly because I was a Yankee, he was afraid to let it go to court," she said happily, forgetting her ice cream. "We can go ahead with the house now."

"And so can the Jacksons and the Marshalls," we echoed.

The cement foundations were already poured and the building started almost immediately. As soon as the carpenters left in the late afternoon (or evening, as it's called in Virginia), I started climbing on the framing and the scaffolding. On the east side, out of sight of my family, I sat on the highest point I could reach and sang.

Meanwhile, back at the cottage, Allison was preparing to leave home before the house could be finished. She had been saved from more schooling by my father, who wrote that a clerk would be needed by his insurance company in late summer and the job could be hers if she chose not to go to college. It seemed to be just what she was waiting for. She and my mother studied patterns and went shopping for material; there was a flurry of sewing despite the heat so that Allison could be properly clad when she went off on her own. On the day she left, she put on the suit my mother had made for her, settled a small hat on her brown hair, worked her fingers into new gloves, and suddenly became a young woman we hardly knew. She left on the train for Chicago and did not come home for two years. At first I think she was happy to be away, occupying a tiny bedroom in my father's small apartment. In time her letters showed a muted nostalgia for the country she had longed so fiercely to leave. "Does Antonio still sing?" she wrote. "Is he staying around?" Antonio was almost the only bird to inhabit our black trees that long, hot summer after the fire. He was a mockingbird of joyous temperament who sang day and night from the top of the one half-alive oak tree left in our yard. Allison had named him, and all that summer we listened to his spilling song, sung in flight, sung in giddy leaps and rolls from the end of a charred branch, sung in moonlight. His irrepressible mocking, which evoked the song of almost every bird now vanished from our farm, must have helped her to bear those months of unrelieved heat and no privacy.

I don't recall what my mother did all day while the house was going up. I remember that she was there most of the time, keeping in touch with what was being built and how it was constructed. When she occasionally had to see Harrison Floyd on legal matters, I now went with her. If she stopped at the Farm Loan Association office, I tagged along and sat, half listening, as she talked to Judge McNeary. When the carpenter she had engaged seemed to be consuming liquor on the job, I went with her as she sought another.

Mother didn't intend to have another house as flimsy as the old one, she said. This one had double floors, plenty of supporting timbers for the walls and roof, and closets, one in every bedroom and one downstairs. She had not had a real closet since she'd moved from Chicago before I was born.

The old house had been held up on brick pillars, and cold winds had swept under it through the latticework around the bottom; this one had enclosing foundations of cement. Also, there would be good weatherboarding on the outside; Mother chose redwood lumber because it was reputed to be fireproof and insect-proof. As far as I know, no one in the country around us had built anything of redwood, and I can imagine Hensley's language when he got the order. Or perhaps she ordered it somewhere else; he could not have been expected to furnish exotic lumber.

As it turned out, the redwood gave everybody a supreme headache. It tended to split with every nail, and she had to order more, slowing up construction. When it was finally finished the house was rose-brown in color, and we knew of no other house that looked like it. Mother decided to paint it, choosing a pale cream color. But the redwood drank the best oil paint, and four coats were required to hide it. Then, of course, it looked like any other house, but it never needed another coat of paint while she lived in it. Two generations later, the love of natural wood may have inspired someone to scrape all the paint off—if they knew what was under there. I've wondered about it but never gone back to look.

By September 1930, my mother and I were living in the new house with its unpainted walls and its sparse furniture, trying to get used to life without Allison. That was when I began writing to her; I believed that I was making my letters sound as if I were at least five years older, though I imagine she had to laugh at a few pretensions. But it began a correspondence that both of us enjoyed; she had a talent for converting ordinary encounters into funny experiences, and I tried to imitate her way of looking at life.

This was not easy because I did not think what was happening to me at the time was especially funny. In the first place, I was discontented with my new room. It was small and L-shaped, and faced south and west. I was much put out that it was not big and square like the room I'd briefly occupied after Daphne left hers. In her old room I could drape myself in her rose-and-cream Spanish shawl that she'd left behind and admire myself in the large mirror over her dresser. Sulkily I sighed for the shadows and presences of that old room, never caring that it had been terribly cold and that its plaster kept falling. My mother's room I considered the only satisfactory new bedroom; it was long, with windows to the north, east and south. It seemed to me that space distribution had not been equitable, and it took two years for me to become happy with mine.

I had not wanted the house that my mother chose to build; I wanted a house from Sears, Roebuck. Different models were shown in their big 1930 catalog and could be ordered along with pots, pans and farm implements. To my eyes, some of the houses shown were pretty and quaint, illustrated, of course, with curving walkways, a husband walking smilingly up to the door, a happy housewife waving from it. I thought those with roof lines sweeping gracefully over entryways would look nice with roses climbing over the door and up to the overhang. I kept showing Mother the ones I liked, but her glances were perfunctory and her answers vague. I suppose the Sears houses were precut and shipped for assembling on site. If so, my mother may have felt about them as she did about clothes bought through their catalog: "Everybody will know where we got it."

The house that my mother decided upon appeared in a magazine from which she ordered the plans and specifications. By the time it was finished, it seemed smaller to me than it looked in the drawing, but its downstairs rooms were ample, especially the living room. This room extended the length of the house on the west side, about twenty-four feet, with a fireplace centered on the inside wall. Stairs went up the middle of the house from a tiny entryway, and the dining room and kitchen were on the other side. Beyond the kitchen was a small, screened back porch with an alcove for a big icebox, and next to that a pantry that was never finished. Beneath was a half basement accommodating a massive wood furnace for central heat, and a stack of wood. Beyond a wall was a root cellar, with steps up to the kind of slanting outside doors children used to slide down.

I don't know why my mother was willing to tolerate five doors in her kitchen: to the living room, to the dining room, to the basement, to the pantry and to the porch. There was not a lot of work space left, even though there were narrow counters on the cabinets she had the carpenters build against one wall. There was a deal table in the middle of the kitchen, but it was never adequate to hold the milk pans, water bucket and whatever mixing bowls and pans were in use during meal preparation. She had no wood cookstove in this house; instead there was another kerosene stove, but not her beloved Red Star. That make had been discontinued, and the one she was able to find balked at burning evenly, heated slowly and its capricious oven sometimes flattened cakes to sogginess or burned biscuits on one side.

The roof of our new house slanted upward to a peak above the first floor, and dormers set into the north and south sides provided extended space for rooms, and windows that opened inward. There were three bedrooms, space roughed in for a bathroom, and a small hallway. The third room could hold only a cot and my mother's sewing equipment. All the rooms were sturdily constructed and snug; in time they were painted mint green or sky blue. My mother was content with how the house turned out, and eventually I stopped wishing for a chaise lounge, a dressing table and a canopy bed.

Fortunately, by the time my mother was painting rooms and staining woodwork she was not noticing that growing difficulty with my life at school was making me suffer, though I don't think it affected my appetite. Probably she had her own suffering to do; she was seeing Daphne and Rob become nearly penniless. As usual, Rob had taken his best cured golden-leaf tobacco to Richmond to sell, only to find, in a city that smelled richly of cigarette manufacture, that prices had plunged and were still falling. He came home on the wagon with little cash and pitifully few groceries. Daphne wrote cheerfully of this to us at home, saying, "I'm sure we'll manage somehow." Unreassured by her tone of optimism, Mother took part of the canned goods and delicacies that my father had sent us and carried them to her daughter. Her gifts were reluctantly accepted by Daphne, who kept looking at Rob stamping in and out of their kitchen.

Mother found that she could say nothing—not that she didn't try—without meeting Rob's stiff-necked silence. "He'll let Daphne go hungry," she fumed mostly to herself on our way home, "before he'll admit they don't have enough to put on the table." She might have kept out of it if Daphne hadn't been pregnant. Mother did not think Rob viewed this condition with proper concern, and was convinced he did not appreciate Daphne's delicacy. I remember her saying, "Rob is an earthy man and he's used to cows having calves and pigs having piglets and he seems to think his wife . . ." She never finished, and I didn't ask what she meant. When I was older I realized that by "earthy" she meant that Rob enjoyed sex and therefore was probably not quite respectable. It did not occur to her, I think, that Daphne could have been earthy too.

With a desperate urge to help them without offending, my mother hit on the idea of asking Rob if he could help her out by building a barn on our place for which she would pay regular wages. She proposed that Daphne live in our new house while he worked on the barn; there was plenty of room, she said, and Daphne could have the other bed in the big bedroom. Rob agreed to build the barn—he could scarcely refuse since his corn crop had been poor and his garden as pathetic as his neighbors' that year—but he balked at having his wife removed from his bed. He would drive the long miles each day to our place after tending his own farm at dawn. It was a daunting round trip for an old car in the 1930s; Rob suffered flat tires, radiator boilovers and regular refusals of his old Model T to keep going or to start after resting and cooling off. He spent a lot of time under the car fiddling with wires or under the hood cleaning spark plugs and coaxing batteries to respond. For him, as for others in those Depression years, even low-cost gasoline was hardly affordable and sometimes he apparently drove the car on no fuel at all but will.

The barn was barely finished when Daphne's time drew near, and she wanted to come home to be nearer to Dr. Chiles for delivery. She also wanted to stay in the cottage we had sweltered in during the summer, not in our new house. By then the wind was coming through the thin walls at night and my mother told her it was no place to have a baby even though she had installed a cast-iron stove.

"It will be fine," Daphne said. "I'm used to the cold; I've become a hardened Scotswoman now." Besides, she said gently, Rob would feel more at ease when visiting her if they were apart from our house. So my mother gladly turned the cottage over to her—anything to have Daphne home again.

For a while, perhaps a week or so, she would come over to have coffee with my mother before Rob got there in the morning. It was like old times for both of them, and as I left to catch the school bus I heard their laughter and knew that my mother was happy. She was not by nature a laughing woman.

Daphne's baby decided to be born on a Sunday, and I found out about it when my mother called me in and said, "Run over to the Marshalls' and see if Mary can come for a while to stay with Daphne. I have to go for the doctor and call Rob."

I raced off and found Mary, dressed in her nice black Sunday dress, just getting ready to walk a mile to her church. She said, "Of course I'll come right now," and reached for her apron. We walked back so fast that Mary was puffing hard when we reached the cottage.

"You wait outside, honey," Mother said to me. I did not object; I was already scared of what was going on. After a few minutes my mother hurried out and said, "Don't go far away. I want you to hear Mary if she needs anything." She drove off and I wandered between the house and the cottage, not knowing what to do with myself. Once Daphne gave a loud groan and frightened me so that I ran to the door and opened it. Mary was patting one of my sister's hands; the other one was flung above her head, holding the headboard.

"What happened?" I said, afraid to go in.

Daphne looked at me over the mound of herself under the bedclothes and managed a smile. "Just a pain," she said.

"Does it hurt?" I asked.

"Yes," she said, "but not too long. I'll have some more pain, so you go on like a good girl and don't be scared. I'll be all right." I withdrew, closing the door quietly.

It seems incredible now that at the age of nearly twelve I had no inkling that having a baby could be painful. Though I read every women's magazine that came to the house (my mother subscribed to four or five), the stories and articles of the day contained no descriptions of womanly functions below the neck. In stories about couples and their first babies, husbands were described as pacing the floor and worrying. Bedroom doors stayed closed, the husband on this side of it. After hours passed and he had shredded his tie, he would hear the wail of an infant; soon someone would bring him the rosy, beautiful newborn and he would have the first glimpse of his child. His wife was tired and happy, with damp curls for hair and he was very tender with her. That's all I learned from reading.

Between my twelfth and thirteenth year, when I was visiting Daphne nine months after she'd had her baby daughter, she handed me a small green pamphlet called, I think, "Marjorie May's Twelfth Birthday."

"Read this," Daphne told me, "and then we'll talk about it."

It was about the onset of menstruation. And it was a measure of my unsophistication that I was enormously surprised that this happened to girls about my age and would undoubtedly happen to me. I had never heard anyone speak of it at school. This did not mean it wasn't talked about, only that I didn't catch on to the terms they used.

Later, when Daphne asked me if I had any questions, I was too embarrassed to voice any, though I must have had some. She understood this and said, "Allison and I decided that we would tell you before it happened to you. Mother never told us. When it happened to us we were scared and thought we'd injured ourselves."

I was impressed that she and Allison had decided to do this for me. "Did Allison send you this?" I held up the pamphlet.

She nodded. "It's not very attractive, but it's the only thing we could find for girls your age. Maybe you'd better not say anything about this to Mother. Just be surprised when she explains it. If it happens at school you can go to the home economics teacher. She keeps stuff on hand in the home ec building." I was in complete agreement about not telling Mother; I couldn't possibly have brought the subject up. Though I read that green leaflet over and over I was still a little unnerved by the event when it did indeed happen. My mother was not surprised and was ready with a little counsel and the protections of the day, now routinely advertised on television but then only mentioned in whispers. Until that moment of truth, she had never given me any warning.

But on the day that Daphne had her baby, I knew nothing of this. I kept looking anxiously down the road for Mother's car, covering my ears so I would not hear the sounds coming now and then from the cottage. They were groans, but not in the voice I knew as Daphne's. There was something deep and wild about them that terrified me, and kept me from going to the door again.

When my mother did come, she brought an old black woman known as Aunt Maggie, who carried something in a bandana. Together they disappeared into the cottage, and I, glad that I no longer had to remain close enough to hear Daphne's cries, went into our new house and shut the door.

My mother had not been able to reach the doctor because he was off in another part of the county attending a patient, and she couldn't find her friend the nurse either. She left a message for the doctor with his wife and picked up Aunt Maggie, who had spent a lifetime as midwife. Aunt Maggie, it turned out, did have some special incantations to help birthing along. She traced a circle around Daphne's bed and sprinkled some powder along it, beamed on by Mary Marshall, who said Aunt Maggie's spells had helped her with each child she'd borne. Aunt Maggie had not finished her magic when the doctor arrived in a hurry. He had hardly entered the cottage when she came out and walked straight to our house, banging on the door with her walking stick. When I let her in she said, "You mama say you fix me some coffee and a couple eggs." I had to help her up the half-step from the enclosed porch to the kitchen, where she carefully lowered herself into a chair.

I lit the oil stove and put on the coffeepot, took down a frying pan and heated it for the eggs. "Do you want them fried?" I asked her.

"Lemme see the eggs," she said. "Is they fresh?" I told her they'd been gathered that morning and she said, "You got bacon grease to fry with?" I nodded, so she agreed to fried eggs, but said, "Now don't gimme no egg that lays down in the pan." The yolks stood up nicely under the salt and pepper, and I left the yellows runny as she directed.

After she had eaten and had her coffee, Aunt Maggie took out a pipe and a little bag of tobacco, poured some in the pipe and lit it. Only then did she seem to notice me.

"That you sister havin' a baby?"

"Yes," I said.

"I been bringin' babies into this world a long time, longer'n that doctor's been alive. I coulda helped her with this one if the doctor hadn't come, but he don't bleeve in my way. Now, when you time come, you remember Aunt Maggie."

I was startled into saying that my time was years away. Aunt Maggie puffed and shook her head. "Be here fore you know it," she said. "You growin' up, git you a boyfriend, git married and then send for Aunt Maggie." I didn't find this reassuring,

but was saved from answering by Mary Marshall coming
in the door. She was stepping quickly and smiled when she
saw us.

"Hi you, Mrs. Woods? I just slipped away whilst I won't
needed to see if you kin go over home with me. I want you
to look at them boys you hasn't seen since the day you holp
them to be born."

Aunt Maggie's wrinkles grew deeper with pleasure and she
said to me, "You, child, tell your mama I be back right soon.
Tell her not to mind about gittin' me home right away. I wait
till she can go."

"I'll tell her," I said.

Mary peered at me. "You all right here by yourself, honey?"
I said I was fine. She helped Aunt Maggie out of the chair,
out of the door and down the path over the hill, Mary walking strongly and Aunt Maggie keeping up somehow. I
watched them until they disappeared, not really happy at all
about being alone. The house was so silent that the Westclox
over the kitchen stove could be heard in the next room. I
wandered from room to room, not knowing what to do with
myself. Usually in such circumstances I fixed myself something to eat, but even this comfort had no appeal. A car was
coming down the road with dust boiling behind it and I
watched it without interest until it turned into our drive and
I saw that it was Rob's. As it quaked to a stop he leaped out
of it and almost ran to the cottage. I thought he would burst
in, but he knocked. My mother came to the door, said something, let him in and all was quiet again.

I did not remember that my mother had said she would call
him, and since I also never thought about telephones, I imagined that Rob had guessed about Daphne. Mother told me
later that she had called him from Jouett, where the doctor's

office was. She received no answer to the two long and two short rings so she left a message with the operator.

With some delight the operator called Rob's neighbor and said, "Bill, you better get over there and tell Rob his mama-in-law just called about Daphne. It's Daphne's time, tell him."

Bill rode over and found Rob in the barn assisting with the birth of piglets. "I'll stay here until she has them all," Bill told him. "You get on up there."

Rob drove as madly as the old Model T would allow and arrived looking as though he'd just come from the pigpen, which he had.

Mother felt that his haste was unseemly and came to the house almost immediately to put a kettle of water on to heat so he could "get cleaned up." Solomon had not come and it was growing late, so she took down the milk buckets to give Rob (our cows had been brought back from Carl's farm as soon as we installed a big icebox). "He needs something to do while he's waiting," she said to me. "Besides, he's a better milker than I am." I would have to get the eggs and water the chickens, she told me. Daphne was all right, but it might be a long time before the baby was born. I didn't understand why it took so long but would not have asked for anything. I told my mother about Aunt Maggie and the coffee and eggs.

"That foxy old woman," she said. "I didn't say a word about your fixing her anything. I never thought of it. But I'm glad she asked you. I felt sorry for her when Dr. Chiles said, 'All right, Maggie, we don't need your magic now. I brought mine.'"

When Rob came in to wash all the way to his elbows before milking, his black hair was standing up because he had been running nervous hands through it, and he smelled ripely of pig. He scrubbed well, took the buckets and left. Sniffing the air, my mother muttered, "I'll have to see if I can find some of your father's trousers he can wear." (For some reason Mother considered the word "pants" to be vulgar.) By the time Rob brought back the milk buckets, she had a pitcher of water, soap, towels, an old shirt and a pair of my father's wool pants laid out for him. I busied myself with straining the milk while he, rather meekly for him, went upstairs to wash and change. It was a rapid affair; he was back down and rushing out of the door before I had finished putting the pans of milk away. His hair still stood up, but the currents of air he left behind smelled of Ivory instead of barnyard.

At school, my social life was terrible. I did not know whom to become and was trying on different personalities. Most of them refused to blend with my real one, which was different from what I thought it ought to be; I was afraid to trust it.

By the beginning of the new year, 1931, a classmate named Charlotte and I became inseparable friends and went everywhere together, arms linked. But the knowing group of girls on whose fringes we both existed began to write her notes and pull her into whispering, giggling circles while I stood watching on the outside. For a time I tried being like the girl who was the center of this group, mimicking her springy walk, her head toss, her experiments with lipstick. This did not gain me admission either; besides, I couldn't do the dance steps she could do. I dared not flirt with the boys she flirted with (all of them), and I didn't know the facts of life that she laughed and talked about so easily. But I was the first to see the new boy who came to our school that year, and I think I was the first to give him my new dimpled smile, one that required me to tighten the muscles in one cheek. I remember that when I gave my age to the teacher, he swung around in his seat and whispered loudly down the row to me, "I'm twelve too." From that we progressed to note passing. Unlike the girls doing this constantly, I couldn't handle the attention and blushed brightly when teased, "You love George, you love George!"

"I don't like him, I hate him," I said, and immediately someone would yell, "Hey, George, Vallie says she hates you."

I refused to look at him as he said, "Do you, Vallie?" but this only made him try harder. Every time I stole a look in his direction he was gazing back; this went on until Mrs. Evans said, "George, turn around and stop mooning over Vallie." All the kids snickered and sharpened their fingers at my red face.

But it was Charlotte's friendship I yearned for. When we were both cast in a play and she was hesitant about doing a dance with a curtsy at the end, I felt it necessary to explain to Mrs. Evans that she was shy. At lunch, when she turned her back on me, I was crushed. I wrote her a note that afternoon on which I think I dripped a symbolic tear, asking, "What made you mad?" She didn't bother to answer, and I rode home full of misery. The new barn loft in late afternoon was a fine and private place to cry, and I went there.

The next day I carefully kept very quiet. At lunchtime, when The Group went blithely off without asking her, Charlotte told me as we pulled our lunch boxes from under our desks, "I didn't like it when you told Mrs. Evans I was shy."

"I'm sorry," I stammered. "I didn't mean—"

"You always do that," Charlotte said. "You always act like you know everything and I don't." She was very cool that day, even though we ate lunch together sitting in a sunny spot on the grassy schoolyard. I invited Janie Parker to eat with us; she needed friends as much as we did and Charlotte and I could talk to her without saying much to each other. By the end of the lunch period we were beginning to giggle a little as usual. But I was growing cautious; I knew it wouldn't last. It never did.

14

The Dance

It was October 1931, over a year after the fire, and Daphne stood in the middle of our long, furnitureless living room, looking at the walls my mother had just painted, at the floor she had just stained, and said, "This would be a wonderful place to have a square dance." By then her baby, Jean, was beginning to walk and Daphne had not had a party since she was married. When she looked at all that new uncluttered space she heard dance music and a hundred moving feet.

"But honey, who would come?" Mother asked reasonably, thinking, I'm sure, that all the people who had once danced at our house had now gone their various ways. Our near neighbors were farmers whose churches taught that dancing was a snare of the devil. Allison was in Chicago, and anyway had never been interested in learning fox trots and shags, and I was not expected to know anyone who danced. (I had seen The Group demonstrate a dance called the "black bottom" at school, but thought it wise not to bring this up.)

Daphne said, "All we have to do is let a few people know there's going to be a dance here and you'll have plenty of guests."

My mother wasn't sure about this. "Oh, I doubt people will want to drive this far," she said.

"Oh, they will, they will," Rob assured her. "In these times people will drive sixty miles for a party just to forget their troubles for a while." The weather had been better for farmers in 1931, but the prices for their crops were worse.

"We can find musicians and a caller," Daphne said eagerly. "Or one of the musicians can call the sets. We can get Rosser and his son."

"What about paying them?" my mother asked.

"A couple bottles of white lightning and a dollar or two," Rob said. My mother said she couldn't possibly pay anybody in liquor, but that she wasn't against the idea of a dance. Daphne thought it should be held on a near Saturday night. Mother said she could make apple cakes and serve cider and coffee; I could see she was caught up in the excitement Daphne always generated. This was my mother's familiar role: staying in the kitchen while Daphne and her friends shook the house with merrymaking.

I hadn't the least idea of what one did at a square dance, but Daphne said, "You'll be fine, Tarbaby, just follow along and do what everybody else does." She said there was really nothing to it; anybody could learn. Privately I believed I *could* dance, though I never had—at least not *with* anybody.

But first they had to discuss what I should wear. Daphne said, "Oh, let her wear stockings, not socks for this," but she said it too late for my mother to order any from a Richmond department store or from Sears, Roebuck. At a general merchandise in Mineral she found some shiny, heavy rayon hose that were rose-colored. No one thought to have me try them on, probably because it was shiny pink hose or nothing.

Solomon and I applied a great deal of wax to the living-room floor and I slid back and forth on it with clean feed sacks wrapped around my feet to bring up the shine. Daphne and Rob came early on dance night and sprinkled granules out of a can labeled DANCING WAX. Dancers were supposed to crush these, get the stuff on their shoes and make the surface even more slippery. We ate supper early and afterward went upstairs to dress. My dress was blue, I think, though my hundreds of blue dresses flow together in memory. I hardly noticed it; I was most aware of my stockings.

My mother could not believe how many people came—so many that not all of them could get into the house. Most were people she had never seen, couples and single men, and quite a few were people she would never have invited: girls popping chewing gum, rough-handed men smelling of whiskey and women trailing the musk of undeodorized underarms (not too unusual in days when the only effective deodorant ate holes in your clothes). There were others too, young women and men of Daphne's age, who made a point of speaking to my mother and thanking her for having a dance in her new house. Daphne and Rob greeted them all; it was clear that Daphne knew and enjoyed a much wider acquaintance than when she had lived at home.

"That's a Hicks, I'm sure," she would say, nodding toward a man leaning against a wall. "And that woman in black is some kin to Rosser's mother."

There were people on the porch and in the yard, and some were looking in the windows. Our lights were dim—Mother had three oil lamps set on tables in corners—and there was a sort of mellow glow over everyone. People came in anything they had to wear; there wasn't a full-skirted, flying-petticoated woman in the lot, and no man in a western shirt and tie stomping the floor in Texas boots. There were made-over dresses, or thin summer clothes on this cool October night, cottons freshly ironed and starched, and perhaps a silk dress

or two. Men wore dark coats and ties and long-sleeved shirts.
Collars might be frayed, and soles thin or heels worn, but
once the music began and the caller shouted, "Honor your
partners," only the movement mattered.

I hugged the wall, amazed that all those people understood
how to move together, and tried to figure out what the caller
meant by "Doe-si-doe your lady. . . . Now your opposite." The
longer I watched the more I knew I could never, *never* dance
the way these people did. I picked out Daphne in her emerald-
green corduroy lounging pajamas of last Christmas; she
moved surely and gracefully, the full pajama legs swirling like
skirts about her feet. Lounging pajamas were high fashion in
the early thirties; they were one piece, like jumpsuits, and the
legs flared widely below the knees. I desired a pair for myself,
but Mother considered them too sophisticated.

I started sliding along the wall toward the kitchen door,
afraid someone would ask me to dance, afraid someone
wouldn't, and terribly conscious of the shiny pink hose sagging at my knees. Even when I rolled them up tightly into my
first elastic garters they did not hold. Every time I took a step
the knee bulges in those sorry stockings grew bigger.

"All hands round," yelled the caller over the sound of his
fiddle, and the dancers started circling. Then the music
stopped. Handkerchiefs came out to mop sweating foreheads,
someone threw open the rest of the windows, and Rob came
toward me to say, "Come on, Vallie, time to shake a foot."

I backed away. "I can't," I said. "I don't know how."

"Doesn't matter," he said. "Just do what I do."

"I can't," I said again.

"Sure you can," he said and dragged me into a group. "Just
listen to the music," he told me, raising his voice, taking his
place across from me.

"Honor your partner," sang the caller, beating time with

his feet to a tune I could have sworn was a fast "Church in the Wildwood." Rob came toward me with a sliding step, and around me I saw the women doing a shuffle step to meet their partners. By the time I got to the center, Rob had already bowed to the place where I was supposed to be and returned to his place, the line I was supposed to be in had left me, and I went back, confused.

"Swing your partner!" and Rob grabbed me and danced around my stiff, unnerved body.

"Doe-si-doe your right-hand lady!"

I was seized, turned around, looking for Rob, forgetting to move my feet with the music, abandoned and then turned in the opposite direction by Rob.

I don't know how I got through it, except that dancers simply moved around me as if I were a puppy that had wandered onto the dance floor. When it was over, Rob led me to where Daphne was drinking cider and talking to several other women.

"I saw you out there," she said, smiling.

One of the women asked, "This your little sister?" and then turned to me and said, "Never mind, honey, I couldn't dance either the first time. They just pushed me out there and said, 'Aw, ain't nothin' to it.' I about died. But I learned, and now they can't keep me off the floor."

As the music started again I ducked and fled into the kitchen. For the rest of the night I helped my mother peel apples and cut the apple cakes she took out of the oven. I put on an apron that covered my shameful sagging stockings and watched the dancers from time to time. Daphne was having a wonderful time; her eyes sparkled, her hair shone auburn in the light and she hardly missed a set.

At midnight the music stopped. Women went upstairs to

get their coats and jackets from the beds, and men stood outside talking quietly as they waited. Some people left without speaking to my mother—Daphne said later they were "backwoods shy"—but most of the women made a point of thanking her, and some of the men did too. The night outside our doors resounded with people calling back and forth, with cars starting explosively and driving away. My mother sent me out with a flashlight to help people find their way across the yard. I watched, fascinated, as nine people stuffed themselves into one car that had no side curtains to keep out the wind. Though they huddled together, they were almost as exposed as they would be in a wagon.

Daphne and Rob were the last to go. They and my mother were looking at the living-room floor, where, down the full length of the room, the stain had been worn off in a blurred rectangular outline. In time my mother put down wine-colored carpet to hide the scars and dents of the only dance we ever had in that house. By the time I had enough friends and might have tried it, my father had come home to live, and he would have been miserable in a house full of dancers. He would have taken a lantern and gone to the barn to read until all of them had gone.

15

My Father the Stranger

My father and I really became acquainted for the first time in 1934, when I was fifteen and he sixty-five; he retired then from the insurance company he had been a part of for over thirty years and came home to stay. Our relationship during his vacation visits over the years had been formal and polite. He brought presents on those visits and I thanked him; then I was expected to take them somewhere else to play.

As I grew older and closer to his age at that time, I tried to understand him as I could not then. Now I believe that he came with an idealized picture in his mind of long days of reading and walking around the farm, with perhaps some cozy, friendly exchanges with my mother and possibly with me, though I do not think he thought much about me at all.

Mother did not prepare herself adequately for my father's retirement, though I am sure she must have had misgivings about it that she did not tell me. She didn't prepare me for it either; perhaps there was no way she could have. I had my own idealized scenario of at last getting to know my father in the way I thought other girls knew theirs. At first I thought that he and I might now become good friends, that he would like the way I was growing up, that there were many things he could tell me about subways, museums and stage plays—the exciting life of the city I wondered about.

That he loved all of us I was sure. I remembered all the barrels and boxes he had sent us in the early twenties. Tins of Chinese delicacies that my mother liked to have on hand—preserved ginger, tinned crisp noodles, dried mushrooms, canned water chestnuts. Food we could not buy in local stores: maple sugar, canned and candied pineapple, canned apricots, as exotic to us then as litchi nuts would be now. There were sweets we never saw in stores in our small towns: Scotch shortbread, chocolate butter creams, butterscotch patties and ribbon candies. Toys shining and smelling of new lacquer, emerging magically from the excelsior they were packed in. We derived a quiet pleasure from the care he showed in making these choices for us.

But the truth dawned on my mother and me after my father had been with us for a few months: We did not know how to welcome a strange man—or perhaps any man—into the life we had created for ourselves; what's more, we didn't want to. In small carpings we revealed to each other that he was an intruder, complicating our satisfactory existence. Of course Mother was aware that we owed much of that existence to his regular checks sent over the years, and she may have hoped that he would be mellowed with age now, glad to be home at last, content to let life go on as it had before he came.

My father did not bring with him much in the way of personal effects: suits and a heavy overcoat, a bookcase, books on psychic research, atheism and religious cults, and two large file cabinets of clippings. But his clothes shoved my mother's over in the closet, and soon hers smelled of his, a curious blend of coal smoke, Chiclets and apartment-house mixed cuisine. He occupied the other twin bed in her bedroom, and he dropped his pocket watch, comb and brush, nail clip and desk calendar on her dresser among her pretty jars and powder box. The combination washroom and linen closet that she had furnished with basin and pitcher, towel rack and chamber pot (we still had no electricity or plumbing) became a place whose primitive facilities he swore at every morning. His filing cabinets and bookcase took up most of one wall in the small room that Mother used for sewing.

The rocking chair in the living room became my father's favorite and he rocked and read there for hours at a time. The only desk was a sturdy mahogany drop leaf that was full of my mother's canceled checks, letters, receipts, account books and, tucked into a pigeonhole, the bit of embroidery she worked on when she found time, so when he wrote anything, he did it on his knees. I don't know if he cared where he wrote, but in our house everyone had had a desk except my father. I don't wish to imply that he was not permitted or encouraged to have one; probably it didn't matter to him.

I found that if I was in the living room when my father was there and made a rustle looking through records I would like to play, or said something to my mother while she worked in the kitchen, I would find his eyes fixing me with a chilly stare over his half glasses. Naturally I left, unable to ignore what I read as hostility and probably was. I usually went up to my room and stayed there until he climbed the stairs at bedtime; then I could go down and play a few records, trying to keep the volume low. That was hard to do with hand-cranked phonographs; the only way to play records softly was to use fiber instead of steel needles and they gave a slightly muted sound to those old 78's. I always closed the doors, but Liszt must have hummed through the double floors anyway.

Sometimes my father was the one to sigh, pick up his book and go upstairs so he wouldn't have to listen to my mother and me talking about dress patterns, what went on at school or her work. She had by then been employed as executive secretary of the Lewis County Farm Loan Association for nearly two years. She enjoyed discussing what she was doing in those years, the people she met and the farms she visited as part of her job, but my father could bear only so much of this before he would say, "Do I know these people? No. Do I want to know these people? No. So let me read and you talk about your job with Mary Marshall or Vallie."

I rarely said anything to my father except when I had to. I tried to at first, but even if I spoke to him directly there would be a pause before he focused his blue eyes on me and said, "Were you speaking to me?" I would clear my throat and repeat the question, and he would shake his head, say, "I don't know what you're talking about," and return without another word to his plate or his book. Anything more I thought to say was swallowed forthwith. After this happened several times, I stopped trying. I think now that if I had been less timid and had insisted on his attention, I might have broken through that barrier. I wonder if it was his slight deafness that kept him from hearing my wispy voice. But of course he wasn't trying either, and felt no impulse to exchange ideas with me.

He had been a solitary man in the city, and he spoke of only one man, dead by then for twenty years, as a friend, apparently the only one he ever had. It was solely letters that had kept him in touch with his children after my mother moved to Virginia, and he barely knew me at all. By adolescence I was as much a stranger in the house he shared with his wife as he was to me in the house I shared with my mother. I could not know that his profound aloneness was what had molded him into the old man he was by then. And I could not recognize that his translation from bustling city to unhurried country must have been unsettling.

My mother was unable to help me appreciate my father's dislocation; though understanding in many ways, she was prevented from seeing it by old antagonisms between them. She felt it was *her* life that was being disrupted and moved from its center. When the two of them had separated and she removed to Virginia—partly because, she said, she could not bring up the children to be targets of his sarcasm—she may have thought he would not live to retire to the farm. He was much older than she, and in those years fewer men lived to be sixty-five. Now that he was home, in seeming good health, she did not know what to do with him. For a while she left him to his reading and went on with her work. It was when he decided he should take part in the running of the farm that matters became uncomfortable. To do anything out of doors he had to communicate with Solomon, and this was difficult for him because he could not get the hang of southern black speech.

"Why can't he talk like other people?" he would say to me testily after I had translated for him, and Solomon was out of earshot.

"He does," I said. "He talks like Susan and other colored people."

From the time that my father started showing interest in the farm, Solomon found himself caught in the middle. He would begin a job, perhaps making a new pigpen, and my father would stand there and watch, wearing one of his old office shirts and worn gray business pants.

"Why are you doing it that way?" he would ask.

"This what Mrs. Bell tole me to do," Solomon would say.

"She *told* you to do it this way?" Incredulously.

"Yes sir. They's a hole s'posed to be here for to pour slops through."

"Pour *what* through?"

"Slops. What we feeds to pigs."

"Slops," my father would repeat a little nastily. "Now that's a nice word." To which, of course, Solomon could give no answer, and he would try to go on with his work of setting a trough in the hole. In a few minutes my father would say, "Don't you ever measure anything before you saw?" or "I knew you weren't making that board the right length," until Solomon was so discomfited that he would suddenly discover it was time to milk the cows.

Later my father would report to my mother about Solomon's sloppy carpentry. "Do you think the pig will mind?" Mother asked more tartly than my father was prepared to appreciate.

"Then you don't care if our money goes for shoddy work?" my father asked severely.

My mother's chin went into the air and her voice became a little harsh. "You know very well we don't pay Solomon much, and we don't need expert builders for a pigpen. I hope you are not telling Solomon how to do things when you don't know what you're talking about."

There were more words between them, impolite words, even ugly words, since my father did not take kindly to being told he was ignorant and my mother was indignant that her judgment was questioned.

Unfortunately, it was not just the pigpen. When my father had read for several hours he grew restless and walked out to check on what Solomon was doing. He hovered around as Solomon fixed a fence, cleaned eggs or washed his hands in preparation for milking. Realizing that Solomon might summarily quit, Mother tried to avert disaster. She started taking my father to Richmond whenever she could—he did not drive—so that he could have lunch in a restaurant, go to the movies and have a beer afterward. But that worked for only two days. She tried a gentle-voiced diplomacy: "You know, hon, we won't be able to find anyone else as capable as Solomon. If you keep standing over him I'm afraid we'll lose him."

My father said, "Himpf" through his nose. Then, "He doesn't even know how to wash his hands. He needs to scrub—*scrub*—before he handles milk equipment."

Mother kept her voice calm. "He's been doing the milking for ten years now and we've never had a problem."

"You don't know; you can't see germs."

"I know we haven't been sick." Then she turned to coaxing. "Maybe while he is doing what he has to outside you could be putting up shelves in the pantry. We really need those."

The pantry had never been finished; it was only a junk room with a window. My father agreed to work on it. He gathered nails, a saw, hammer and boards, laid them all out neatly, put on old clothes and brought a level. After he had put up wooden braces he cut the first shelf. It was a quarter inch too short. My father swore mildly and tensely cut another. This time it was not short enough and he had to trim it. It was the nailing that undid him; he could not drive the nails he chose to use straight down. They curled without going through the boards. He tried four times to pound them in, each time with the same results.

We—or at least I, who was in the dining room—heard the crash of his hammer as my father flung it against a wall, and a string of swear words that I did not know were in the language. He told my mother later, "That lumber is no good. I can't drive a nail through any of those boards." He put up one precarious shelf and quit. This did not deter him from overseeing how other work was done, however, and my mother worried.

"If only your father could meet someone he could talk to," she said to me several times.

"How about Mr. Ford?" I said. Mr. Ford was a local minister who did not press his religious views when he called.

"Oh dear, no." She was emphatic. "He would crucify Mr. Ford. Your father would be sarcastic about his church and beliefs, and I can't have him doing that."

We really couldn't think of anybody. All my father wanted to talk about was his dislike of churches, his scorn of organized religion and how stupid people were to believe there was a God and a heaven and hell. He liked to tell visitors in solemn tones: "When the fire burned our old house all my books burned except my books on religion." When the visitor made sounds of amazement, he would say smugly, "All my religious books were in Chicago," and enjoy our guest's weak smile.

Finally, in the days and months after Solomon had resigned (for the reasons my mother feared) and gone to work for a neighbor who was delighted to hire him, my father, who now cleaned the eggs brought in by a hired man who came for two hours a day, found a friend—an improbable friend whom we expected would be chewed up and spat out after half an hour in our house.

He came to our front door with a Bible under his arm, and I looked at him in surprised recognition. He was Robert Dunlap, a farm boy who had been two classes ahead of me in school.

"Hello, Vallie," he said when I opened the door. "Your father home? I'd like to talk to him if he has time."

"Certainly," I said. "Come in, won't you?" I was mimicking my mother, and wished I could tell him to hide the Bible. I walked ahead of him to the living room, said, "Father?" and waited for him to turn his head. "This is Robert Dunlap. He lives on a farm near here and he wants to talk to you."

Robert put out a hand and gave my father a warm, firm shake. "Do you have a little time for me, sir?"

"Time is what I have the most of," my father said, noting the Bible and getting a gleam in his eye. "Sit down, sit down. Not many people want to see me. Most of them want to see my wife."

That was when I left; I decided to go out and take a long walk down the pasture that now had lush green grass where once there had been ashes. I went across the creek into the woods, which were gradually sending up bushes from the burned stumps, to a place I liked to sit when I wanted to be really alone. I stayed there a long time and hoped my father would not gloat later over his attack on Robert's beliefs, which I presumed were strictly Southern Baptist.

But when I came into the kitchen, Mother, starting on supper preparation, put her finger to her lips, and I could hear Robert's eager voice, and my father's equally eager one answering him. They were talking, not arguing, and my father was listening politely. When Robert said well, he had to go

home and help with the milking, my father went with him to
the door and said, "Young man, I have enjoyed your visit very
much."

"I'd like to come again next week, sir, if that would be all
right."

"You come whenever you like." My father actually
sounded pleased. "This is the first intelligent conversation
I've had since I came to Virginia."

Mother and I stared at each other in disbelief. My father
came out to the kitchen and poured himself a glass of wine,
obviously in good humor. "Now there is a fine young man,"
he said. "I brought out some of my clippings on biblical
history and he wanted to hear what I thought about all of it.
We didn't agree on all points, but he read the Bible versions
of the same history and we compared them. He's coming back
next week."

Robert was back as he had said he would be, polite and
smiling as before, and for months thereafter. He and my
father sometimes strolled outside on pleasant days, Robert
with his Bible, my father with copies of *Truthseeker,* a publication for atheists. They were often still deep in talk when I
came home from school. Most of the conversation seemed to
be about what was in the Bible, but frequently I heard my
father talking about the city he had lived in for so long, telling
Robert all the details I used to wish he would tell me.

I know now that it was Robert's gentle persistence and
innate dignity, impervious to ridicule, that could bypass my
father's outer defenses to touch his terrible need for a friend.
Robert was still coming to visit when I went away to college,
and continued to do so until he volunteered for the army in
1940. My mother said that my father was as desolate as if he
had lost a son. Until Robert was killed in the Pacific, they

exchanged letters, and Mother made cookies that my father could send him. When Robert's family came to tell my father of his death, they came in a body: his one brother who farmed and his three sisters, who had never married and stayed on the farm. My father subsequently made a rare gesture—he visited Robert's family as they awaited the return of their brother's body. Mother said later that it was the only time she had known my father to reach outside of himself to others in pain.

16

A Little Something Coming In

In 1933, when my mother became executive secretary of the Lewis County Farm Loan Association after Judge McNeary's ill health overtook him, she at last had a business address.

The judge had left her an office of sorts over the only drugstore in Mineral, consisting mostly of his old rolltop desk, a typewriter, some stationery and loan-application forms. The job paid little and was not full-time. Its major requirement was that she fill out the infrequent loan applications for farmers seeking financial help, and that she know enough to inspect their farms and assess their worth. The work suited her; it carried a little prestige, it gave her a chance to see more of the county and, as she said, "The salary's not much, but it's a little something coming in." She clung to it gratefully when my father retired and she was not sure they could live on his retirement income.

Mother liked to have me ride with her during the summers, when she had to visit farms, and I liked going because most of the farms we went to had owners' sons with whom I could flirt demurely as she talked with their parents. These were purely practice sessions for me; I would not have known what to do if one of those overalled boys had spoken to me.

I had little interest in the work my mother was doing, though there were times I could not escape knowing about it. There was the first time that we drove into the yard of Hector Ruffin, scattering chickens, geese and dogs. It was a hot day and I did not want to wait for my mother in the car, so I walked with her to the door. It was wide open, and inside chickens were wandering through the high cool hallway. At my mother's knock a well-endowed woman of about thirty-five in unconfining clothing stode toward us, shooing chickens before her and yelling over her shoulder, "Hector! If you don't put this door on we're all going to walk in chicken mess . . . How do you do?"

"Mrs. Ruffin?" my mother said. "I'm Alice Bell and I came to talk with your husband and you about your farming operation here. You know that Mr. Ruffin has been in and applied for a loan?"

"Hector!" bawled Mrs. Ruffin again toward the back of the house. "Excuse me, I have one time getting him out of a book. Come on in, he'll be here in a minute."

"We'll just wait here," my mother said, probably because of the chickens in the hall and their visible excrement.

"Well, you all might as well sit in the grape arbor, then, where it's cool." She pointed and we went toward the inviting arbor behind us, which had old wooden benches beneath it. We sat there in a faint breeze, and in time Hector Ruffin appeared, smoothing his hair and hitching up his pants. He shook hands with my mother and acknowledged me.

"I suppose you'll want to see the barn. What else?"

"Your outbuildings and some of your near fields." He

glanced down at her shoes. "Don't worry," she told him. "I'll put on boots."

I stayed in the arbor as they went off. I looked at the fine old brick house that had sagging, paintless windows with one or two broken panes, and a porch with beautiful columns, also paintless and warping. I wondered if a farm loan could help to retore it all.

Mrs. Ruffin came out, shooing chickens again, bringing a pretty, delicate glass with something greenish in it. "Here," she said, "I made some peppermint tea yesterday and it's cool to taste, so I thought you'd like some." I thanked her. It was like a breeze on my tongue.

"This is a pretty glass," I said.

"Yeah, it is. Not many left. They were Hector's grandmother's . . . everything's breaking or falling down around here. Well, I'm going out and see what your mother and Hector are talking about."

I waited in the hot afternoon, watching bees in the blooming clover, a rooster stalk into the house, an old dog dig a cooler place under a lilac bush. I could hear the voices of my mother and the Ruffins and decided to find out myself what was going on. They were standing near the barn, a large red building with a mammoth manure pile to one side. I knew it was old, well-rotted stuff because it didn't have an unpleasant smell. When I lingered at a distance I could hear Hector saying, "My real love is teaching, Mrs. Bell. When they cut the staff at Monroe College, I had been there only two years and was one of the first to go. I knew the only other thing I could do was to come back here and make this farm support us."

My mother said, "The only way to do that, unless you have outside help, is to work sunup to sundown and sometimes beyond. Unfortunately, that doesn't leave much time to read books."

He threw her a sharp glance and said, "You sound like Betty here." Betty was nodding her head. "And you sound like my neighbor Ben Bolton. He says he won't allow himself to look at the almanac until after the first hard frost." He rubbed the bare circle in the crown of his dark curls. I realized I liked his face, with its slightly arched nose, dark eyes that looked sleepy but were not, a crease forming between black brows, and a slow, faint smile.

My mother folded the papers she held and said, "I'll be sending these on in a day or so. I'll let you know as soon as I can what the bank's decision is."

"What do you think?" he asked her. "Are they likely to think we're good risks?"

My mother hesitated. "Basically, you have quite a bit in your favor, but—"

"Mrs. Bell, we need to know about the *but*s," Betty said.

"All right, here they are: You need to put more time into what you're trying to do, you need to use that manure piled up there, probably on your corn, and"—she gave them a half-amused look—"for making a good impression if for nothing else you ought to put that door on its hinges. If one of our land bank members decided to call on you, that door would ruin your chances right there."

"See," Betty said, "I told you."

Hector put his hands up over his head. "I'll fix it today, absolutely. You ladies have convinced me. And Betty, you lock the bookcase."

About five miles down the road, Mother said she liked Hector; he had good potential. "I think Betty will see that he works hard, and she's got the will to work right along with him. He knows what to do, if he'll just do it."

"But the house," I said. "It's going to pieces."

"First they have to take care of the land. It has to provide meat and grain for their own use, with enough left over to sell. In these times they will probably just get by, but they'll eat. The house can wait for a couple of years."

Mother knew what she was talking about. I remembered how our old house had needed paint for years while she built new chicken houses.

I went to other farms with her, some of them immaculately kept, with every shrub trimmed, fences cleared of honeysuckle, privies whitewashed, walkways swept, stables cleaned, and no manure piles at barn doors. These were good risks, my mother said, but I found them uninteresting.

One of the people who had gotten a loan was the husband of Edie Stonebrunner, the friend who had cared for Allison after the fire. Mother was notified that Leo had made no payments for several months and that she was to call on the family and then report to the home office. She was troubled about this; she knew she had recommended the loan because of Edie and because Leo was known to be a hard worker and skilled with sheep. He and his sons wanted to try new breeds and needed pens, sheds and lambing quarters. The last time my mother had visited everything had been going well; the buildings were under way and there were new sheep in the fields.

The day my mother drove to their place, I was out of school and went with her. Their farm was pretty and somewhat quaint; the low porch was covered with wisteria, the old barn a silver-gray building with red doors. Beyond it were the new sheep quarters.

As we went into the long driveway my mother mused, "I've never known Leo not to cut his hay. There must be something wrong." I saw that it was high with ripening grasses, already past its time for green hay.

At the house Edie came to the door and invited us onto the porch. As we sat down she excused herself, and in a moment we heard the low rumble of a male voice at the back of the house; then a door shut. Edie came out and said, "Alice, Leo is too ill today to see you. Is there anything I can help with?"

"This concerns both of you, Edie, and I'm sorry he's ill. Maybe I should come back in a day or two?"

"I don't know when he'll be better," Edie said, her eyes focused in the distance. "He's been sick so much . . . I can't tell you when to come." Her voice was tired, even defeated. She swung to face Mother and said, "He hasn't made the payments, has he?"

My mother looked directly into her eyes and shook her head. "I thought he might be having trouble, and apparently he is."

Edie gave a short, mirthless laugh. "Yes, indeedy," she said, and looked down at her hands. At the back of the house a door opened. "Excuse me," she said and left us. Then we heard her say sharply, "Leo, I told you to stay in bed."

"I do what I damn please," Leo answered. There was a sound as if a body had bumped against a wall, then a shuffle.

"Leo, please. Alice doesn't want to see you like this."

"But I want to see Alice. Always like to be nice to Alice." Now Leo appeared at the screen door, wavering drunk, and stumbled out onto the porch. Edie caught his belt, steadied him into a chair and turned to my mother. "I'm sorry. This is the third month he's been unable to work."

Leo looked us over, having trouble focusing. "Alice, I'm gonna pay that loan off when . . . when . . . God, Edie, I need a drink! Get me a drink."

"No." Edie's mouth was grim.

Mother stood up and said, "I'll come back when you're better, Leo. You can't talk business today." Her hand was insistent on my elbow as we went down the steps, Edie following us.

At the car Edie said, "You see?"

"I do see," my mother said. "It's bad for you and the boys."

"What about the loan payments?"

"I don't know. I may be able to buy a little time. Can you get him on the wagon?"

"My God, Alice, if I could do that I'd have done it. You know drinking men—or maybe you don't. If they don't do it themselves, it doesn't do any good."

"Try anyway," my mother said. "He's risking a lot."

"Everything we have."

"Edie, come here," Leo groaned from the porch. I stole a look, not really wanting to, and he was sliding off the chair.

My mother said quickly, "What about the boys?"

"Joe's disgusted, says he's leaving home. Ed's too young to really help. David and I do a lot, but—"

"Dammit, Edie, I need you—where are you, dammit!"

Hastily my mother started the car. Edie leaned in the window and raised her voice over the sound of the motor. "Seven years he's been on the wagon. I don't know what happened." She pulled back and turned away.

My mother shifted gears and swung the car around. "I'm sorry you had to see that," she told me. "A man loses all dignity when he's drunk." I remembered John Nicholson, but this was worse.

Mother went on: "It would be best for Edie's sake if you don't say anything about this to anybody."

"I wouldn't," I said, wondering why she thought I might. I was getting too old to consult Susan or Mary Marshall, and it wasn't the kind of thing I talked about at school. "But if it does that to him, why does he drink?"

"I suppose he can't stop once he gets started. That happens to some people, and not just men, either. Poor Mrs. Emlaw . . ." She stopped, obviously deciding she had said enough.

We talked no more the rest of the way home. The late evening was getting chilly, and though we now had a car that produced some heat, it wasn't much. My mother was deep in her own thoughts, and I huddled into the seat not wanting to ask any questions. It was not only that I knew my mother believed it was better for us not to know the uglier facts of life; there were doors that I was reluctant to open wider for myself. Glimpses through them were so unsettling that I slammed them shut and looked the other way.

I knew the Stonebrunners were on Mother's mind for days and nights. I would hear her trying not to wake my father and me as, unable to sleep, she went quietly down the stairs at night to drink warm milk and read. I put Edie and Leo out of my mind and did not ask about them. My mother, usually so eager to talk about her work, did not mention either one. She had a few triumphs; the Needhams had paid off their loan. "I'll have to take you out there some day," she said. "They've built up that place from nothing."

"What about the Ruffins?"

"He did qualify for a partial loan. His wheat is in and he did a good job, and his corn did well. He's keeping up with the payments, but his wife says if they don't make clothes out of feed sacks this year they won't have any. It doesn't seem to bother her."

There were people who came up the drugstore stairs to see my mother, hoping desperately that their applications could be approved. The ones who left silently, their shoulders hunched and their hope gone after talking to her, were the ones who cost her pain and sleepless nights. She knew that the land bank was their last resort; there was nowhere else for them to go. Sometimes an older couple whose youth and vigor were diminished would come in, and she had to explain gently that there was no use taking their application. One of the women, clasping and unclasping her rough hands, said, "It don't seem right after we's worked so hard all our lives and paid all our debts that we cain't get no help now because we's old."

"I wish it were not so," Mother told them. "I may think you can handle a loan, but the bank won't consider it when they see your ages."

On November 1, an unseasonably warm day, my mother was informed that she was expected to meet Edward Cary, the land bank executive for Virginia, at the Stonebrunners at 4:30 P.M. I did not want to go, but my father was away, Mary Marshall was ill, and my mother would not leave me alone on the farm. She met me at school because she could not wait for the school bus, which is why I remember the date. It was a brilliant day with a sky filled with scudding clouds and gentle winds.

When we arrived Mr. Cary was already there, sitting with Edie on the porch. The scene was a cheerful one, with Mr. Cary smiling and Edie in a good mood. One of the boys had gone to bring Leo up from the sheep shed. When he appeared he was thinner and much fitter than the last time we'd seen him.

I don't think my mother realized what was coming. After a discussion that I barely listened to because I could see their son David, the sun on his blond head, trimming honeysuckle along a fence row a few hundred yards away. I came to attention when Leo said, "Now Mr. Cary, I can't possibly do that. How can I make full payment when I'm just trying to catch up on the monthly payments?"

"Mr. Stonebrunner, when you and your wife signed for this loan you read the conditions. Right here it says that when you default on any payment the entire loan becomes due and payable. We've given you about five months' grace, and we can't continue to do that."

I looked down the porch length and saw Edie with her head down, looking at her hands in her lap. Leo was staring at Mr. Cary and Mother was sitting tensely to one side.

"If you can give us a couple more months . . ."

"We've already given you extra time because Mrs. Bell felt you needed it to catch up," Mr. Cary said.

Leo's eyes flicked to my mother and back. "I was sick for . . . for some time," he said.

"I know that, and I'm sympathetic. But we can't give you any more time—perhaps a week more if you think you can borrow the money from a relative or a friend."

Leo's eyes followed his son's bending back and then lifted to the horizon. "I don't know. I can try. That's all I can do."

Mr. Cary put away his pen and some papers he had taken out of his pocket, stood up and said, "I hope you folks can get some help with this. If you can work it out, get in touch with Mrs. Bell—"

"I haven't time to drive that far to get in touch with Mrs.

Bell," Leo said angrily. "It will take all my time to do my work here and try to find the money for you."

"Mr. Cary?" Edie, who had been silent the whole time, raised her head. "Are you saying we are about to lose our home?"

Mr. Cary did not flinch, though my mother did. "Yes ma'am. But if you and your husband can borrow three hundred doll—"

Bitterly Edie said, "You might just as well ask us to borrow a million."

Mr. Cary put on his hat and went down the steps. At the bottom he said, "Mrs. Bell, I will send you a letter on this," tipped his hat and turned away. As he drove off, Mother, her face set, said to Edie, "I'm sorry. I didn't want to see this happen. Is there any way—"

"Not a snowball's chance in hell," Edie said. Then, her eyes brimming, she whispered, "I thought you were my friend." She turned roughly away and went into the house, letting the screen door slam.

Leo got up painfully and set the chair carefully against the rail. He looked at my mother, who said, "I'm so sorry," her voice unsteady, but he could only shrug. We left him then, going too loudly down the steps and driving away.

The first week after that meeting my mother was tense with worry for Edie and Leo. The week passed, but she heard nothing. Halfway through another week she was informed by a copy of a letter to the Stonebrunners from the land bank office that foreclosure proceedings were being initiated. It was her duty to go to the courthouse and make arrangements with the lawyer who usually handled land bank mortgage defaults in the county.

Mother never saw the Stonebrunners again, but sometime in the 1940s she received this note from Richmond; I found it after her death among the letters she kept:

Dear Alice,

It has taken the war and the loss of one of our sons to make me realize how empty possessions can be. I think of you and your girls and have come to know you had nothing to do with our losing our place in Courtney. We did it to ourselves. I know you tried to help us but I wouldn't see it then. The move was painful for me but in the end Leo found a fine job in the Patent Office here and we live comfortably. I have wished I could take back the last words I said to you. They have haunted me all these years. Please forgive me for saying what I did—you were indeed my friend.

Edie Stonebrunner

17

Daphne

To me, my sister Daphne is forever young, forever fair. She is still the lovely young woman with the fine straight nose, faintly cleft chin and wide gray eyes in the photographs my mother took of her sixty years ago. These are the only pictures I have of her except for the ones in my mind. In my mother's photographs she is looking off dreamily to the right; in my mind she is laughing, a wide, white laugh that creases a dimple in one cheek. She still looked much that way when she died at the age of thirty-one, still eager for life, surprised by death.

Marriage and privation changed Daphne from the late-rising girl she had been in our house to the woman she became in hers. Nothing quenched her laughter, though she usually had little but old and faded clothes to wear. She scrubbed clothes in a washtub for her husband and child, and her once well-tended hands grew rough and red.

The Depression was no more cruel to Daphne and Rob than to millions of others, and less so than for many who suffered hunger and the loss of houses and land. She ate every day, if not always well, and Rob's farm had plenty of wood to keep warm by. But it was hard for my mother to see her first child, who had been so vivid in pretty clothes, looking, she said, "like a washerwoman." She could not offer to make clothes for Daphne without implying that Rob was unable to provide for his wife. Once she took her a blue gingham dress she'd made, and later learned that Rob resented the gift so much that it was put away. It was never seen by us again.

When Allison wrote from Chicago to say, "My friend Rosalind gave me some clothes I can't wear. Maybe Daphne can use them, or maybe Vallie, so I'm sending them along," Mother took the whole box on her next visit. Rob could not possibly mind second-hand clothes, she reasoned, and in this she was right. When she took out black cocktail gowns, Daphne said, "I remember when I'd have loved wearing these," and put them aside. There were slinky lounging pajamas and an evening gown, but also some simple flowered dresses that she put on and wore. In these she was the earlier Daphne, cool and lovely.

But if she had lost her carefree girlhood of pretty clothes, in marriage Daphne had acquired a large, warm, raucous family, and her enjoyment of them made up for all she had put behind her. When I visited, I was briefly a part of it all.

Rob had five older brothers, each of whom was married and had, it seemed to me, quantities of children. On every Sunday they all came back home from their jobs in Richmond, bringing wives, children and food. In summer, which was the only season I was there as a child except for the three months I stayed after the fire, large tables were set up in the yard under oak trees and the food put out in bowls, on platters and plates. I was astonished by the rapid consumption of everything: Cakes were reduced to crumbs, bread to a crust in a wrapper, salads to a few shreds of cabbage left in a bowl, chicken to bones and my sister's enameled pan of potato salad to emptiness within an hour or less. I forget what we children drank, but the adults all consumed pots of hot tea. When I expressed surprise at so much tea, Rob said, "Braw brecht Scots drink only tea or whiskey." There were no bottled soft drinks; nobody could afford five cents a drink for all those children when there was free water and milk around.

Daphne loved those Sunday gatherings, and she moved lightly among the trees and between benches and chairs, working with the women, attending to small Jean, sometimes sitting long enough to talk and sew. The men and older boys played baseball, or the men stood around and told stories while the boys listened, learning how men expressed themselves. There were always babies and lap children casually tended by the nearest adult or older sibling, so that mothers had freedom to move around and visit.

Rob's father and mother (known as "the Ma" and "the Da") seemed very old to me as they sat in chairs under the trees watching the flow of life they had begun in another land spilling over now into this one. There was a great deal of tussling that went on between the male cousins, and I was often in the thick of it because Daphne was unable to convince me that girls didn't roughhouse. Finally the grandmother said to her, "Let her play, Daphne, she will have to be a lady soon enough."

There were shouts of laughter, yells, the screaming of babies and small children, and all of this ebbed and flowed through the long summer afternoons. When dark came, the children were fed lightly and packed, sleepy or already asleep, on beds and couches in the house. The older ones stayed up to sit on the porch steps and railings, listening to the men talk. I don't remember where the women were—probably cleaning up—but I wanted to be where I could hear the stories, which were of the brothers' boyhoods, of pranks and ghost sightings, and of a trip to the local bootlegger for white lightning when all the brothers piled into the car together and were apprehended by the sheriff on the return trip. As the evening grew later, one of the brothers could begin a World War I song, usually "A Long Way to Tipperary," and the others would join in. All but Rob had been old enough to go to France in 1918, and those war songs were the only ones I ever heard them sing. They would go on to "Over There" and others and end with "Keep the Home Fires Burning." As the final notes died away there would be a pensive silence in which I, with a poor sense of timing, once asked, "What was the war like?" wanting to hear about battles, blood and beautiful Red Cross nurses. This was greeted with heavy silence, until finally a baritone out of the darkness that I knew to belong to Rob's brother Alex said, "We can't tell you." And another voice said grimly, "And we wouldn't if we could. It's not anything we want to remember." Surprised into a silence of my own, I wondered why, and did not learn how terrible those memories were until I was much older.

Rob would come in from having fed and milked the cows by lantern light because he had played baseball until dark. In another hour or so one of the brothers would stretch and say, "Weel, it's aboot time to head back," the wives would be called, the children stuffed into cars still asleep and they would be gone. The drive to Richmond was twenty-five miles and they probably drove no faster than thirty-five miles an hour. There was not a wholly sound, unpatched car in the family, and they were the only traffic jam in that country neighborhood on Sunday night.

Even if the weekend proved rainy, the brothers brought their families to the homeplace anyway. Most of the children were sent to play in the barns, on the porches or in the rain, with mothers yelling from the doorway, "Jim-mee! You come in here and take off your new shoes. I just paid three ninety-eight for those shoes." Or "Alan, come back in here and take off your new shirt. If you're going to get wet do it bare."

On those days the brothers sat around after dinner in the big room and talked about conditions at the tobacco plants where they worked or about politics. Voices rose louder and louder, the arms of chairs were struck, and it sounded as if at any moment a brawl would shatter the dishes still on the table. Once, coming down from a little hall bedroom upstairs, I heard them and went in fear to my sister, who was fixing supper in her kitchen. "You'd better do something," I said. "They're in there yelling at each other. It sounds like a fight." She looked at me in surprise, then went into the long hallway to listen.

"It's all right," she said, laughing at me. "They're having a good time." I couldn't believe that men could have a good time yelling angrily at each other. Of course she told Rob what I had said when we sat down to supper, and he, who had been yelling with the rest, found my discomfort very funny. He went back to tell the others, and there was a shout of laughter while I sat with Daphne feeling embarrassed. She patted my shoulder. "Never mind, Snub Nose, you just don't know that when a bunch of Scotsmen get together they'd rather argue than anything else."

Alex came to the door and said to me, "Come on, Vallie, come into the big room. I'll protect you from those wild men and you can see the fight." I shook my head. "Come on," he insisted, "it's about to start."

"I can't," I said, grasping any excuse. "I have something to do upstairs."

"You're going to miss a good fight," he said and left, not wanting to yield his place to anyone else.

I got up and told Daphne, "I do have something to do upstairs; I'm going to read."

"After you and I do the dishes," she said. "Or rather, you do them because I have to get the eggs ready for Rob to take to our customers tomorrow."

I was supposed to help Daphne when I visited, and in fact this was one of the reasons that I was sent to visit her. I was considered old enough to wash dishes, tidy up, weed the garden, shell peas, gather eggs and occasionally mind small Jean. It was not until several months later that I understood from Mother that Daphne was expecting another baby and was suffering from a tiredness that made it impossible for her to work all day without rest. It was in her kitchen that I learned to use a strange iron that had a little burner in it for heating. I do not know what the fuel was, perhaps alcohol, but it made a subdued roaring sound that made me very touchy about handling it. I stood at the ironing board while Daphne napped on a cot under the kitchen window and Jean slept in a screened outdoor crib that Rob had made.

I was thirteen and not yet well broken to housework. I longed to be outdoors or curled up somewhere reading a book. The year before I had given up my old work of helping Rob pull caterpillars off of tobacco plants. This was a dreadful job but it was vital part of tobacco farming and I had felt important doing it. The worms were smooth, cool, as large as a man's index finger, and so close to the green color of the leaves that they were hard to see. One had to look for the dark droppings and then search for their source. As the caterpillars were pulled off, the tobacco juice, sticky on their feet, eventually covered one's hands. As I remember, these horned green larvae of the sphinx moth were dropped on the ground and dispatched under one's shoe. My shoes became coated with tobacco-leaf juice, green-worm juice (the same thing, I suppose) and dust. They were an appalling sight.

Daphne had her second child in the fall and named him Bruce. This one was fair, as fair as his sister was dark. While Jean had black hair, dark ivory skin and brilliant blue eyes like her father, Bruce was pink and white with a faint suggestion of blond hair. Rob looked at the baby's hands, said, "They'll never be big enough for baseball," and smoothed his tired wife's hair.

Daphne said, "He's fine, he's perfect and I won't send him back."

My mother told Mary Marshall that Daphne had her second baby too soon after the first, but I'm sure she did not say this to my sister. She was learning to be careful with motherly comments to her oldest daughter. Jean was by then two years old, but Mother believed Daphne had not yet regained her strength. But then Daphne had never been particularly sturdy. Now two children crowded the quarters that Rob and Daphne had in the big house, and when, a year or two later, a small tract of land with a house on it became available, somehow with his parents' help they bought it. It was thinly built and cold in the winter, but in that it was no different from other Virginia farmhouses, except that it had been roughly constructed besides. Rob continued to do the farming on his parents' land as his father declined in strength, but Daphne was happy to have a whole house at last, poor though it was. She and Rob raised turkeys and bees on the new place, and, looking like an Old World goose girl, she was sometimes out waving a white apron at the gobblers and hens. She was a little thin and pale but was having a wonderful time.

By then I was old enough to want to help in Daphne's kitchen without coaxing. She watched my growing up out of the corner of her eye, aware that I was no longer interested in pulling caterpillars off tobacco plants because now I was interested in keeping my dresses and shoes clean. She recognized this as outward evidence of hormonal activity and was sure I would be showing a growing interest in boys. I was, of course, but less than she guessed; I liked mild, distant flirtations, but that was all. She made sure I was invited for swimming picnics when Rob's older nephews were along, and we would all pile into cars and go to a place on the river a mile or so away. It was a small river, with a bottom of leaves and sand that made the water look brown, but it smelled fresh and leafy, a delight on hot summer days. I had never seen a sand beach or the ocean, and a muddy path down to the water was fine with me. Sometimes in the group there would be a visiting girl from the city who would look around at the old shoes kicked off at the water's edge, at the farm boys in the water with hair dripping in their eyes, and at the mud stains on her suit and then decline to join the fun but instead sulk on a log or in a car. The rest of us stayed in until our lips turned blue and then rode home in our wet suits, so cool that the hot air made us subdued and drowsy.

Daphne seemed changed to me too, no longer the elder sister with the powers of a parent but someone more like me, or more like I was becoming. She told me about keeping a notebook describing the country men and women she lived among. These portraits were material for a book she planned to write, and she said about them, "I never knew what some people go through just to live." She talked to me about my social life too, something I had never discussed with anybody, not even Charlotte, although she and I both wistfully talked about boys. At the age of fifteen, I didn't have any social life of real consequence, not even the church contacts my classmates had.

"I hear that at school Larkin Chasen has a crush on you." Daphne looked sideways at me to see my reaction.

"Larkin? He's a senior."

"Well? Don't seniors have crushes?"

"He's just nice to me," I said. "Do you want these biscuits to be drop or cut? Besides he's . . . Well, he's not too old, I guess, but I'm too young."

"Use the biscuit cutter. And you'll grow up."

"By then he'll be somewhere else."

Her eyes brightened. "Why don't I ask him to come down here—"

"Oh, no!" I was startled. "Don't do that; he'll think I put you up to it."

"If he likes you he won't care."

"No," I said. "Anyway, I don't like him that much." Which surprised me by being true; I did like Larkin, who had rich, dark red hair, freckles and a friendly smile, but I realized in that instant that my idea of romance had to do with the men I imagined, not with the boys I knew.

"I'm not like you," I said, searching for a way to explain. "You always had boys around. Nowadays if they don't have money for gas they can't go anywhere. You had beaus that could come on horseback." We both knew that in these hard times hardly any parents could afford gas for their sons' courtships. Larkin's father was a minister and he could never use the car.

"Well," Daphne said, "you can't date now anyhow. I know Mother would never let you."

"But I don't care. Maybe someday when I'm older and

there's some man I like, but I don't really want to date boys much."

Daphne's eyebrows went up and she laughed. "You don't want to be a little old granny in a corner, do you?"

I looked at her and said, "I won't be. I know I won't be."

She shrugged and said, "All right, I guess you do. I can feel certainties in myself sometimes too."

After my father came home to live, Daphne and I used to talk about what was happening to our parents. There was no one else to whom I could say, "Do you suppose they ever loved each other?" Allison was too far away to talk to, and in any case I wasn't sure that she would want me to describe the tense atmosphere in our house.

"They did once," Daphne said. "But Father needs to see her as a submissive wife, and Mother could never be that. Goodness knows, they should never have married."

"But they did produce us."

"True, and I wouldn't miss life for anything," Daphne said, picking up a crying Bruce, whose sister had just pinched him. Watching her, still with some of my mother's point of view, I could not grasp how she loved her life as it was then, devoid of luxury and marked by drudgery that never ended. I did not understand the joy she derived from seeing the promise contained in her unlikely surroundings. She and Rob would turn the unfinished upstairs into two rooms, she told me, one for Jean and one for Bruce. The backyard, with its tipping sheds and weeds, she saw as it eventually would be, planted with flowers and the sheds replaced with a neat house for poultry.

I did not want Daphne's kind of life; I wanted to have a nice house in the country, one room filled with books, a barn with a horse in it for riding, and fields that stretched toward mountains. I did not tell her this, and I wish I could laugh with her about it now.

Two years later I went to the college that Daphne had attended, though I did not enjoy the experience, left it early and eventually went to work. I saw Daphne only now and then. We wrote to each other and I saw her on Christmas holidays, and once when she wanted me to go to a dance held somewhere. On those winter visits I stayed on a couch in her living room, where they stoked the fireplace before I went to sleep. By morning it was bitter cold, and I could barely shiver into my clothes and head for the kitchen. There the fire would be roaring in the cookstove and a great enamel pot of coffee was perking. Rob was already reading by the stove and Daphne was giving Jean and Bruce cinnamon toast. She poured coffee and I made the breakfast as I drank it; it was a nice cozy family scene. The only problem was that Rob had a terrible time pulling himself out of *Gone with the Wind* to head for the barn. I remember how bright Daphne's eyes were with interest and energy; her happiness touched us all.

Then I did not visit my sister for a long time, though I don't remember why; probably by then I had found work that did not give me much vacation time and I was dating. On one of my weekends at home my mother told me we must make time to see Daphne, who had written that her doctor had sent her to bed. Though Mother had some difficulty saying it, I think she implied that Daphne was bleeding during another pregnancy. When we arrived, she was indeed in bed, looking wan and discommoded about having to be "lazy." Rob had just brought her a late lunch and she looked at it without enthusiasm. I could feel my mother deploring its sodden look and wishing she could cook something appealing, but she made no comment.

My mother's mission was to urge Daphne to see a specialist in women's diseases in Richmond. It required some courage for her to do this, knowing of Rob's sensitivity to any interference.

"There is a Dr. Jameson," she told them, "who is supposed to be very good. And," she took a deep breath, "I will make up any fee beyond what you would pay Dr. Grant." She leaned forward. "You must let me do this, Rob. Daphne's trouble could be very serious."

Daphne looked at her husband; he was gazing out the window, and I realized that since he and Daphne had married he sometimes had difficulty meeting my mother's eyes. I felt the painful indecision in the room—or perhaps it was Rob's pride that was hurting—and I turned to examine the cosmetics on Daphne's dressing table, a pink-skirted packing box. There was a lacquered box holding perfume, delicious sandalwood, under its hinged top. My father had given it to me and I had passed it on to her because it was not right on my skin. There were creams and powders, but nothing like the array of scents and bath salts that had once filled her dresser at home.

"I can take her any day you can get an appointment," Mother said, and let her case rest.

In the silence Daphne's spoon clinked, and we could hear her children calling to their grandmother down at the big house, where they were staying. Rob turned and said a little stiffly, "I can see that she gets to see Jameson."

"Would you like me to call the doctor and then call you?" Mother pressed him. He did look at her then, his eyes telling her that he knew what she was thinking and that he was offended by her doubt.

"I will call him from here," he told her. "Daphne and I will make the arrangements."

He took Daphne the next day, Sunday, to Dr. Jameson, who had been alerted by the symptoms my sister gave him

over the phone. After his examination he scheduled an operation for that same afternoon. Rob called the postmistress at
Frederick Station to give her the message, and she sent her
husband to tell my mother, who was in the kitchen canning
late tomatoes. We still had no telephone and it was probably
one of the few times in her life that my mother wished for
one. She told me we were leaving immediately for Richmond,
took the hot jars out of the canner and put a few clothes in
a suitcase; we were out of the house in thirty-five minutes. She
left me at my boardinghouse and went on to the hospital,
sure, she said, that Daphne would do well in Dr. Jameson's
hands. She arrived just before Daphne was taken to the
operating room.

"She climbed on that stretcher as easily as a child," Mother
said later, trying to understand what had happened. She
waited out the hours with Rob until Daphne was wheeled
back on the stretcher and lifted into bed, still unconscious,
still smelling overwhelmingly of ether. There was no recovery
room then in that hospital, perhaps not in any hospital. My
mother stayed by the bed while Rob talked to the doctor, and
when he came back she did not tell him that she could hardly
bear the still whiteness of Daphne's face on the pillow,
though it is probable that he was as shaken by it as she.

Both of them watched the nurses come and go with their
starched, expressionless bustle, taking Daphne's pulse, calling
her by name, easing her head on the pillow. Finally my sister
opened her eyes groggily and Rob leaned over to say, "It's all
over, sweetheart, how do you feel?"

Daphne croaked, "Now I can go home," and fell asleep
immediately.

An older nurse of greater tenderness felt Daphne's feet and
legs, said, "Her feet are cold," took a blanket out of the
wardrobe and spread it over her, tucking it in lightly. Then

she smiled at Rob and my mother and said, "It's going to take quite a while for her to come out of the anesthetic. Why don't you folks go and get some supper? We'll be watching her." But neither of them could leave her so pale and distant against the sheets. In the quiet that followed, Rob told Mother what the doctor had said; somehow she had been unable to ask.

"He said," Rob told her, "that with rest Daphne can regain her strength. She's anemic from blood loss." After a pause he added, as if he had to, "He said I should have brought her sooner, but Dr. Grant back home seemed to think . . . He thought she was improving." His voice faded and he sat there, leaning forward, hands clasped between his knees.

"Who is taking care of your cows and livestock?" Mother asked, partly to spare him the pain of his thoughts and partly because she was always aware of cows lowing at the gates, chickens pressing against a yard fence waiting, pigs howling for food.

Rob shook his head. "Nobody. The Da is laid up with a bad foot, and he can't do much anyway. I didn't have time to arrange for anyone else."

"Well," said my mother, "the pigs will eat in the dark, and you can milk by lantern light. If you go home now, maybe by the time you get back Daphne will be less groggy. I'll stay for a while until she's more awake, but I need to get home too."

So Rob drove the twenty-five miles to do what had to be done at home, ate a sketchy supper and then headed back. My mother stayed and watched Daphne begin to stir; finally her head turned and she said, "Rob?"

"He's gone home to milk and feed, and then he's coming right back," Mother said, patting her hand. "Are you comfortable?"

"No. Some water." My mother held the glass for her to

take a swallow or two. "Just want to wake up," Daphne said thickly. "Can't."

"Then sleep until Rob comes, honey," my mother said. "I'll be going home soon because your father will be worried. The nurses are taking good care of you and I'll be back in the morning."

She said that Daphne gave a slight wave of the hand and tried to smile, but it faded out in sleep. My mother kissed her, smelling the ether still issuing from her lungs, and waited another half hour to see if she might rouse again. The nurse came in, gently shifted Daphne's position, checked her pulse and said to Mother, "Good, she's sleeping quietly; she'll be fine." Because there seemed nothing more to do for the time being, my mother left quietly. Passing her in the hall the same nurse said, "We'll watch her, don't you worry. The doctor will be by in a little while."

"Her husband will be back too," Mother said, and left.

Sometime after that, before Rob's return, a clot shaken loose in her bloodstream blocked the oxygen to Daphne's heart. The nurse found her just as she had been, seemingly deeply asleep, but there was no pulse or heartbeat. The nurse dropped Daphne's hand, rushed to the head nurse, and the resident was called. Dr. Jameson arrived a few minutes before Rob, and it was he, himself shaken, who had to break the news. "She just slipped away from us," he told Rob. "She never really came out from under anesthesia; she never knew." It was the only comfort he could offer. And it did help all of us that laughing, life-loving Daphne had no idea she would die so young.

Rob came straight from the hospital to our house. Mother had not been able to sleep and was in her robe, reading, when she heard his car. "I knew," she said later, her face showing the stricken realization. "I knew before he said anything." She reached out to him at the door and he broke down in tears in her arms, the first he'd cried since childhood. Later, when he was quieter, sitting hunched in a chair, she blew her nose and told him, "You don't need to reproach yourself, Rob. You made Daphne happy, and you must remember that." It was her opinion that Rob had waited too late to seek good medical help, but she knew it was because he had barely cash enough to pay the local doctor. She could not look at his misery and add to his pain and guilt. "You have to think about the children too," she said. "You'll have to bear up for them."

"I know. They still have the Ma, but I . . ."

My mother had to wait until early morning to call me before I left for work. Her words were something like, "Vallie, honey, Daphne's gone. Last night a little after I left." Her voice barely shook.

"Mother, no! She couldn't have." Mine shook more, broke at the end.

I could tell she was fighting tears to say more. "Take the bus—I'll meet you."

"All right," I said, and she had to hang up. She sent Allison a telegram and the answer came back: COMING SOON AS POSSIBLE. LOVE ALLISON.

I told my landlady, Mrs. Britten, a southern gentlewoman fallen upon hard times and renting rooms.

"Oh, Miss Bell," she said in distress, "your poor mother." She had lost a daughter younger than Daphne, a daughter so present in her memory that I had come to know the girl as a living personality. Her eyes brimmed with her own loss and ours.

The day stretched so forlornly ahead until time to catch the bus that I told Mrs. Britten I might as well go to work.

"Oh, child," she said, "you simply can't do that. It would seem disrespectful to your sister and your mother." I went back to my room and stood staring out the window into the alley. Mrs. Britten came up softly behind me and said, "Miss Bell?" I turned. "You must eat something, child. Try to swallow a little toast and coffee." She held a tray and on it the delicate china of her better days, a cut-glass dish of preserves, the toast buttered, the coffee steaming. Usually I had to go out to a restaurant five blocks away for breakfast and I was touched to easy tears.

I don't remember what I did that day beyond calling my supervisor at work and telling her, and then calling Monty to cancel our date for the weekend. He was the man I eventually married, but I hardly knew him then, and when he asked if he should come to the funeral I said no. I knew he would have to be with me and my family and I was not ready to face what that could imply. He wanted to take me to lunch, but I said I didn't want any lunch.

Carl Stevens brought my mother to meet the bus I rode to Jouett. The ride to the farm was almost totally silent.

"Is Allison coming?" Carl asked, his only words except for greeting me.

"Yes," my mother said. "Late tomorrow. I'll meet her, Carl. I need to do something." That was all that was said for four miles. Once home, my mother and father and I did not trust ourselves to speak of Daphne, and we talked of what to fix for supper, what to do about tomorrow.

"People may be coming by," Mother said.

"Then I'll have to shave in the morning," said my father. "Is my suit pressed?"

Our nearest neighbors, told by Carl of Daphne's death, called the next day. The Woodfords, the elder Painters and Quinton, Robert Dunlap, Mary Marshall (who immediately took over the kitchen) and Solomon, concerned about my mother though no longer in her employ.

Mother picked up Allison, who arrived by train, tense and exhausted. We spent another evening of not speaking of Daphne but of Allison's trip home, of the time we would have to leave for the funeral, of how one of us would ride with Carl. If we wept, we wept alone. I could not.

Daphne's funeral service was in the largest room of Rob's parents' house. The casket was open, and the shell from which Daphne had fled lay there white and still and utterly unlike her. I had never seen a dead body before; I looked once and then away, knowing that this was not really Daphne but choked by the sight nevertheless. Rob sat with his head down, his arms around his children and Jean's arms around him. He could not bear to look again into the casket, which he would have to do if he raised his head.

I don't remember what the minister said; I don't think I listened. He was there because of local custom, summoned by Rob's sister because neither he nor Daphne belonged to a church. After the short service most of us walked behind the hearse into the field where was a spot that Daphne had loved under an ancient tree. The minister read the Twenty-third Psalm and commended her spirit to God. As earth was shoveled over the plain coffin, Rob broke from among his brothers and threw himself into the grave, calling Daphne's name. Hands pulled him out and restrained him. We could see that

his black hair stood up wildly and the rich color was gone
from his face. His children were not there, at least not with
him. Probably they were with his sister, Evelyn.

What else happened there after my mother and father
spoke to Rob's parents I cannot bring back to mind. We
drove home, my mother, father and I in our car, and Allison
riding with Carl, who could say little. I remember that later
we sat tensely in the living room as visitors began coming by.
My mother, though haggard from sleeplessness and unshed
tears, was able to talk; my father did not know how to, and
sat erect and silent in his dark suit and stiff collar after greeting callers and shaking hands. I sat numbly beside Allison,
wondering if there was something wrong with me because I
could not grieve. I did not know that grief for Daphne's death
would visit me later, when I realized what I had lost. Allison
answered questions about what she was doing, how she liked
the big city, when she was going back (soon, she said; she had
to be back at work), and was given compliments on how well
she looked. I studied her with pride; she wore a black dress
with pale blue collar and cuffs that made her skin look lumi-
nous, and in that setting she seemed to radiate urban sophisti-
cation.

As they left, callers murmured their sympathies. One
woman said, "I always knew Daphne was too good to live
long; the good die young, you know."

Upstairs, after our visitors were all gone, after from habit
my mother had made sure the chicken houses were locked,
the dog fed, the cat out, after we heard her climb the stairs
wearily, surely to lie awake again, Allison and I sat on the bed
in my small room, and she smoked a cigarette. The windows
were wide open so that the smoke could go out; our parents
would not approve.

"God, this house is so full of emotion . . ." she said. "I can't wait to get out of here."

"I guess all funerals are like that," I said, but I really didn't know. It was the first one I'd been to, and I doubt that Allison had been to any others herself.

She blew out a cloud of smoke. "Why did Rob have to be so dramatic—throwing himself into the grave like that in front of all those people?"

I had no answer except to say, "He must have been so upset he didn't know what he was doing."

Allison finished her cigarette and mashed it into a candle holder, one Daphne had given me. "I never could understand what Daphne saw in him. She wasn't brought up to live like that."

All I could think then was that Allison had grown so far away from all of us that she could not feel herself a part of our lives anymore. At the time, though, I also hadn't lived long enough to appreciate how Daphne could have been as happy as she was with her life. I did know better than Allison what she had seen in Rob, but I couldn't bring myself to say so.

We slept together in my double bed that night, and the next day my mother drove Allison to the railway station at Fredericksburg. I sat in the middle. We watched her walk, tall and slender, up the steps, her heels clicking, and saw her take a seat near the window on our side. As the train pulled out, she waved and smiled, a tiny black hat and a veil tipped over one eye. My mother said wistfully, "I think she was glad to go." She and I drove home. It was time for my father's afternoon coffee and I had some with them. Nothing seemed changed then, except for a deeper sadness in my mother's face. It never quite left her for the rest of her life.

18

A Mushroom House
and Frogs Singing

The land that I live on now is on top of a hill; the house that I live in grew out of the earth like a mushroom and is about that color, tawny and gray. It has four windows looking south to the scallops and peaks of two nearby blue mountains. It has taken me sixty-odd years to find this house, which lay hidden in my future while I was thinking that I did not want to live as Daphne lived, as I said good-bye to an early farm, and as I tried to shape a life in the Blue Ridge Mountains.

I sometimes dream that my mother has coffee with me here at my breakfast table—coffee is much connected with her in my mind—and that we talk more than when she was alive. I have tried to imagine Daphne in this house but she eludes me, as she has for most of my life; I can never translate her from the time I remember her into this one. She lingers still in the years before everything changed: before World War II, before penicillin, before atomic fission, before television, before colored people became black people and could sit anywhere on the bus, before Rob turned into a well-to-do farmer. But I still hear echoes from wherever she is of her astonishment and delight in life and, I have no doubt, in what we call death.

On the tax books I am registered as owner of these particular meadows and this hill on which I live. But the true possessors are deer—three large doe and progeny of various sizes. In the fall they visit my garden at dawn, and I notice their coats turning from golden to the gray-brown color of bare branches and leaf-strewn earth. In spring they frisk on the damp ground, leaving the garden soil pitted with heart-shaped prints. Dawn is their time, and they are there when the dog is let out in the morning, sometimes with mist swirling around them. He goes charging from the door and they stare at him with noses twitching until he is halfway to them, then lift their tails like white handkerchiefs, vanishing as though they had stepped off the edge of the hill. He is diverted by the heaviness of their scent in the garden, and by the time he has tracked them around it several times they can be two miles away. I doubt that they are, though; more likely they have slipped into the woods nearby and stand deep in briars hoping that the dog will give chase. Then they will leap fences that he must crawl under on his belly and circle back to bound through the garden again. By the time he returns from the chase, his tongue dripping, his thirst prodigious, they are lying comfortably downwind, preparing to chew their cuds.

When this house was taking shape, a workman said to me, "You gonna live up here with all them wildcats and bairs?" and I said yes. No animal will notice me, I thought; they will think my house has grown here or been heaved from the soil like a rock. Its basement is backed into the side of my hill, with glass panels across the front so that to stand just inside is to be at one with a wide sweep of earth but to feel unseen. The house's wooden beams show—rough, weathered timbers supporting light, open steps and a wall made of shelves for books. The roof slopes steeply to accommodate a loft bedroom on one side and a high-pitched ceiling over the other, a long room where meals are fixed and eaten and where friends sit and talk in armchairs at the end. There are windows on three sides; in winter, sunlight pours in to light and warm the floor, the meal laid on the table under windows, wine in the glass, sewing dropped on a chair, a book left open. The walls are white and the house is filled to the brim with light.

This land of deer is full of silences and sounds that I had not known for a long time: the crisp taffeta swish of the crow's passage overhead, the whistle of dove's wings, the low urgings of parent birds with their young in the dogwoods, the grasshopper's exuberant dance in the air, holding himself up with a frenzy of papery wingbeats until he falls heavily into the grass. Between all these are moments of silence, like rests in music, when the mind sharpens its attention.

Once before I thought I had found all these things on the eastern slope of the Blue Ridge. There was a cottage with a fireplace at each end, a rocky purling stream out front, fifteen bearing apple trees, and by five o'clock every summer afternoon it was shaded by a blue mountain. It was, I suppose, too good to be true. The cottage was set back from a narrow blacktop road marked at its beginning only by a brown wooden Forest Service sign that read, TO BLUE RIDGE PARKWAY. From there the road climbed six miles into clustering mountains where the parkway wound along the top. There were a few houses scattered along the road, including mine, and one small combination store, service station and dwelling.

Each spring the entrance of this road was invaded by frogs drawn by freshets from the hills that poured down the ditches on either side. Small ponds appeared in fields nearby. In late March and early April thousands of female frogs swarmed in answer to the calls of males already staking out pools and puddles. Overnight the road was alive with small gray-green frogs hopping toward the music. Those of us who lived there drove slowly and dodged them as best we could. As we veered drunkenly to miss the heedless and the amorous, our heads vibrated to the overpowering frog song. It was a sound to make the brain quiver, and at a distance it becomes a sweet lulling piping, a music buried deep in the psyche of the country-born, along with the scent of apple trees in bloom.

But for me and the frogs, the song was ending. Within two years the development of a ski resort began four miles above my cottage. The narrow roadway to the Blue Ridge Parkway was widened, straightened, flattened and given a 55 MPH speed limit. Its traffic grew great with flatbed trucks, cement mixers, culvert carriers, fleets of gravel trucks, fine cars, limousines and finally buses. The snowy morning that I looked out and counted twenty-six buses going past was the day I decided to sell. And when nine of them were waiting for the traffic to clear, parked panting and smoking in front of my house, I called a real-estate salesman.

The frog ponds were drained, of course, but the frogs came back, as programmed as salmon to return to the waters of their birth. They were squashed without thought and probably without notice by people heading for the resort four miles up the mountain. I had to drive over their flattened bodies when I came home at dusk on weekends, the only time I could escape from the city a hundred miles away. Even if the frogs had somehow been spared, I knew I wouldn't have been able to hear them for the traffic.

Another blacktop road now winds through other mountains below this house. In winter, when the dirt lane that ends in my backyard is slippery with freezing and thawing, I sometimes have to walk nearly a mile to reach my doorway. My small truck will not negotiate the long hill even with cinder blocks and wood holding down the back for better traction. So before winter shuts down for good, I lay in basic supplies. Then I need only a backpack to bring up groceries from the truck, which I park near the highway. It is a fair exchange: a long walk for a place to hear bird wings flying, grasshoppers dance, and, come spring, in a small cattail-fringed pond at the bottom of the hill, frogs singing.

19

Flood

September has come in chilled and soggy. It seems to have been raining for days. The yard is awash and the cat stares from the doorway as if looking from a window in the ark. When I drive down the road toward the post office, a sheep farm half a mile from my house has a large lake where ewes grazed and their lambs walked unsteadily a week ago. Doubtless they are in some safe sheepfold on higher ground; surely they would not be out on a day like this.

Rivers and creeks have spilled over their banks, drainage ditches are full and even with the roadway. The postmaster greets me with the ancient "Think it's gonna rain?" I am mailing my letters from the post office because my mailbox is wet inside. That's all I do; I'm afraid if I stay too long the tiny seasonal creek between the highway and my house will wash out the bridge. When I return the highway where I turn off is already two feet deep in water on the low side and a stream is flowing across the blacktop. I can hear it spray against the underside of my truck as I go through it.

On such a day one is grateful for shelter, for a stove with

a fire and a tea kettle steaming. I remind myself that this time last year the weather was dry and hot, and we and the forest rangers eyed a cloudless sky and sniffed the air for leaf-smelling smoke that strikes fear into the hearts of people who live in or near woods. I'd rather have the rain, even when there's too much, than live with the fear of fire day after day.

But when I go to bed and the rain is still rushing down the spouts, I think of the people in Rockfish Valley, the beautiful stretch of country at the base of Virginia's Blue Ridge Mountains where I used to live. I know what the older ones are doing—at least those who live along the creek that flowed seventy feet from my front door; they are lying awake listening to great boulders being tumbled about by the powerful muscles of that rushing water, a knocking, grinding rumble. They try to tell themselves that what happened once is not going to happen again, not for a thousand years, but the memory of vast waters descending is too unsettling. They get up and turn on lights and go to the door and listen. The creek roars in the night and they walk by flashlight to its banks to see how high the water is. Toward morning, if the rain slackens, they can finally get some sleep. If the rain does not relent, husbands and wives sit hunched and listening, or they go look at their sleeping children, or they turn on the television, but the creek steals their attention. Only when dawn comes and they can see what is around their houses can they relax and perhaps doze awhile.

They do all this in memory of an unforgettable night in August 1969 when Hurricane Camille, moving upward from the South, came across the Blue Ridge Mountains, met cold air from the north and formed a massive, boiling storm over Nelson County. In less than eight hours an incredible volume of water fell on the county's mountains and valleys, pouring down hillsides in sheets and torrents, turning valleys into great rivers. People awoke to feel their beds moving like rafts in the water filling up their houses, and when the walls burst asunder with the pressure, they were swept out into flood-waters, clutching at mattresses, bedposts or whatever they could. People who went through it say they never saw such rain. One of them described it to me two years later: "It won't like regular rain, it come down solid, like water poured out of a bucket, only it was like that all over. No raindrops, just solid water coming down ever'where."

Lights went out in house after house as the waters rose, but people could still see because great lightning bolts were strik-ing continually, showing the frightened, astonished people high, raging waters that they couldn't believe. Thunder crashed like mountains being torn up by their roots and hurled into valleys. Later this was joined by the roar of earth slides.

On Davis Creek, where hills were divided by a little stream a few feet wide, people had built their small houses on the slopes: steep homesites but pleasant, home to kinfolk, par-ents, grandparents, young couples, children. When the mas-sive rains came, the hillsides were already soggy from an unusually wet summer. Davis Creek became a torrent so quickly that sleeping people had no time to flee. The land under their houses became liquid, and the houses with their occupants were swept in one vast mudslide, gathering speed as it went. Trees, houses, furniture, great rocks and human beings were smothered in a towering wall of mud that jammed against the bridge where Davis Creek ran under Route 29. Fifty-three residents died in the slide, and two miles of High-way 29 was obliterated that night.

In the hollows and verdant groves of the Rockfish and Tye

River valleys, there were people who had gone to sleep despite the storm and woke to find their houses moving off their foundations. One man, finding water on his bedroom floor, thought that a pipe had burst until he felt the house move. His wife rushed to pull their two children onto the bed with her, calling to him. He couldn't hear her over the sound of ripping boards. Rising water carried the bed up to the ceiling, the house broke apart, and the bed with his wife and children was carried out into the darkness. He himself was swept away, his clothes torn off and his naked body deposited in the top of a tree still standing. When he was rescued he had to be hospitalized for severe bruises and so much loss of skin that grafting was required to replace it. Another man watched helplessly as his wife and three daughters were swept up by a surge from a rampaging creek and disappeared.

Children were torn from their parents' hold. Grand-parents vanished into the swirling currents and were never seen again. One man who owned a sawmill stood on his porch in the night smelling the sap of freshly cut wood, puzzled by why it was so strong. It was the smell, he learned later, of living trees being torn off mountains as the thin dirt around them became mud and flowed away from their roots. They fell and were smashed by boulders as large as houses that rolled down with them.

People wading and stumbling through rising waters were terrified by rumbling sounds that were not thunder, and by the puzzling smell of turned earth, like newly plowed fields. What they heard and smelled were the sides of mountains, earth, trees and rocks, collapsing and pouring into the valleys below, churning into the floodwaters, thickening the rivers and piling up in bottom lands.

The rain stopped in the early morning hours. Gray daylight

came two hours later, and only then did the surviving people of Tyro, Massie's Mill, Roseland, Wood's Mill, Beech Grove and Lovingston realize what had happened. Even then, with telephone lines down and roads impassable or no longer in existence, each community believed it was alone in disaster. Only when rescue workers in helicopters started to survey the damage and hunt for survivors did separate settlements learn the extent of the storm.

Some of those who survived were caught in trees or marooned on islands of mud and debris. One girl had been thrown with her sister into the flood when their house turned over. She was heaved by waves into a treetop. All night long she could hear her sister calling for help. Just before dawn the cries stopped, and by daylight she could see no sign of the girl. She herself was not rescued until nightfall, and her sister, Nelson County's junior beauty queen, was not found for days. She was dug out of the mud by a student who used to take her to dances. He had noticed something white in the mud; it proved to be her knee.

That was the evening and morning of the first day of the flood in Nelson County. On the second day, Camille's clouds were gone, the August sun shone hot, the air was clear and full of birdsong. In that clean sparkling air, fathers started digging for their lost children and for their wives. Women waited for word of their husbands and brothers while trying to fix meals for rescue workers, or prayed that a child might be found alive. Surrounding counties had been asked for help and some came, but eastward along the James River other communities were also calling for help. Floodwaters were rising to their houses, waters thick with mud, pieces of dwellings, trees, fence posts, children's toys, the bodies of cattle and occasionally of people.

The Mennonites came to Nelson County to help before the clouds were gone, quiet, efficient men and women making up relief teams who did not wait for bulldozers or back hoes before heaving away trees and broken timbers in the search for bodies. Some were from the Shenandoah Valley, some from other states or Canada.

In the fierce August sun bodies decomposed so rapidly that within a few days they could be identified only by comparing dental charts and checking bones for known fractures. County doctors understood that people wanted to be sure they were burying their own kinfolk, and they conducted the sickening examinations doggedly. In the heat it was heroic work indeed.

By this time help had come to the county as churches mobilized, the governor flew in by helicopter to view the damage, the Small Business Administration sent workers and the Red Cross moved in. One hundred and twenty-five people were lost in that storm in Nelson County, but few by drowning. Most died from being battered by great rocks and timbers. When meteorological experts studied what had happened to that lovely land they confirmed the unbelievable: In less than eight hours at least thirty-one inches of rain had fallen on Nelson County, and in the Davis Creek area it was probably as much as forty inches.

I moved to that county two years after the flood and saw it for the first time. The small place I bought in Rockfish Valley at the foot of a mountain was without topsoil on its lower half. It looked like a field of bare stones, its once-rich dirt by then somewhere at the bottom of the Atlantic Ocean. But by another summer it bloomed with the vivid blue flowers of a weed called viper's bugloss, a prickly, beautiful plant that thrives in barren places. Honeysuckle put forth a few tendrils and thorny, leguminous locust trees sprang up. What they grew on I cannot say, unless they thrived on bits of pulverized weeds, molecules of powdered grasshoppers and granite dust.

Even then raw scars of the flood's rampage were fast disappearing under vines and lush growth. Half of a stone house had been dropped on the lower end of my land, several of its rooms sheared away. Inside one could see an old sewing machine unaccountably left behind by surging waters. This house had belonged to neighbors who were visiting in another state when the rains came. They returned to find everything gone except for that piece of house washed off their land onto mine.

The 1969 flood has become a county legend. Nothing people tell about it can be more astonishing than the facts. I am told, though, that people are building new homes again on the slopes above Davis Creek. One young man there is quoted as saying, "The weather people said a storm like that can't happen again in a thousand years. I don't reckon I'll be here to see it when it does."*

*I heard many of these stories directly from survivors. For basic facts in this much abbreviated account I am indebted to an article, "The Flood," by Ken Ringle in *The Commonwealth* magazine of December 1969, and to a detailed book about the catastrophe, *Torn Land,* by Page and Jerry Simpson, published in 1970 by J. P. Bell Company, Lynchburg, Virginia.

20

The Way It Was

Maris is at my door at four in the afternoon saying, "I'm dying for a cup of coffee. I've been trying to get a patient into the hospital all afternoon."

Maris is a registered nurse in the home-health-care team at a community hospital. She comes in and throws her coat on a chair as I move the kettle over the hottest part of the wood stove.

"Who this time?" I say.

"Old Mrs. Hughes. Her daughter hit her in the stomach yesterday with a telephone book and is refusing to admit that her mother needs to go to the hospital. Of course she needed to go earlier, but now she says she just wants to die."

I know Mrs. Hughes. For a while I worked under Maris's direction as a home-health aide, and the situation is as bad as she says at the Hughes house. Mrs. Hughes's only daughter, Geneva, visits rarely, and sometimes Geneva's husband holds the old woman's arms behind her so she can be struck by the daughter. This is punishment for her complaints about their neglect. When eighty-one-year-old Virgie Hughes told me this while I fixed her lunch one day I was indignant. "You don't have to stand for that," I said. "I'll call Social Services and they'll send someone out to talk to your daughter."

But Mrs. Hughes said in her thin old voice out of her old bowed frame, "No, honey, I don't want you to do that. I wouldn't a told you if I'd thought you'd report it. Geneva's my only child; I can't bear to have the law after her." She made me promise never to speak of it outside of her house. But here is Maris and she knows. I fix her coffee and get cookies and we both enjoy our caffeine.

I tell her some of my stories of Mrs. Hughes—for example, how she likes to write her name over and over on pieces of paper that she then tears up.

"Why do you do that?" I wanted to know.

"Oh, honey, I've seen them people at the dump goin' through them trash bags. They're not goin' to find Virgie Hughes's name in there."

Bent, white-haired and not strong, Virgie was no longer able to drive the truck she kept at a local garage. "I go down and visit it sometime," she said. "You kin take me down there someday." She was confined to the house and yard but she managed to see much of the little that went on around her. I arrived one day when the street in front of her small house was being repaired, and after she had with difficulty unlocked three locks to let me in, she said, "Come here, honey, and look at this." She led me to the window overlooking a ditch being dug in the street and pointed. "I never seen the like," she said. "That man diggin' has titties."

I leaned over her bent back and saw a person in a hard hat tossing shovels full of dirt out of the ditch with a hefty swing. I studied the figure and said to Virgie, "Mrs. Hughes, that's a woman."

"What? A woman? Now I never seen a woman on a road

crew. You sure?" She stared hard with old blue eyes intent. "Well, if that don't beat all. I thought sure that—"

"She has 'em all right," I said, "but on her they're normal."

Mrs. Hughes had mourned for her husband for twenty years. Because her greatest need, more than food or health care, was for someone to talk to, I asked her about her wedding.

"Jake was sixteen years older'n me," she said. "I was just fifteen—or was it fourteen?—when he told my daddy he wanted to marry me. He had to wait, you know, because my daddy wanted me to finish school, and I did too.

"The Christmas I was sixteen we was settin' around talkin'—Jake came over to sit with me every Sunday and holiday—and he said, 'When we goin' to git married?' And a notion just took me. I said, 'We kin go to the church right now and the preacher'll marry us.'

"So I told my sister Orleen to put on a sweater so she could stand up with me, and we didn't tell anyone else. We just walked up to the church—it was open for Christmas, you know—and the preacher married us.

"Then we come back and Jake went on to his house and I stayed at home. I was terrible shy, you know, and he didn't press me. It was three months before we slept together, and even then he stayed on his side of the bed and I stayed on mine. It was a long time before we got any closer."

Maris shakes her head now and laughs, then puts down her empty coffee cup. "I wish you'd come back to work," she says.

"I'm working on this book . . ." I say.

"You gonna put all those poor patients in it?"

"No," I tell her, "but I might put you in it."

"Well, say I finally got that pitiful old woman into Adventist Hospital in spite of her bitchy daughter."

Maris drops by my house occasionally without announcement. She is the only black woman I really know in this western part of Virginia, where there are few blacks. Only among her poor white patients is Maris called a "nigger." She is a deep cream color, with a dusting of freckles. She can speak black English or she can sound like a professor of nursing, which she was at one point in her career. She is old enough to have watched the Selma march on television, to have been proud of Martin Luther King, even to have cheered for the integration of Little Rock.

"What was it like for you when you went to school? Were you made to feel second class?" I ask her.

"No," she says in a slightly surprised voice. "I went to school in Verona, and I did what everybody else did. I went to pajama parties and proms just like my classmates. It was just different there. I was never called 'nigger' in my life until I took this job." Her hometown is about fifty miles away, in the Shenandoah Valley.

When Maris leaves we hug on the promise that she will come back soon. She is careful to go before sundown; once she stayed until dark and had to call her husband to explain why she was late. That time she made a wrong turn at the end of my road and drove for miles into the mountains. Her husband phoned to ask about her and said angrily, "I wish she'd never started working with you mountain people," lumping me with Mrs. Hughes who, with other poor stricken ones, feels shame when a black nurse comes to the door.

I never talk to Maris about the black people I knew in my childhood and girlhood, but I do tell her that my mother never let us use the word *nigger*. "It is disrespectful to the colored people we know," she said. "Besides it's a common, vulgar term. Don't let me hear you use it."

As far as I know, that's about as far as my mother's early

sensitivity about black and white relationships went. When she moved to Virginia there were many black families near our farm. Some of the restless younger ones left home for the excitement of Philadelphia and Washington and found jobs there, but back home there were mothers and aunts, older brothers and fathers, who did not want to leave. If it had not been for this labor pool, my mother could not have managed a farm, raised a family, sold cookware, done fine sewing, and for a time developed and printed her own photographs.

I think the way we lived is sometimes called "the simple life." It was certainly uncomplicated by labor-saving devices. Water was pumped by hand from a well. Washing was done by scrubbing clothes on a washboard, in big round tubs requiring two people to empty, then filled again with rinsing water. Clothes were wrung out by hand.

I used to play at the feet of the woman who ironed all the dampened cotton clothes, table linens and sheets for our family of four females. "You move now," she would say. "I might drop this iron on you head." Three irons were kept heating on the hot wood stove, and she picked up one with a wooden handle that clamped on. She would use it until it became too cool to *ssst* when she touched it with a licked finger. Then she set it back on the stove, unclamped the handle and moved it to another, hotter iron. There was an art to using these instruments without leaving scorch marks on clothes. Each one weighed five pounds or more, and they smoothed garments with weight as well as heat. After a day's ironing a woman was as tired as if she had been digging potatoes or hoeing.

"You mama the first lady I ever knew don't want to tear up the house for spring cleaning," Susan said once. Her tone was one of approval. "When I worked for Mrs. Oberman, she got to wash every strip of cloth in the house and git the dirt out between the planks in the floor before Easter.''

My mother did not believe our house needed to be spotless. She considered preoccupation with cleaning and polishing a waste of time; "Life's too short," she said. Perhaps a little at Christmas, or when a visitor from Chicago was coming, but even for a wedding in the living room I doubt that my mother would have dusted the spiders from behind the tall bookcase in the corner. The necessary work of each day just to keep the farm going required all her strength and more. Though her kitchen was occupied half a day by a black woman, Mother was the one who shivered into the kitchen before dawn in winter to start a fire in the big cookstove. When temperatures dropped into the low figures she often had to break the ice in the kitchen bucket to get water for her coffee and for the breakfast cereal.

For these early chores she wore a bathrobe of heavy blanket cloth, totally utilitarian, the only kind of heavy bathrobe shown in the catalogs of the time. It was a dark garment with a shadowy print, a shawl collar outlined in silvery cord, and tied with a matching heavy tasseled cord. As sharply as when I was five I can recall today how that robe smelled comfortingly of her nighttime warmth, woodsmoke and coffee.

Mother started another fire in the living room for us to dress by and tended the one there and in her bedroom in between sewing our clothes, keeping the farm accounts and cooking. Any unused room stayed unheated; before the dining room was built we studied in the kitchen on cold winter nights. A small fire was lit in the stove in Allison's room when her studying was done, just big enough to warm a space around it so she could undress. The sheets were icy cold, and if I was sleeping with her I had to get in first because I slept next to the wall. The wall was cold too.

"Come on," I would say, "I'm freezing."

"Don't think you can put your cold feet on me," she would warn, which of course was what I'd had in mind.

Then Mother would come upstairs with two hot irons wrapped in towels for our feet, or a flat soapstone heated and wrapped in newspapers to slide under the sheets. Even so, when we curled up under the covers there was a period of shivering before our bodies finally warmed an envelope of air around us. These were the only times that Allison and I snuggled together; we had to in order to warm that bed. In our sleep we moved apart, and we hardly ever slept together in summer.

Winter began in November, never mind what the calendar said. It was then that my mother talked to Solomon about our hogs. It was time to put up the year's supply of pork. When frost lay white over the fields and the ground was frozen hard underfoot, a neighbor was summoned to help Solomon kill the pigs and scrape them so free of hair that their skins shone in the cold.

I was not allowed to go outside during hog-killing hours, nor did my mother. The pigpen was so far from the house that it was mostly a quiet affair, at least where we were. I was allowed out only after the pigs were cleaned and hung by their feet, stiff and pink in the frigid morning. By afternoon Mother was cutting them up on the kitchen table, using great knives and a cleaver. This was before *Charlotte's Web*, so I was able to view the pigs' carcasses with interest as food, not as animals I had known. The day had a certain festive air. Parts from the two pigs were given to Solomon, his helper and the woman assisting in the kitchen, and their pleasure was contagious. The liver, feet, some of the side meat, the brains and some of the fat went to them. The whitest fat my mother rendered into lard over the lowest heat on the stove. She used it for biscuits, yeast bread and even for cakes. Lard is an animal fat much out of favor today, but it lent a subtle flavor to breads that cannot be obtained any other way.

Any skin that was cut off went to our helpers, who could make it delectable. Out in the yard the men cleaned the intestines with many washings; afterward these were divided among them and they took them home to roast into chitterlings. It was a fairly stinking process that ended in crisp, delicious bits of pork.

Susan salvaged all the tiny bits of fat. "What do you do with those?" I asked.

"You ain't had cracklins? I make cracklin bread and bring you some."

"That's bread's much too fat," my mother interposed. "She can't digest it."

"It's mighty good . . ." Susan said, but my mother had spoken, so I had to wait until my twenty-third year for my mother-in-law to give me cracklin bread that she had made. I ate it without a qualm. Bits of fat fried until they were crisp were incorporated in thick corn bread and baked on a greased black pan. They were eaten hot on a cold day, preferably with turnip greens boiled with thick bacon or fatback. It was food that stuck to the ribs, and probably to my in-laws' older arteries, but it tasted good and remains one of the dishes that southerners still remember when they talk of "down-home cooking."

For days after hog-killing time my mother rendered lard in pots on the wood stove. She ground meat for sausage, cooked and canned it. Pork loins that we could not eat immediately she canned in jars set deep in boiling water for hours. The house smelled chokingly of hot fat, and my mother's face was red with heat. Susan washed up the mountain of pots and pans and sometimes sang under her breath.

Outside Solomon was stringing up hams and squares of bacon in a smoker. The smoker was made of a large bottomless barrel suspended within a teepee of poles over a very low hickory fire; we must have used green wood to produce so much smoke and so little fire. The meat was dangled from the crossed poles and hung inside the barrel. The process went on for days.

A few years later my mother discovered a mixture called Hickory Smoked Salt, and after that simply buried the ham and bacon in tubs of the stuff. It contained nitrates to hasten the drying of the meat, but we did not know these might not be good for us; the cured meat tasted as though it had been smoked for days.

The first black woman I remember in our house day after day was Aunt Alice Winslow. She introduced herself this way, pronouncing the title "Ant." Her husband was white-haired Uncle Peter, born into slavery seventy years before. Aunt- and uncledom was conferred on aging slaves by white folks, and the custom persisted for several generations after they were free.

Aunt Alice wore many petticoats, baked a cherry roll that could bring angels to earth and told wonderful stories. The ones I loved were about a rabbit belonging to the Philadelphia family she had worked for. This animal had some of the cunning of Br'er Rabbit and was constantly in mischief. I asked for these stories over and over, and each time I was bent, curled, speechless with laughter.

As she grew older, Aunt Alice could go no farther than to the nearest white family to work, but when she was dying it was my mother who took her food and sometimes medicine. By then Aunt Alice had almost nothing but a house and a tiny amount of money sent her by her nephew in Philadelphia. A great-nephew stayed with her, but he was hardly more than a child, and it troubled my mother that he was trying to care for a dying woman. She went to see if Aunt Maggie Woods, who lived half a mile from Aunt Alice, could help. Aunt Maggie was the midwife she had brought to Daphne. She had a reputation as a conjure woman, and she listened impassively to my mother, her black eyes darting sharp points of light from her copper-colored face. After a pause she took her pipe out of her mouth and said, "I kin make a charm to ease her some. One dollar all it cost."

My mother said, "I don't think charms can help her now. But your kindness will help her know that somebody is looking after her." She offered Aunt Maggie payment if she would bathe Aunt Alice and do what she could for her several days a week.

There was another pause. I stood behind my mother watching the smoke from Aunt Maggie's pipe seem to curl up through her straw hat. We stood there for so long that chickens were beginning to peck around our feet. Finally she said, "I reckon I kin take my stick and go over to Mrs. Winslow's. But," and she smiled a toothless smile, "I make her a charm anyway. Won't cost you nothin'."

When we got home my mother wrote to Aunt Alice's nephew in Philadelphia telling him the sick woman needed whatever help he could send—the boy staying with her, Mother said, could not care for such a sick woman. And until Aunt Alice died, her nephew Albert sent my mother one or two dollars every week to ease the old woman's last hours.

With that my mother paid the doctor for the strongest pain-killer he would prescribe. She herself gave the first dose to Aunt Alice, and then explained to the boy living with her exactly how and when to give more.

"Do you think you can remember this?" Mother asked him. He nodded. "It's important," she said.

He nodded again. "I know," he said, so low that she could barely hear him. "I do it so she won't moan so bad."

After Aunt Alice, Susan came to our household. She was a gaunt woman with shining dark skin marked by smallpox and an enjoyment of life that bubbled under the surface of her workday self. She allowed Allison and me to see it, but I don't think she ever gave way to it in front of my mother. Once when she carried some eggs for my mother's customers out to the car and did not know where to put them because a neighbor was in the passenger side, she just stood there holding them.

"Where must I put these?" she asked, peering around the armful of boxes.

The neighbor reached up and told her, "Put all them boxes in my lap; this here dress is old as Adam anyways."

"So I put 'em in her lap," Susan told us, "and I guess she was right—she sho' had on Eve's shoes," and she doubled over with laughter that we joined. She told this story frequently, but I don't think she ever repeated it to my mother.

Allison and I both loved Susan, but I was the one who followed her when she went to the barn to talk with Solomon as he milked, who trailed her back to the house and who then accompanied her home when she left for the day. I didn't stay; I went along as a friendly puppy would because I liked trotting along with her and racing back at top speed.

Susan's room in our house was the kitchen. Though I

would try to entice her into the living room to sit, and later into our new dining room, she would only come in, look at what I had called her to see and then return to the kitchen.

"Why don't you stay in here with me?" I asked her.

"It ain't right. You come out here with me in the kitchen. I has to watch the fire."

I knew that neither Susan nor Solomon ever entered the front door, and that they never went beyond the kitchen except when work demanded it. When I asked Mother about this, she gave a characteristic answer: "It just isn't done," she said. That told me nothing except that the subject was closed: no more questions.

So it was because of Susan that I also spent most of my house time in the kitchen; Allison was often there too. I don't remember that we did anything except listen to Susan. She would read to us out of *Grit*, a small newspaper that she subscribed to. She slowly read us the jokes, the stories of strange people and of amazing happenings something like those in tabloids now featured on grocery checkout lines.

"Do you really think that's so?" we would ask.

"Yas, it's so," she would say, a little offended. "They wouldn't put it in the paper if it won't so."

We saved the comic pages for Susan from the *Chicago Tribune*, which arrived two or three days late at our house. Allison and I read them first, but looking at them again with Susan made them freshly funny. She read them aloud, panel by panel, telling us what was happening: "Maggie's gettin' madder and madder at Jiggs—look, she got one eye closed and her mouth turned down, she gone hit him in a minute— there she go! She done bounced that rollin' pin offa his head!" She was especially fond of Rachel, the black housekeeper who was once a character in *Gasoline Alley*. That Rachel was exaggerated and unrealistically thick-lipped did not occur to her, or to any of us at the time. She was just a comfortable mammy sort who delighted Susan by talking about her "pillow-slip teef." Susan knew exactly what she meant: Front teeth were indispensable when holding a pillow slip so that a pillow could be stuffed into it with both hands. She also liked Mushmouth, the black man in *Moon Mullins.* To her and to us all the characters in comics were celebrities; it pleased her that some of her own race were represented. Barney Google and his mule, Mutt of *Mutt and Jeff,* Andy Gump and the squat, bowlegged Jiggs were all caricatures. I don't believe she felt demeaned by Rachel or Mushmouth, any more than Allison or I were by Maggie with her rolling pin. Our social consciousness had not been raised.

Those were the years when my mother was away from home four or five hours a day selling Wearever pots and pans. On such days Susan was with us until late afternoon, and I hung around listening to her talk with Solomon when he brought the horse to drink at the well trough, when he came in to get the milk buckets and wash his hands, or when, on April days, they both sat outdoors on the ground on empty feed sacks cutting up potatoes to plant.

They talked a great deal about two churches, Ebenezer and Rising Sun, perhaps six or seven miles apart, where the social life of the black community centered. In August, both churches held revival services (as did many white churches) and there were baptisms of all the people who "came to Jesus" during revival. Listening to Solomon and Susan I had the feeling that the August revival season was a joyful and extended festival, for them more exciting than Christmas or any other holiday. They talked of the people who had left to work up north; all these, they said, would be coming back to the churches where they grew up. It would be a time of reunion with children, brothers, sisters, uncles and cousins. Many of them would be riding together in big cars, with American flags fluttering from their radiator caps, and they would stream back home from Philadelphia, New York and the District of Columbia.

Both Susan and Solomon had time off from work for those weeks in August, as did workers on other farms around. We were affected by the festivities in another way: Our sale of frying chickens increased noticeably as church members prepared feasts for eating on the grounds after services.

As that time drew near, Susan sang hymns that I hadn't heard before, along with old ones she sang every day. She had a plangent, bluesy voice, and the twists and turns she gave each line of music were strange to me and sometimes sad. I tried singing the ones I could remember, but I could never imitate the intricate modulation. I didn't know then about soul music, and I realized later, when it became well known, that Susan was an early and accomplished singer of soul.

Susan usually did not swear, and Solomon never did. At moments of mild surprise Susan said, "Dah Jesus!" but in times of real tension she said, "Shit!" This was three generations before the word came in from barnyards and outhouses to join casual conversation. I didn't know its meaning, but it spat nicely between the teeth when something went wrong.

One Saturday night we were all at dinner; Rob was there with Daphne, and Daphne's friend Winnie was seated next to her fiancé. I was between my mother and Allison. There was laughter and talk, my mother's dinner was delicious, and I, struggling with a chicken drumstick I was supposed to eat with a knife and fork, sent it slithering into my lap. It was the appropriate moment for me to say, "Oh, shit!" Loudly, the way Susan said it.

The talk stopped. I saw my mother's astonished face and

was paralyzed by the sight. "Where," she said coldly, "did you get that word?"

"Susan says it all the time," I offered, my voice thin and small.

"You are not to use it again, ever, understand?"

I nodded. The meal was ruined for me; I could not touch the drumstick, which was now back on my plate. Talk resumed among the adults, and Allison looked hard into her plate trying not to laugh. I could not even eat dessert. When the others rose from the table, Rob came over to me and said softly, "Why don't you come along and show me the new calf?" I just shook my head. As soon as my mother was talking in the kitchen I slipped out the door into the summer twilight and went behind an old haystack to cry. I thought of staying there forever until they grew frightened and sent someone out to look for me, but when my mother called me twice I went slowly back to face her.

She met me outside the door, wiped my face with her apron and said, "You understand, don't you honey, that you mustn't use that word anymore?" I barely got out a yes, snuffling. "You come on in and eat your dessert and we'll forget all about it."

Before she forgot, though, she evidently talked to Susan about the word the next day, for Susan mended her ways. From then on her burnt finger, a smashed cup, the rip in her dress, brought from her, "Shit! I mean shucks."

During the worst of the Depression, Susan worked two days for us and two days for another family. In between, Mary Marshall came to wash dishes and do general cleaning so that her family would not starve.

Mary's husband, John, had recently died of appendicitis

because he refused to go to the doctor or the hospital until the pain in his side changed to a raging tiger in his belly. When he reached the surgeon fifty miles away it was already too late. His death left Mary in despair over bringing up five boys and a girl. We were her nearest neighbors, and after she had used up her tears crying on Mother's shoulder we did not see her for a while. She and big John Marshall had "scuffled," she said, all their married life, and had a home, a cow and pigs, a few chickens and a garden.

John had been a trusted sawmill hand who managed to work most of the time. One winter day a chimney fire had ignited their roof and the house burned down. John and Mary hastily built another, and then it too was engulfed in the forest fire that burned our house, along with their cow shed, chicken house and store of hay. Once more, as soon as lumber was delivered from Hensley's Cross Corners mill, John and his older boys had put up yet another house. He never seemed to rest; late at night and early in the morning he was nailing boards, building a chimney, putting on a roof. Then in the fall, when he was digging potatoes, his painful appendix, poulticed by Mary and dosed with strong laxatives by John, finally ruptured.

When Mary appeared at our door on a cool October day, John had been in his grave a month. She looked thinner and very tired, though she smiled—or tried to.

"I'm so glad you came over," my mother said. "The pullets are beginning to lay, and I have a lot of eggs too small to sell. Why don't you take them back with you to fill up those big boys?"

Mary thanked her with dignity, but then had to wipe her eyes with her apron. "I come to see if you . . . if you could let me have a little milk today."

"Of course," my mother said.

"I can't pay you right away," Mary said, her voice unsteady. "I thought I might could holp you out some in the house."

Getting out a milk pan, Mother evidently heard more in Mary's words than I did. She said, "You don't have to pay for milk . . . are you folks going hungry over there?"

Mary hesitated. "We still has a little cornmeal," she said. "And some turnip greens."

"Is that all?"

"Yes ma'am."

"Was John able to leave you anything, Mary?"

"Just six children and four walls. You know he didn't never mean to leave us like this, Mrs. Bell."

When Mary left she carried eggs, milk, cornmeal and flour. My mother added a jar of bacon fat for flavoring the turnip greens. The next morning Mary was at our door by eight o'clock wearing a fresh white apron, and she went right to work cleaning up the kitchen. It was not a small job. There were always dishes from the night before and from breakfast. Before she could get to the dishes, she had to take soaking pots out of the sink and find a place for them on the end of the stove or even on the floor. My mother was usually there skimming cream from milk and putting it in the churn. If the milk was "turning" it was dumped into buckets for the chickens and pig. Then the milk pans had to be carefully washed and scalded so that no trace of sour milk remained.

Mary was more equal to that kitchen than anyone else, though she must have quailed at the door whenever my mother said cheerfully, "There are quite a few dishes this morning." But her face never lost its look of bright expectancy, even when she looked at the sticky aftermath of Mother's jam making, which overflowed all available surfaces.

When she finished and all the pots and pans were put away, the kitchen was neat and clean beyond anything my mother and I were able to accomplish. Mother always became bored halfway through a big dishwashing job and left the hard things to soak. I liked to do more, but she would tell me, "That's enough now; you don't have to stay in here all morning. Let the rest go for now." In her eyes the time spent in cleaning for what she considered appearance's sake was a terrible waste. But when Mary did it, singing, Mother would say, "You make this kitchen a pleasure to work in."

Mary Marshall became my mother's only close friend nearby; I was too young for her to confide in and Daphne and Allison could not be talked to except through the laborious route of letters. It may have been her quiet, listening look, her way of folding her hands in her lap and being still. Whatever it was, only Mary could come into the house, walk through the dining room, saying to me, "I goin' tip upstairs to see you mother," and call on the stairs, "I'm comin' up," prompting my mother's answer, "Fine. Come right up." She would walk into my mother's room softly, saying, "How you this mawnin'?" and sit down to talk, knowing she was wanted. In any stage of undress (though she never emerged from the washroom in less than her slip) Mother welcomed her, and they would talk for an hour or so. Only to Mary did she confide her fears about Daphne having more children than she should, or talk of Rob's shortcomings as a son-in-law. In turn Mary treated her to slightly jealous gossip about Susan (she could never quite accept Susan's still working for us), and told her something of her own troubles with her boys since John's death. Her daughter, always called Sister, was a good girl, she said, but hadn't ought to have just boys around.

My mother talked of Allison and how long she'd been away

from home because she couldn't manage train fare home. "I wanted to send her money, but she's got this idea that . . . Well, she just flatly said she wouldn't take anything from me. You know she used to say when she left that she was never coming back, and I think it's her pride."

Mary answered the pain she recognized under the words, saying soothingly, "She git over that, you just wait."

By coming silently to the bottom of the steps I heard my mother talking to Mary about my father. "He retires in two years," she said. "I don't know what he will do here; he's a city man."

"I reckon he will res'," Mary said. "He been workin' a long time."

"I'm afraid . . ." my mother said. Mary made a sound of sympathy. "I'm afraid he may have a hard time learning to live like we do," Mother finished.

Mary sighed. "We just has to do the bes' we can," she said. "And hope."

"And hope," my mother echoed. But she never mentioned these fears to me.

For her work and her friendship, Mary received the standard pay for black women, but it was barely enough pay to keep her family in cornmeal, molasses and fatback. If her few chickens refused to lay, she could get eggs from us free. When she had to sell her cow, my mother had milk to spare. She did have a garden, but how she managed to clothe six children I do not know. When her daughter was ready for high school, a way had to be found for her to live in the county seat, which was near the only available high school for blacks. Black schoolchildren were not provided school buses then, and Sister would have to walk. She told Mary, and Mary told my mother, that her daughter didn't care what she had to do to go to high school, but she was determined to get her diploma. Sister had her eyes set on a future different from her mother's.

Mother found a family in that town who would give Sister a basement room and meals in exchange for her help with cooking and housekeeping, and Sister became a live-in servant whose time at school was part of her pay. My mother told me, "You don't know how lucky you are. You just have to get up, eat your breakfast, dress and ride the bus each morning. Sister will have to cook breakfast for Mr. and Mrs. Crizer, wash the dishes, clean up the kitchen, sweep the walk, fix her lunch and then walk to school."

I did not dwell on the inequality of our circumstances. At the time I was struggling with the perils of adolescence and a growing awareness that some of my classmates also suffered from unequal opportunity. There were girls who rose every morning to help their mothers with other children before they came to school, and who went home to do half a day's work on the farm before finally opening their books and wearily trying to study. Writing assignments terrified them, and one or two would catch up with me between classes and ask, "What can I write? I don't even know how to begin." Sometimes I could provide skeleton outlines for filling in— general titles like "My Family and Our Farm" and "What I Have to Do on the Farm"—and once primed they could produce a page of material, even when they made lists instead of paragraphs. But what I liked best were the short essays I wrote for them, trying to make them sound like something they might write. The fun was in changing my mind's gears to think as they thought and choosing words they would have used. I don't know if I could do it now, but it seemed easy then. Our English teacher was an exceptionally good one for such a small school and I grew smug thinking that he never suspected my under-the-desk writing service.

I think now of one girl in particular. Quiet Janie was the oldest girl in a family of ten children. By the time she reached high school she was already cooking meals and sewing for the younger ones. When she stepped from the school bus at the road to her house, she faced ironing, cooking, attending to younger children if her mother was ill (as she often was) and cleaning up the supper dishes before studying—all this without benefit of electricity or indoor plumbing. The other children helped, but Janie was older and steadier. When she finished school with little distinction in any subject except math and home economics, I believed she would never escape the family.

But Janie, taking herself in hand, had other ideas. In the summer after graduation she got a job at a local cannery, but one week of hard, mind-dulling work there was enough. She left, and with her week's wages in hand journeyed to Richmond and signed herself over to the Medical College of Virginia as a nurse probationer. In those days first-year nursing students were required to perform the most menial tasks about the hospital for their board and tuition, but Janie, released from a life of constant work, had more time to herself than ever before—time, as it turned out, to be young for the first time since childhood. She finished nursing school just before World War II, was recruited into the army and ended the war years as a captain in the United States Air Force, caring for badly wounded men flown in from the battlefields.

Mary Marshall's daughter, Sister, grown sturdy on corn bread and greens, more beautiful than her mother had ever been, finished high school with ease and went to the same nursing school as Janie, in a "separate but equal" class with other black students. After she was graduated and capped, she was called "Nurse Marshall" rather than "Miss Marshall" by her white supervisors in medicine. Though she may have outperformed or equaled white students in her profession, custom decreed that no black woman could be addressed by the same title as her white colleagues. Sister lived long enough to be called Miss or Mrs. by white physicians, supervisors and patients, but her mother, Mary, died before this honor could astonish her old age.

I do not talk of all this when Maris comes, throwing her blue, soft-lined coat across the couch, putting her feet to warm in the oven of my wood cookstove. The stove is partly for old times' sake, though it is airtight and Amish-made and its grave simplicity could have been designed by Shakers. Its eight-inch-wide stovepipe soars straight through the cathedral roof fifteen feet above, a lovely black column against the stairs and the shelves behind it.

It is as much Susan, Aunt Alice, Mary or Sister as I who greet Maris, and who listen to her quick words and high-pitched laughter. She talks about her youngest son; she is disturbed because at eleven years of age he keeps to himself, is interested in nothing but taking radios and televisions apart and putting them back together, or in reading everything he can find on electronics. "I decided he needed a birthday party," Maris says, "and I invited a lot of kids, even though he said he didn't want a party. I said, 'You gonna have this party and you're gonna have a good time.'

"Well, we had it, and about an hour after the cake and presents he came into the kitchen and said, 'I want you to know I hate this party and I'm not having a good time and I wish they'd all go home.' Can you beat that?"

"And?" I say.

"Well, all the kids were having a great time except him, so I took a deep breath and told him, 'If you'll go back in there and be polite for another forty-five minutes I'll never give you another party, okay?' And he said okay. After they'd gone, he dusted off his hands and said, 'Well, that's that. What a waste of time.'"

"Are you sure he's only eleven?"

"My husband says he hasn't been a child since he learned to read directions for putting toys together. He didn't want to play with them; he just wanted to know how they worked."

We're having coffee and cinnamon buns. She says, "I'm gonna miss this. I came to tell you I'm quitting this job. Moving back to Georgia." I am not surprised and say I thought the stress of her work would get her down.

"Not job stress. Husband stress. My husband says he's tired of cold winters. He says that Virginia ain't south like the rest of the South, and besides I come home too tired and too bitchy when I travel all day."

Our good-byes at the car are restrained; in our minds we have already parted. She tells me to visit them in Brunswick and I say she must come back to this house whenever she is in Virginia, but neither of us expects to see the other again.

I watch her car disappear over the hill and know that sometimes I will remember her laughter and the laughter of Susan, though in different rooms.

21

Search

"In Iowa," my mother once said, "the wind blew cold across the prairies and we didn't have enough wood to burn so we burned corn." That's my memory of what she told us. There was so much corn, she said, that it was cheaper to burn than coal or wood. That was probably only one winter, or even only a few weeks during one winter. Or perhaps, as people tell me now, "It couldn't have been corn; it must have been corncobs." But ever since Mother talked of burning corn, I have clung to a vision of her keeping warm in Iowa winters by a stove in which corn is popping like firecrackers and turning into coals.

I have an old photograph of my mother sitting on the top step of a porch in Ainsworth, small chin in hand. She is about three years old, in a dark dress, black stockings and high-button shoes. Her still babyishly rounded face is solemn, her brow wide under pulled-back dark hair, her straight brows as faint as feathers. Near her sits her bearded father, holding a straw boater, the only sign of summer in the picture. His fine, straight nose, which she inherited, is his best and strongest feature. Against the wall an older woman sits; she is probably about sixty, my mother's maternal grandmother. The child's dress has many tucks in its long full skirt, a pretty detail that allows the dress to be lengthened as she grows.

When I found this photograph among my mother's things after her death, I studied it, as one will, searching for the person she became in that small, unsmiling child. The year it was taken was 1886 or 1887. My mother's mother had died two years before with the birth of twins who did not survive. "You see, she had whooping cough when the babies were coming," my mother once said. "It was so weakening; she would cough and cough until she gagged and couldn't keep anything down, my grandmother told me. The babies were too tiny to live and my mother had no strength left. Nobody could do anything for any of them."

Mother would talk about the mother she could not remember, and we would look at the tintype she had of a delicate-looking young girl with a rose in her hair. "She must have been strong," my mother would say wistfully. "She could ride any horse in the country. She rode horses men couldn't ride; she had a way with them." Her grandmother had told her this too.

In the grandmother I found much of my mother. She had married an artist in the East, and for a while life was comfortable. But in his thirties the artist began to suffer more and more from illness and a doctor recommended the climate of the Ozark Mountains. Eventually the artist and his family went west from New Jersey and homesteaded near Rolla, Missouri, where they farmed with much difficulty. Their only draft animals were oxen, and they used them to pull the plow, to pull the crude harrow set with wooden teeth that broke up dirt clods, and to pull the wagon. It seems that only his wife and probably his older son actually farmed. The artist continued to paint, reduced by hard times to exchanging his paintings for cornmeal or whatever else they would bring. Only two of his works survive in our family, and they are good oils. He was probably most proficient as a portrait painter, though that could not have taken him far in the Ozarks of the 1800s.

But his wife, my great-grandmother, approached it all with a fierce practicality, soothing her children when they heard cougars crying like infants in the forest at night and trying to find enough for the family to eat during the day. She was desperate enough to catch turtles that local mountaineers did not eat, and to kill and cook them. When neighbors asked how she, a woman, could do such grisly butchering, she answered, "I'll do anything I have to to keep my children from going hungry." She, who rode through Confederate territory to reach their homesteading land, a Union flag at her horse's head, was not daunted by their distaste. I look at her small and unafraid face in the old faded photograph; the eyes have seen birth, death, hunger, illness and hard labor, and have accepted them all. What she called her "French nose" is prominent. Playing the old game of "baby's eyes, baby's nose," one of her children touched hers, saying, "Mama's nose—Mama has plenty nose." She told this, amused and completely without vanity, to my mother, who liked to repeat it to us.

My great-grandmother wryly called Missouri the "State of Misery" as she and her family went through repeated bouts of malaria. That was before drainage made the beautiful setting of their farmhouse free of mosquitoes and turned it into healthy country. She lost her husband and eldest son there, and left their graves to join her daughter and Scots son-in-law in Iowa. There she stayed to bring up my mother.

When my mother brought in the first lettuce leaves of spring from our garden on our farm in Virginia, she would eat a leaf in ritual remembrance of a childhood yearning for green food. "My grandmother gave me the first head of lettuce she could find every spring, and I would sit down wherever I was and eat the entire thing, plain. We had almost no green food in winter out there, and I suppose my growing bones needed the iron and calcium." Nobody seemed to connect the aching of her young bones with diet. She was told she had rheumatism, and when she wept with pain her grandmother would comfort her with warmed poultices and her father would hunt for whatever remedy there was to rub into her knees and ankles.

In Ainsworth, my grandfather put his modest savings into a seed-and-plant business, and published a monthly magazine called *The Floral Instructor.* My mother remembered walking amid the flowers, among which he hung cages of canaries to sing for customers. For a while all was well. His early training in horticulture in Scotland made him a sought-out expert on fruits, flowers and vegetables. But her next vivid memory was of the entire business block of Ainsworth in flames, and of watching fearfully with her grandmother as her father's building, with its seeds, plants and birds, was consumed. He came home exhausted after it was all over, covered with black cinders and reeking of smoke, a man of valuable property no more. He did not have enough savings to start again. Within a few days he knew he must try to find work in Chicago; she could not tell me what he did there except that he left on the train after telling her to be a good girl and help her grandmother. So at age ten or eleven my mother learned to take more responsibility from the older woman, who was losing her strength and zest for life. "She was worn out by the hard life she'd lived," Mother said. "All of a sudden she could barely stand at a table and teach me to make bread. She tried to keep up with the clothes I needed, but sometimes I had to finish those, and they looked like a child had worked on them. She'd say, 'Try to make your stitches smaller, Alice. I'm sorry I can't help more.' But she just couldn't. I had to learn to do almost everything, and when I was thirteen she died. That was when I went to Chicago to keep house for my father."

When I commented from my fourteen-year-old perspective that she hadn't had much fun in her girlhood, it seemed to surprise my mother. "We didn't really expect fun," she said, looking back into those years. "But I did have some, you know. When I was fifteen and sixteen, I and a friend used to go tobogganing in one of the Chicago parks. And skating. I loved skating."

"A man friend?" I asked.

She said, "Oh, dear, no, we didn't have men friends at that age. I didn't even have my hair up yet. My father wouldn't let me have any friends except girls my own age."

I could not imagine her, a tall girl with her hair down her back, young and laughing. Somewhere she'd seemed to lose the free laughter I liked to believe she'd had. Surely one could not toboggan without it? I used to wonder if marrying my father had quenched the gaiety in her. She met him at a church social, a wildly improbable place for my father to be. He was still in possession of most of his black hair, handsome, blue-eyed, just a little taller than she and fifteen years older. "He was very charming to me then," she used to say. "It wasn't until later . . ." and her voice would trail off, leaving us to insert our own experience of his sarcasm and ridicule, his way of frowning coldly when we giggled. My father had an abhorrence of giggling, and until I was grown he used to

consider me the most empty-headed of his children because
he found the way I laughed deplorably silly. It was not unlike
Daphne's, except that I would sometimes get carried away by
it into gales and smothered explosions.

"If you don't learn not to giggle," he once told me, "you
will never attract a husband." Since it was my only way of
laughing I really could not comprehend his pronouncement.

Had Mother perhaps been prone to titter occasionally, or
tried to tell my father something that she found funny, only
to be told coldly that she was not attractive when she talked
and laughed at the same time? That could dampen a good deal
of ardor, I would think. She was only twenty-one when she
married, and doubtless my father felt it necessary to remold
her nearer to his heart's desire. He tried to do the same with
us, but by the time Daphne was ten years old and Allison five,
he was at the disadvantage of not seeing us often enough or
long enough. This may have been in my mother's mind when
she decided to move to Virginia and begin a life without ease
or convenience.

As I grew older and achieved some sense of pity for my
father, who seemed to miss so much of the joy in life, I wanted
to understand how he became that way. It was too late when
at last I became mature enough to be able to talk to him. He
died when I was twenty-eight, but my psyche required another six years to mature. I do remember that he had only
bitter memories of his mother. He was born when his only
brother was nearly grown, he said, and was made to feel he
had not been wanted. He told us that his mother gave him
only an old ink bottle to play with, and occasionally beat him
while she prayed for his soul. Mother scoffed when I repeated
this, telling me she had known his mother, a sweet little old
lady with dainty habits and pink-and-white cheeks in her old

age. Yet it may be true that she had not wanted him, and that he was scarred forever because she was unable to love him. Perhaps it was out of the memory of such a bleak childhood that he understood so well what gifts would charm us all: the magical Japanese paper flowers that looked like bits of confetti—dropped into water they bloomed into roses, peonies and lilies; the satin-smooth wooden lap desk he gave Allison so she could write in bed, where she was forced to spend so much time; the filigree watch and ring of abalone he gave to Daphne; the plates, vases, small pitchers, delicate cups and saucers, selected at pawnshops or estate sales with a sure sense of beauty for my mother. They so delighted her that she had a plate rail built for them around our dining room. As a child I loved big beach balls, and he brought these for me several summers in a row. When I was thirteen he gave me a small, wooden twelve-inch upright chest of Japanese make. It was lacquered red and held four miniature black drawers behind two red doors. The whole was decorated with gold-and-black leaves and birds. I kept hairpins and makeup and bits of jewelry in it for years. His later gifts for me were chiefly books; they were what I wanted most.

There were rare occasions, I remember, when my father seemed content, even happy, within his family. At such times he knew that we found pleasure in the objects he had selected for us; at these moments my mother warmed to his unusual affability; we children could approach and touch him, lean against him and safely love him without being frowned away.

But these were rare moments and ceased as we grew into adolescence. By then he seemed wary of us, and we shied away from his criticism and his demand that we not be an embarrassment to him. His strictures, communicated by disapproving comments to Mother made loudly enough so we could hear, included not talking boisterously or much at all, not running (our knees showed immodestly), not expressing euphoria in giddy ways, not giggling, and bringing home only impeccable friends. Of course, it was easier for us simply to stay away from him when he was home, knowing he would be leaving in a few weeks, and giving him the living room for himself and his books. He never missed us, I'm sure. When he retired and I was the only child at home, I largely avoided him. He did not notice this, either; as far as I know, he never asked for my presence any more than I asked for his.

In later years I wondered: Had my father ever wanted friends for himself? There was only one man whom he spoke of as a close and valued companion, and that was early in his life, before he married. As nearly as I could tell, he never had another until the too-brief friendship with Robert Dunlap, who came to our house with his Bible under his arm. Even after Mother moved to Virginia there was no evidence that he sought or made friends in Chicago. I imagined him in those years as a lonely figure moving along the crowded streets of Chicago, buying his morning paper, having his black shoes shined, going to work, doing his actuary's job well, watching other men of the company talking together and telling himself he didn't want to be part of irrelevant conversations. At the end of the day he went out into the press of the homeward bound, sometimes walking to his apartment, later eating his evening meal at an inexpensive restaurant. Sitting there with his newspaper or book, he checked his water glass and coffee cup for smears. If he found any, he summoned a waiter and pointed out the dirt. When others were brought, he examined them too. He read while he ate, paying no attention to anyone else unless there was a disturbance, tipped carefully and left. On certain nights he went home and wrote to my mother; they maintained a constant exchange of letters all those years. Not one letter survives, not even those from the few years after the fire and before he retired.

What else my father did during all those years in Chicago is a mystery I wish I had been bold enough to ask him about. I think he must have spent hours browsing in pawnshops and second-hand stores. I believe he spent as much time in the public library and in bookstores. Yet the books he brought with him when he came to Virginia were paltry and of little worth compared to the volumes lost in the fire. Those books and the bookcases that held them remain in my memory as part of the mystery of my father. Did he buy them one by one in bookshops or pick them up in sets at sales of fine household goods? Why did so many that I opened seem so untouched if they had been owned before? It is possible that book collecting was a passion of his youth and subsided with age, and that he could never bring himself to open those ponderous classics.

There is much that I will never know. All that I imagined may be wrong. He may not have been a lonely man at all; he may have been very content in Chicago. Other people may have truly bored him enough that his greatest pleasures were enjoyed alone.

If that is so, he must have suffered from his retirement as much as my mother and I, and felt an anomie at being cut free from the city, where he was never censored for being himself because nobody cared. He was not ready to live with family members who cared too much that he was not what they expected.

My father was not a happy man at the end of his life, but looking back I cannot see how any of us might have made him so, except by loving him unconditionally. Of that my mother had no conception and was unable to do. Such a difficult charity I did not know either, and did not learn until long after his death. I am not at all sure I could have practiced it with the living man and offer it now only to his restless shade if it has still found no peace.

22

A Late, Late Blooming

All through high school I knew I would be a writer. Or rather, I believed I *was* one. Two of my teachers thought so too, so when graduation loomed I told my mother I wanted to go to the University of Missouri School of Journalism. I think my English teacher had told me this was the preferred school for writers. At this announcement, my mother felt it was time to trim my expectations; Missouri was too far away from home, she said. She wanted me to be closer, telling me that she had lost Allison to distance and big cities and did not want her youngest to lose touch with home. In fact she had decided that I should go to Daphne's college, which she considered close and adequate.

After I had digested this enough to look at their catalog, Mother said, "You will notice they are offering a commercial course now that can give you an edge in finding a job."

"Mother, I'm only good at writing. It's all I want to do. I'll never be any good at business."

"Child, you can't possibly know how many thousands of writers are going hungry these days. You need to learn something practical to live on, and you can write in your spare time. Besides, you will need to know how to type, and you will learn other skills that will open doors."

It sounded reasonable, and since I really had no knowledge of the world outside of the farm, I had no argument except an inner certainty that did not impress her. She knew about breadlines and the misery of people who could not find work. She also mentioned white slavery, which turned out to be a fear that I might be enticed astray by men who "used" girls. She did not explain how they used them, but I, who knew nothing of prostitution, heard vague shadows in her voice. I was unsure, and afraid to entrust my future to myself.

So I enrolled at the Fredericksburg State Teachers' College, where the dean of women was the same one Daphne had known. My mother was confident that there would be no danger of my being led astray by men while Mrs. Baldridge strode the halls. An erect woman firmly encased in foundation garments, her gray hair set in steel-cut waves, she paced the floor of the dining hall at dinner barking directions over our heads: "Young ladies, you do not tip your soup bowls. It is correct to leave a little in the bottom. . . . Keep your left hand in your lap except when you must use it to hold your fork when you cut meat. . . . Now this young woman has perfect manners except that she slumps. Stand up, young lady. No, that's not *standing*—pull in your stomach, now lift your shoulders, now hold your head up. There, see—*that's* what I mean, girls. Now I'll count to three and I want every girl sitting straight, spine against the back of your chair, feet flat on the floor . . . one, two, three—that's better." The sound of feet flattening on the floor died away, and she turned smartly to address her own dinner at a table up front, leaving us feeling cowed.

·   ·   ·

My first shock was having to share a dormitory room with two other girls, one of whom threw her dirty socks into the closet that she and I shared. She left them there until she ran out of clean ones. In time my clothes and hers reeked of sweaty feet. To open that closet door was to let a miasma loose in the room and into the hall. At this time I laid much store by personal daintiness, having discovered it not many years before, and wanted to suggest it for her socks, but I did not know how to broach the subject. Now I realize that the direct method of holding my nose and saying, "I think your socks have died in here," would have been the best approach. Instead I held my tongue.

At home I had a room to myself, a bookcase and a writing desk. In our dormitory room there was one small table for the three of us. It was usually occupied by the owner of foul socks. She was red-headed and big-boned and said it hurt her back to study on the bed.

"It's sure nice here," she said thoughtfully more than once. "Back home there was five of us in one room. This is the first time I ever had a bed with nobody but me in it."

My other roommate was quiet and thin, and has otherwise vanished from memory. I found I could escape them both by going to the typing room to practice, or to the library. At the library I briefly struggled with bookkeeping, while from all sides came the siren calls of unopened books. When I succumbed and opened a book of poetry, I was lost to bookkeeping forever.

In the long typing classes I spent all my practice time making up stories. Probably no one else had as much practice using quotation marks, and the teacher never checked my papers, which were filled with conversations. Shorthand I enjoyed; business English I scorned. After classes I went for long, brooding, solitary walks on the landscaped campus, wishing for dirt paths, the smell of pines, the sound of running water. Back at the library I wrote plaintive letters to my high school English teacher, who was sympathetic. "I never thought the commercial course was the right choice for you," he answered. He had never gone so far as to say this to my mother—not that it would have done any good.

A brown-eyed senior with smooth red braids around her head, who introduced herself as Estelle, was assigned to our dining table of callow freshmen to remind us to lower our voices and moderate our speech. She had a calm and tolerant gaze as she went around the table the first night, asking each of us about ourselves. It proved to be her most endearing quality; she wanted to talk about you, never herself.

"And your name is Vallie?" she said, getting around to me. "Is that for 'Valerie'?"

"No. It's what I used to call myself because I didn't like my real name."

It was like her not to ask what that was. "And where's your home?"

"In the country," I said. "A farm. Where I wish I was right now."

She laughed. "What would you be doing on the farm right now?"

"I'd be reading or going for a walk or listening to music."

"You mean," the freshman across from me said, "you wouldn't be milkin' the cows or cleanin' out the stable?" She had just told us she was from the city of Norfolk.

"No." I looked her in the eye. "I finished that at four o'clock." I had never cleaned out a stable in my life or milked a cow, but I wasn't going to ruin my image.

In Estelle's suite in senior quarters, I found my second

campus refuge and a friend. She read my fumbling poetry with respect and we took long walks, talking or not talking as we liked. At the time I believed that her friendship was the only relationship of worth I found in that school. But of course the whole experience was more: It was the splitting of the cocoon of the farm, and a rude emergence into a life of rubbing elbows, which, liking my virginal state, I would not have willingly chosen.

Without a backward look at the end of the term, I left that college, and all colleges, unpersuaded by another former teacher that I should try for a scholarship elsewhere in the state to study what I wanted to. At that point what I'd had of college life was nothing I wanted to continue. I would go out into the world of the city, find a job of some kind and write in my free evenings in my rented room.

After a long search for work, that's exactly what I did. My mother agreed to provide my board plus three dollars a week for spending money until I found work. While I was looking and after I began working, pages and pages flowed from my pencil and from rented typewriters. When I wasn't dating I wrote, and for a while men gave me ample time for it. Hitler began his march into Poland while I wrote obliviously of love. War was burning down Europe and there were rumors of war in this country, but I wrote on, starting a collection of rejection slips.

One evening a young intern named Shannon MacPhail, who had an evening free from hospital duties, drove the two of us out into the country in his father's Dodge and parked under vast, beautiful oaks in the moonlight. "This is my grandfather's house," he told me. "He died two years ago and I'd like you to see it." We walked up a drive, where the scent of honeysuckle from a hedge smote me with longing. Ahead was a house brooding within its trees and shrubs, a graceful, slender house pale in the moonlight, with tall windows, dark shutters and a curved flight of steps at each end of the long porch.

"It's lovely," I said.

Shannon stopped and said, "I'd like to carry you over that threshold."

Alarm clutched me as I tried to fathom his meaning. Now? On future dates? He didn't notice and went on: "If we get married, Vallie, we can furnish this house during our engagement. It will be all ready to move into when I go into practice."

I looked at his close-cut, slightly crinkled blond hair tipped with silver light, and at his eyes, which were not on me, but on the house. "Shannon," I said, "you've missed something." He turned to look down at me, puzzled. "You haven't mentioned love, and you haven't asked if I'd marry you."

"Oh, sorry," he murmured, as if his mind were just coming out of the door. "Of course I love you, Vallie, or I wouldn't have brought you here. Actually," he added, turning toward me, "I've been trying to control an impulse to kiss you." Then he wrapped long arms around me and kissed me firmly on the mouth.

No sparks ignited in me, but I felt him tremble slightly. I said, "I can't be engaged now, Shannon, because I'm giving so much of my time to writing."

"Being engaged to me won't keep you from writing."

"Not intentionally. But I'll have to go out when you want to go, I'll have to meet your family and all their friends and go places we ought to go—all that."

"But you will want to if you love me, won't you?"

I wasn't strong enough to say, "But I don't love you

enough." Instead I patted his arm and said, "Just wait a little while. I'm not ready to be engaged." I was working on a long poem then, one I believed might be published, and it was taking most of my ardor. If Shannon's kiss had roused the deeper, primitive response that I had once felt with Todd, I might have forgone that poem for one with him. But it didn't. As we drove back to the city, he told me of another girl ready to marry him whenever he asked her, but I was unable to feel the proper jealousy. Apparently he did find her affections less absentminded than mine later that year, but I, intent on creation, hardly noticed.

The day finally came when, sitting at a typewriter staring at the fifteenth page of a story I was working on, a merciless realization obliterated the page: What I was writing—indeed, all that I had written—was not good enough. Nothing I had done had adequate depth or breadth or sure knowledge. I had not lived enough to know how the people I created in my mind would bring up children, love one another, live together, face devastation, share laughter, know hardship, grow middle-aged, grow old, die. Sitting there, I saw my certainties about writing drop into the revealed hole of my unknowing. Shaken, I stood up, covered the typewriter, tore up the pages I had just written, threw out two hundred more pages of something I once had thought promising, and went for a long, sorrowing walk. As they say, something within me died. For a long time afterward I wrote nothing but the poetry that my mind kept composing without my willing it, but it wasn't good enough either.

Eighteen months later, when I was twenty-one, learning began with marriage. I had a child when I was twenty-two, and another four years later. Marriage proved to be a crash course in much that I had not understood. In the year that a third child was born, my marriage ended. In time I supported the four of us by writing a great many words for a volunteer health agency, some of them good. By the time I reached forty years of age, I had all the material I needed, but found that some of it lingered on, too painfully unresolved to write about with detachment.

It has taken me almost a lifetime to be ready to write about what I have learned.

23

Good-byes

In 1940, Allison moved to Washington, D.C., to become a government employee. She spent vacation time at home, no longer so depressed by farms and small towns. Sometimes we were there together. I found her laughter easier, her tolerance expanded, her speech lively. Mother made some effort to curb her use of "My God!" so frequently, but her heart wasn't in it; she had resigned the job of mothering Allison. Of course she still had me to shepherd as much as anyone could who saw her youngest only on weekends. I was still living in Richmond and engaged by then, with the wedding tentatively set for November. Monty was in Georgia working as managing assistant for a radio station. My mother was trying to build up my strength—or at least my girth—by feeding me well when I was home. Apparently she believed it was desirable to approach the trials of marriage with a reserve of added flesh. Though my weight would not budge from ninety-eight pounds no matter how I was stuffed, it didn't seem to matter; I was rarely sick.

Once in a while Allison and I saw Mary Marshall when she

came to straighten up the kitchen. Her sons were grown, her daughter married, and she came partly because she needed the easy friendship she had with my mother. She could no longer "tip upstairs" to spend time there talking because my father now owned half the bedroom. Sometimes they talked quietly in the kitchen. Mary said her oldest son was in the army, the others were working in Cincinnati and the house sure was empty. Allison and I hugged her and noticed that her hair was becoming gray. Mother took her out into the garden to talk as they gathered vegetables. Their closeness was to end only at my mother's death.

I am not sure where or when we lost track of Susan. After I left home for work, Mother no longer needed her and she went to work for someone else. I saw her once when I was home on vacation, when she came to buy eggs. We talked with pleasure for a few minutes, but someone was waiting for her in a car and she could not stay. I have a vague memory of Mary Marshall saying a year or two later that Mrs. Coleman had gone to live in Ashland, Kentucky, when her husband retired from the railroad. In the 1960s, I tried to write of her and my regret at losing touch with her. I never finished and she has not left my mind since.

Two years after Allison's move, Mother and I rode the train from Richmond to Washington to attend her January wedding to a tall, gentle sandy-haired Mississippian. By the time she met him she had wearied of flat midwestern accents and the hard, curled r's of the North. She warmed right away to Morgan's dropped g's and soft speech. "And I knew he was a southerner before he even said anything," Allison told us. "He opened the door for me."

The train we boarded was filled with soldiers; in 1942 all passenger trains were filled with servicemen. My mother and

I found separate seats, each next to a young man in uniform. The one beside me began talking right away.

"Where you from, miss?"

"Richmond," I said. "Virginia."

He told me he was from a small town in Nebraska and was homesick. "You look kinda like my sister," he said, and brought out a picture of a dark-haired girl who did not resemble me at all. Then he handed me his wife's picture, his father's and mother's, his niece's and nephew's. It took him the slow three-hour trip to D.C. to tell me where he'd met his wife, where they honeymooned, how they had two weeks in their new apartment before he was called up, how she had given him her cross to keep him safe from Nazi bullets. He was not interested in me except as a woman who would listen and murmur appropriately. In a way this was a relief. I had been sure that every soldier would want to hold my hand and make overtures; they were supposed to be sex-starved and lonely.

Allison lived in a miniature apartment she had secured before the city of Washington bulged with government workers. We walked to the church that damp afternoon, Allison, her cheeks pink, her eyes shining, dressed in a dark suit and hat with a veil, and Morgan wearing a serious expression. Behind them walked Morgan's cousin and her husband, the only representatives of his family near enough to be present. Mother and I trailed behind. My father, who was not well, did not come.

I spent the walk remembering my own wedding. On the surface it had been ordinary enough.

My father, happy to give me away, escorted me down the aisle to the wedding march from *Lohengrin*. My wedding gown was made by my mother-in-law-to-be, my veil was borrowed and my bouquet overwhelmed me with the scent of gardenias.

"Keep time to the music!" my father muttered fiercely, feeling that I was ruining the dignity of the moment with my agitation.

A few minutes before, Rob, my widowered brother-in-law, had appeared in the minister's study with his and Daphne's daughter, Jean. I had not invited him. I had seen him only once since Daphne's death. My Mother had felt it was her duty to occasionally visit Rob's mother, who had the care of the grandchildren, and she usually took some prepared dish since Mrs. McClough, by then in her seventies, found cooking burdensome. Whether Rob came in from the fields to greet and talk with her I do not remember her saying. He and the children surprised us one Thanksgiving when we were sitting down to a small roast hen, and I think we barely had enough to feed everybody. My father, never comfortable with children, found conversation difficult and ate in silence, but the children ignored him happily. Rob sat between Jean and Bruce to prevent quarrels, and in the end my mother and I were glad they came.

I never expected Rob to appear at my wedding since I had not told him about it. That it was callously bad-mannered of me to slight a man who had been so kind to me and dear to my sister occurred to me later—shamefully later. It was a mark of my obtuse immaturity that I did not realize it then.

The chapel held a maximum of seventy-five if they stood, and the guest list had been trimmed to fit. When someone came to tell me that Rob was waiting to see me, Allison, my only attendant, gasped and whispered, "If *he* comes, I refuse to go out there!"

This scared me into last-minute panic, and when Rob greeted me I did not tell him to join the standees already gathered. I hugged Jean and lied to her father that there was no room in the chapel. He wished me happiness anyway, and I left in my cloud of veil. No one knew that I was ashamed of myself for this lack of grace under pressure. Allison's reason was that not long (perhaps ten months) after Daphne died, Rob had proposed marriage to her. Offended that he showed so little respect for Daphne's memory, she refused, though Mother told her, "It's because he loved Daphne that he came to you."

I think my own first reaction when I heard this from Mother was that Rob was being too hasty in trying to find another wife, more because he was still not over his grief than because it was unseemly. At no time did I feel it was an insult to Daphne; I had been too aware of the love between them. I thought then and think now that what he was seeking more urgently was a mother for his children who would be as much like Daphne as possible. I believe the need to fill his marriage bed was of less importance to him.

I understood and sympathized with Allison's response to his overtures. I would have turned him down had he asked me, even though I liked him, but given her outspoken distaste for Rob she could not have acted differently. She was still feeling indignation about it all at the time of my wedding.

All this lingered in my head as Allison and Morgan made their vows. Afterward the wedding party was taken to dinner at the Shoreham by Morgan's cousin, and our mother watched in concern as Allison and I both drank sparkling burgundy. Mother believed that nothing good could come of the consumption of alcohol and drank only coffee; she knew she had to remain sober to steer herself and me back to the train.

Mother and I waited on the unheated Union Station platform that night for our train, which arrived four hours late.
As it crept from the station, we were told that the rails were
covered with ice. The train moved slowly and stopped frequently. Servicemen walked the aisles or sat or slept, and the
air was blue with cigarette smoke. It was six A.M. before we
reached Richmond, and my mother still had to drive home.
I tried to persuade her to wait until the ice cleared, but she
refused. "I can't telephone your father and he's already worried, I know," she said.

"But you could have an accident," I pointed out.

"You forget I've been driving all these years in all kinds of
weather and never had an accident." It was her old I-will-live-
in-the-chicken-house stubbornness.

I waited that day to hear the worst, but there was no word.
Two days later a letter from her said that hers had been the
only car on the road from Richmond, and that she had driven
the whole distance in second gear without incident. It was a
good thing she'd come home, she said; my father had not fed
the chickens and nobody had milked the cow that morning.

THE VIRGINIA BOOKSHELF

Garrett Epps
The Shad Treatment

Donald McCaig
An American Homeplace

Ivor Noël Hume
*The Virginia Adventure: Roanoke to James Towne:
An Archaeological and Historical Odyssey*

Virginia Bell Dabney
*Once There Was a Farm . . . :
A Country Childhood Remembered*

Cathryn Hankla
A Blue Moon in Poorwater